BEAVERBROOK

Maple, Ontario: the birthplace

BEAVERBROOK

*A Study in
Power and Frustration*

TOM DRIBERG

WEIDENFELD AND NICOLSON
7 CORK STREET LONDON W1

First published 1956

PRINTED IN GREAT BRITAIN BY
WILLIAM CLOWES AND SONS LIMITED
LONDON AND BECCLES

CONTENTS

LIST OF ILLUSTRATIONS

Illustrations 1a, 1b, 2, 3a, 4a, 4b, 5, and 6 by courtesy of the Daily Express; 3b of PA-Reuter; and 7 of Baron and the Camera Press.

ACKNOWLEDGEMENTS

MANY other books must be read or referred to when a book of this kind is in preparation. Some of the most useful have been Sir Winston Churchill's *World Crisis* and *Second World War*; Sir Harold Nicolson's *King George V: His Life and Reign*; Mr G. M. Young's *Stanley Baldwin*; Sir Austen Chamberlain's *Down the Years* and *Politics from the Inside*; Sir Charles Petrie's *Life and Letters of the Rt Hon Sir Austen Chamberlain* and *Walter Long and His Times*; *Memories and Reflections* by the Earl of Oxford and Asquith; Dr Thomas Jones's *A Diary with Letters*; Mr Stanley Morison's final volume of *The History of The Times*; the Duke of Windsor's *A King's Story*; Lord Reith's *Into the Wind*; Mr David Farrer's *The Sky's the Limit*; and the Report of the Royal Commission on the Press (with the evidence given before the Commission). Precise references to these and other books are given in the text and footnotes; but I have not thought it necessary, in a book intended for the general reader, to provide the elaborate apparatus of sources appropriate to a work of primary historical scholarship.

Mr Robert Blake's biography of Bonar Law, *The Unknown Prime Minister*, and Mr Frank Owen's life of Lloyd George, *Tempestuous Journey*, both appeared when this book was nearly complete. Invaluable as these are in their respective ways, nothing in either of them has caused me to revise an interpretation of certain episodes and relationships which differs in some respects from theirs. The fact that at one crucial point—the account of the overthrow of Asquith—I differ also from Lord Beaverbrook's own interpretation of the evidence does not lessen my debt to his *Politicians and the War*, which contains the most important of all the raw

ACKNOWLEDGEMENTS

material for the study of that historic operation. For data on the earlier part of the inter-war period I am equally indebted to his smaller work, *Politicians and the Press*.

While I was a Member of Parliament, I was able to use the excellent library of the House of Commons; and the staff of the library and its research department were most helpful.

I must express my thanks to Mrs Bambridge, Messrs A. P. Watt and Son and Messrs Macmillan for permission to reprint the passage from *Stalky and Co* on p. 200; to Sir Harold Nicolson and Messrs Constable for permission to include the long quotation on pp. 113–14 from *King George V*; to Mrs Bambridge and Messrs A. P. Watt for permission to print for the first time the verses by Rudyard Kipling on p. 10; to the *Toronto Globe and Mail* for permission to reprint the extracts on pp. 46–9; and to Lord Beaverbrook and the *Express* newspapers for their permission to include the numerous quotations from material of which they are the copyright owners. I am also most grateful to the *Express* for supplying and giving permission to reproduce many of the illustrations.

It would have been impossible to give the source of every statement in this book: much of the material in it is derived from my own memory and observation, much was learned in conversation with friends and associates of Lord Beaverbrook. Lord Beaverbrook himself, however, is in no way responsible for anything contained in it. It has been checked for factual accuracy, so far as possible; but it is an unauthorized and independent work, and the writer alone is to blame for errors of fact or interpretation.

Finally, I am grateful to Miss Laura Kilcawley for her patient typing and retyping of the manuscript.

T. D.

CHAPTER ONE

A DAY IN THE LIFE OF A PRESS LORD

In private business his commands prevail,
On public themes his reasoning turns the scale;
Assenting silence soothes his happy ear,
And, in or out, his party triumphs here.

GEORGE CRABBE

THE HEAD is too big for the boots. It is a powerful head, broad, rather flat-topped, bulging—almost as if its contents were pressing the bone-structure outwards. The brow is deeply furrowed, there is a skirting of wispy grey hair.

The face is dark in hue, a mottled tan, permanently sunburned. The mouth is just as in every cartoon of him by Low or Vicky, a satchel-mouth, bisecting the face in an enormous grin; when something is said which appeals to his sardonic humour, the mouth suddenly gapes in a harsh thunderclap of laughter. Sometimes, when he laughs, he throws his head back and the eyes are as wide open as the mouth, staring as if in astonishment, white glaring above iris. When he is pensive or angry, the eyes narrow nearly to slits. They are 'piercing' eyes—perhaps through deliberation, as an element in the tycoon mask. In friendly or in formidable mood, it is a magnetic face. The Sutherland painting and the Karsh photographs show that he likes to be portrayed, like Cromwell, 'warts and all'.

Long years of public life in England have not modified at all the Canadian resonance of his voice. Sometimes it is loud, grim, and rasping; sometimes it sinks to a melancholy or a coaxing purr. There often seem to be echoes of its intonations in the voices of those who have worked much with him; and they affectionately imitate him in conversation with each other.

1

B

When he is dressed (in unobtrusive dark-blue suit, with plain white shirt and plain sombre tie, rather like a humble dissenting minister in the days before Methodists wore Roman collars), the rest of his appearance is an anticlimax. He is five feet seven inches in height, slight of build, with a suspicion of a paunch. The short legs taper to small, neatly shod feet.

He takes no interest in men's clothes, his own or other people's. He likes to see the women at his dinner-table elegantly gowned: he does not notice if the men are in evening dress or not. Mostly they are not; for many of those whose company he enjoys prefer not to put on dinner-jackets or white ties, and they are often bidden to dinner at short notice: Frank Owen, for instance, unkempt, snarlingly argumentative, red tie flying.

Dinner is the social climax of Beaverbrook's day, and almost its only period of purely social relaxation. There are rarely fewer than seven or eight guests. He is a good and a genial, if a dominant, host. When he is at his house at Cherkley, near Leatherhead, Surrey, he does not sit, as most hosts do, at one end of the long table: he sits in the middle of one side, and can thus take part in all the talk and control its theme. He will take pains to make a new, young, shy guest feel at home, to draw him or her out. Some say that this is like being taught to swim by being thrown into the deep end of a bath; for Beaverbrook has no 'small talk', and his idea of a conversational opening is to fire direct, searching, often intimately personal questions at novice and expert alike. The impulse is genuinely hospitable; the technique also digs out fodder for the insatiable, wide-ranging curiosity which has helped to make Beaverbrook the most successful newspaper publisher of the century. The process may be a test of character, too, more severe than those to which candidates for posts in the Foreign Service or commissions in the Army are subjected: a young man who keeps his head, answers

2

concisely and vigorously, and says when he disagrees with his host, and why, may pass with honours and be invited again; the flounderer or the stooge may be rewarded with a grunt of disgust or a surprisingly violent tirade against some person or institution with which he has to do. Most acceptable of all are those who can contribute some item of hard news to the discussion, though they may be startled to see their host leave the table when they have spoken and scribble a note on a writing-pad on the sideboard—a particularly disconcerting procedure if the story has been embroidered for effect.

The food is of the finest quality—the most delicately flavoured Scotch salmon, a saddle of the most tender lamb, Demeter's cornucopia of young fresh vegetables, a pudding that would have won gold medals at any of the most grandiose gastronomic tournaments of the nineteenth century; and it is prepared by a *chef* who can have few, if any, equals in the private houses of England today. Yet Beaverbrook eats little himself, and must reject some of his *chef*'s most lyrical offerings.

The wine matches the food. Many bottles are collectors' pieces. All are scrupulously catalogued in a massive cellar-book. From this cellar, on many a Sunday during the Second World War, two bottles of Niersteiner Auslese 1935 would be sent to the War Cabinet offices, where Beaverbrook used to lunch with Winston Churchill, and put on ice for them.

In this respect at least, he is not merely a rich man who has bought the best of everything. He has a true appreciation of wine. Duff Cooper once said: 'If anything could reconcile Max to Belloc'—to whose Catholic and European culture he had a congenital, irrational, and bristling antipathy, no doubt richly and hilariously reciprocated—'it would be Belloc's *Heroic Poem in Praise of Wine*'. He knows that carefully cellared champagne, like the company of some women, can be enjoyed at a more mature age than is popularly supposed.

Most rich men of seventy-five leave it to their butlers to open and pour wine: there are three menservants waiting, yet he himself gets up from the table, uncorks bottles, and replenishes glasses. If it is a bottle of champagne, he will stand up in his place, grip the bottle by its base and point it at each glass in turn round the table, pouring accurately in each: no mean feat. An epicure, if ungratefully critical, might say that he fills the glasses rather too often and fast for wines of such quality; few guests are known to object.

He himself also mixes the cocktail before dinner. It is usually a *daiquiri*—the West Indian cocktail of rum and cracked ice. He mixes it in a machine which makes a noise like twenty electric razors. He has one of these machines in each of his houses.

It is only in the evening that he himself takes wine, or any alcohol. Even then, he takes it in moderation, though he has one of those apparently iron-clad insides which can absorb champagne and whisky in alternate doses. In the spring of 1954 he gave up alcohol altogether for a time—to the distress of his associates, who found that, without it, he was able to relax even more rarely than before.

His constitution seems to have grown stronger, and his health to have improved, in the past decade. At one time he was spoken of as a hypochondriac; and there was some truth in the assessment. He did worry a good deal about his health, and the worry in itself may have aggravated the asthma which has been his chronic complaint. It was partly cured by a stay in the dry desert climate of Arizona; but his and his valet's day is still punctuated by frequent inhalations and applications of drops and douches.

If, however, hypochondria means completely baseless worry about completely imaginary ills, it was an exaggeration to apply the term to Beaverbrook. He had solid grounds for anxiety, especially about any complaint affecting his throat. Few of his present friends or employees know that in 1918 and

4

1919 he was ill with a rare, often fatal, fungoid infection of the throat, actinomycosis. For a time cancer was suspected; the rumour ran round that he was dying of it. His bitterest enemies began to forgive him; even Mrs Asquith, whose husband's downfall he had helped to engineer, wrote to say that she regretted some of her tarter epithets.

Mr Wilfred Trotter, an eminent cancer specialist, operated twice. The operations were not successful; the fungoid growth returned. Beaverbrook was advised to see a Portuguese doctor, Gomes by name. His treatment, as Beaverbrook recalls it, was simple, drastic, and agonizing: he poured four hundred drops of iodine down Beaverbrook's throat daily. Then there was another, minor operation. The throat healed. Beaverbrook did not die. Long afterwards he said: 'It had not been my intention to die'. A secondary pleasure of his recovery may well have been the knowledge that his enemies would now be cancelling their forgiveness, and Mrs Asquith regretting her remorse.

He used to worry about his eyesight, too. It seems to serve him adequately now, though he does not like to waste it, or his time, on long letters or long articles. 'Keep it short' is a maxim of his; and short articles are therefore preferred to long in his newspapers.

From his 'hypochondriac' period dates a general instruction to news and feature editors that stories of disease and medicine, of strange plagues and new cures, should be given prominence. 'People like reading about them', he would say. If his editors were able without too much difficulty to identify the 'people' in this dictum, they were not so foolish as to question it. It may well, in any case, be true. At least, when asthma obliged him to give up smoking, there is no evidence that the newspapers were ever instigated to an anti-tobacco crusade. Had they been, there is little doubt that the efficient men who run the business side of them would have pointed out, as it would have been their duty to, that much of the

5

advertising revenue was derived from the sale of space to cigarette manufacturers.

There is little or no smoking after dinner at Cherkley—not because Beaverbrook, like some fanatical non-smokers, dislikes it in his presence, but because, as soon as dinner is over, he steers his guests firmly into his comfortable private cinema, in which smoking is forbidden by the safety regulations. Most of the good films of the day are shown here; it is one of the incidental, though not one of the least important, duties of one of his film-critics to select films likely to entertain him. The films are gladly lent by the companies making or distributing them. It is one of Beaverbrook's idiosyncrasies that, just as children's presents are supposed to be 'a surprise', he prefers not to tell his guests in advance what films he is going to show them. An attempt seems sometimes to have been made to choose films likely to please particular guests. Beaverbrook's own taste includes a *penchant* for good 'Westerns'. His favourite film is *Destry Rides Again*; he owns a copy of it, and is said to have seen it sixteen times.

When the film is over, he may sit for a while in the drawing-room with his guests and the old chow dog, probably in order to tidy up items of work with those of them who are also his employees. The hours in the cinema may have been, in a sense, an escape from the conversational obligations that normally follow a dinner-party. Merely social chatter, or balanced discussion of general principles, bores him: light gossip is beneath him (unless it is personal and of political or business significance); abstract, philosophic, artistic or antiquarian argument is beyond his competence; his passionate obsession is with the concrete, the 'human', the financial, the topical. He may play a few records on the gramophone (the latest batch from New York, or calypsos from the West Indies); or telephone to a night editor his comments on any important late news, of which he will have been notified; or dictate a few memoranda into the dictaphone near the grand piano, one of

6

many such machines in the various rooms of his various houses. Mr Percy Cudlipp once said that Beaverbrook's two favourite musical instruments were the gramophone and the telephone; he might have added the dictaphone, possibly the dominant instrument in this machine-age trio.[1]

If the dinner-party has not been a formal one, and he is in convivial mood with a few cronies, he can sometimes be persuaded to sing: songs of the Canadian lumbermen and the Scottish metrical paraphrases of the Psalms are his favourites, and of the latter he likes best *The Lord's my Shepherd, I'll not want*, to the tune *Crimond*.

Soon, however, he will be off to bed, gravely offering his guests the full-arm's-length handshake characteristic of him. A vigilant servant will have seen to it that the lift is down in the hall for him. It is an unusual lift. Because it was installed long after the house was built, it has no shaft: it descends, silently, straight into the open hall. If an unobservant guest is standing underneath it, he may be alarmed but he is in no danger; some magic device causes it to hover and stop an inch above his head.

The lift carries its master slowly up to his bedroom. He is asleep by midnight or one o'clock. For he wakes early, and he has a busy day.

It starts between five and seven in the morning, whenever he happens to wake. He reads, voraciously but fragmentarily, the books, magazines, and newspaper-cuttings which are piled on and around his enormous bed. As he glances at the cuttings, he throws nine out of ten of them to the floor; they are done with. The tenth he puts aside: there may be an idea for an editorial in it, or something he wants to check.

Soon the carpet looks like the scene of a paperchase. The same phenomenon attends Beaverbrook wherever he is, if he

---

[1] The machine that Beaverbrook now mostly uses is a Soundscriber; but 'Dictaphone', still strictly a trade-name, has almost passed into the language as a generic term.

is on his own ground (and he stirs from it, nowadays, as little as possible): whether he is at Cherkley, or at his penthouse in Arlington Street, Piccadilly, or at his farmhouse in Somerset, or at his villa, La Capponcina, at Cap D'Ail in the south of France, or at one of his three Caribbean houses. ('He has seven houses,' a friend has said of him, with a not-altogether-misplaced note of pity, 'and no home . . . Every one of them is a glorified office.') The same phenomenon occurs when he is in his car: cuttings, cuttings, Kleenex tissues, memoranda, cuttings, reports. Most of them go on the floor, some to his secretary, sitting in front by the driver: 'Here y'are Miss Rosenberg, here y'are . . .'; and every minute or two again, 'Here y'are'. The same phenomenon occurred, too, in the caravan—specially built on a 'bus chassis, and now sold—in which he used sometimes to travel to his west-country farms, entertaining his guests *en route* to luncheon. Paper is Beaverbrook's element. It is almost as necessary to him as air. His campaigns against the restriction of newsprint supplies correspond psychologically with his own limitless appetite for his essential raw material, as they do economically with the interests of his newspapers. For his own private letters and memoranda, he often uses the thinnest, cheapest flimsy, innocent of engraved or printed address and of the pretentious coronet with which less powerful peers adorn their notepaper.

At about eight o'clock, after he has done his deep-breathing exercises, he rings. Breakfast is brought to him, with all the morning newspapers—the direct cue, of course, for a new orgy of paper-tearing and paper-discarding, for the dictating into his bedside machine of several dozen messages to his staff.

By ten he is on the telephone fairly continuously, collecting news, exchanging views with business and political cronies, giving instructions to stockbrokers and secretaries and editors, issuing abrupt summonses ('Will you come and see me at 11.30 . . . Good-bye to you.'). Similar activities occur in the early evening, or indeed at almost any time during the day or night: he has under his control, after all, newspapers published every weekday morning, every weekday evening, and every Sunday. There is never a moment when some column is not being compiled; some editorial onslaught is always brewing. There are always relays of people available to see him: he dislikes being alone. Transport is provided for visitors as a matter of course, however far they are coming—an elderly taxi from Leatherhead station or an air fare from London to Nice. He paid the transatlantic fares, by air or sea, of guests who came from Canada to his seventy-fifth birthday party in May, 1954. His friends are useful to him as sources of news, but it is not primarily because they are useful that he cultivates them: his feelings of friendship are genuine. He is, however, hypersensitive: a slight mistake, or a joke that he does not care for, will sometimes antagonize him disproportionately. He is also naturally, and cannily, combative. 'When a man hits me,' he once said, 'I wait until he's not looking and hit him twice.'

When some political or personal quarrel ends or interrupts a friendship, or when a close acquaintance, for some reason, cools off and ceases to seek his company, he is not the man to shrug his shoulders and forget about it: he is apt to feel, passionately, that he has been bereaved or even betrayed. His reactions to such experiences, however, are neither simple nor uniform. In some cases he will inveigh against the lost friend sonorously and cumulatively, with the sombre fury of an Old Testament prophet castigating human wickedness: 'Ah . . . what a scoundrel! Did you ever know such a scoundrel? Never was there such a rascal . . . ,' and so on. In such cases it is unlikely that the erring friend will receive favourable publicity in Beaverbrook's newspapers.

In other cases, the parting is an occasion of sorrow rather than of anger. Rudyard Kipling was for many years an intimate of Beaverbrook's: their ardent imperialism was a link;

they were congenial companions. Kipling's name (with those of Tim Healy and Bonar Law) is on the first page of the first visitors' book at Cherkley, dated July 13th–14th, 1912. This book was a gift from Kipling, and he inscribed in it verses composed by himself:

> This is the prayer the Cave Man prayed
>   When first his household fire he lit
> And saw the solemn stars o'erhead
>   Contemptuously look down on it—
> The sweep and silence of the night,
>   The brooding dark on every side
> Oppressed his simple mind with fright
>   And, 'Heaven send me friends!' he cried...
>
> And that is why I send this tome
>   Of virgin pages fitly wrought
> To hold the names of all who come
>   Beneath your roof at Cherkley Court.
> O long, long may the record run,
>   And you enjoy until it ends
> The Four Best Gifts beneath the Sun
>   Love, Peace, and Health, and Honest Friends.

These agreeable verses were certainly written without ironic intention; yet it may be doubted whether so generous a share of the 'four best gifts' has fallen to the man to whom the verses were addressed as falls to the average citizen of modest means. The record has run long indeed; but Kipling himself was not to see it to its end. Some years before his death he was estranged from Beaverbrook—because, oddly enough, in one respect Beaverbrook was a less thorough-going imperialist than he: Beaverbrook favoured Home Rule for Ireland at a time when this issue provided a sharp test of Tory loyalty, and Kipling never forgave him for it. Years after the quarrel, Beaverbrook sought reconciliation. Kipling answered him coolly. Those who knew both men throughout those years cannot recall any occasion on which Beaverbrook spoke harshly of Kipling.

Sometimes his son Max will spend an hour or two in the morning sitting by his bed: Max helps to run the newspapers, and much of Beaverbrook's other property also—for instance, the Cherkley estate—has been made over to him. Beaverbrook is a proud father: Max Aitken's wartime record as a fighter-pilot in the Royal Air Force was something to be proud of; but, at the time, the knowledge that he was in almost daily danger was a sore anxiety to his father. Always, on returning from a sortie, Max would telephone to him: if the call had not come by the expected time, Beaverbrook's nervous distress was acute. Beaverbrook's unremitting concentration on his work as Minister of Aircraft Production was so important that Winston Churchill at one time seriously considered relieving him of this extra anxiety by ordering that Max should be transferred to a safe ground job. Somehow Max learned that this was being considered: his protests were so furious that the idea was dropped.

In 1945 it was decided that Max should enter the House of Commons, and the Conservative candidature at Holborn was procured for him, not without some resistance by elements in the local Conservative Association. As a candidate, he was 'sold' to the electors in one of the most slickly organized campaigns of that year, when many of the local political machines were rusty from wartime disuse. In addition, of course, to the usual thorough canvass of individual dwellings, he toured the local pubs in the company of prominent officials of the Licensed Victuallers' Association; and it is believed that influential Roman Catholics who were aware of Max's fine personal qualities induced many of the congregation of the Italian Church in Clerkenwell to vote for this personable (and divorced) son of a Presbyterian father. The decision to stand may not have been taken by Max alone and unprompted. Beaverbrook may well have felt that it would be useful to have a voice in the House of Commons, to supplement his own—now rare—appearances in the House of Lords. Max Aitken remained in Parliament for five years. He did not, however, settle down comfortably to the Parliamentary routine; the political club atmosphere of the House, the intricacies of its procedure, the lobbying and intrigues and exhibitionism were not congenial to his straightforward and rather conventional business mind; and in 1950 he did not stand for re-election.

By about eleven o'clock the main work of Beaverbrook's morning is over. In his bathroom an open fire is burning. After his bath—reclining in which he has, on occasion, dictated editorials and interviewed employees—he dresses quickly and goes downstairs (passing on the way, if he is at Cherkley, Eric Kennington's vivid portrait of Max Aitken in RAF uniform). He is still a keen walker: every morning, and sometimes in the afternoon as well, he will walk for several miles, talking all the time to some congenial companion. In London he walks in the Green Park; at Cherkley a car takes him up to the top of a hill and meets him three-quarters of an hour or an hour later at the other end of a path—the Long Gallop—that runs along a fine, open, well-wooded ridge, part of a property that he gave some years ago to the National Trust. (He regrets having done so, for he now disapproves of the National Trust and has often denounced it as a device for enabling hereditary aristocrats to live in houses that they cannot afford to maintain, and rich men to avoid spending as much as they should—citing especially the case of one of the socially exalted families with whom he is always feuding, the Astors.) It may be that these fresh, unspoiled uplands, rich with conifers, remind him of the country he knew as a boy in New Brunswick; when he first acquired the property, he named two of the woods Upper and Lower Canada.

Wherever he is, Beaverbrook goes for his walks. Most of all he likes to have someone with him to whom the scene is

new: in country or in town, he is an enthusiastic and inform-
ative guide, pausing frequently to draw attention to the excellence of the trees in this plantation or of the houses in that
street. A friend walking with him once in Toronto was puzzled
by the vehemence with which Beaverbrook exclaimed again
and again, pointing along street after street of ornate but
characterless skyscrapers, 'Look at that! Isn't that beautiful?
There now . . . Beautiful, beautiful'—until it dawned on him
that, beauty being in the eye (or mind) of the beholder, the
special beauty of these busy modern streets lay in the fact that
Toronto was the most prosperous city in Canada. Prosperity,
to Beaverbrook, is not merely an indispensable material condition: it has a positively aesthetic appeal. It is no accident
that his own best-selling book was called *Success*, and that its
main theme is success in making money. When he is reminis-
cing about his boyhood, and the games of marbles which he
used to play with the other boys, he boasts: 'I knew the value
of every marble in the place'. To him, 'value' is synonymous
with 'price'. He is profoundly cynical about human character
and its weaknesses: in this respect he conforms with the classic
definition of a cynic—'a man who knows the price of everything and the value of nothing'. He is almost a pure material-
ist, in the western, non-dialectical sense of the word—yet only
'almost', for his materialism and his hard-boiled cynicism are
relieved by impulses of generosity and personal loyalty. He
will go to some pains to buy good presents for every boy and
girl invited to a children's party; he keeps on his pay-roll
many old employees who are long past useful work; there are
a few old intimates in public life—outstandingly, Winston
Churchill—whom he will never attack in print or speech even
if he disagrees with their policies.

Many rich men indulge in public benefactions, and it is
never easy to be sure of the integrity of their motives in doing
so: Beaverbrook has been a lavish public benefactor; but he
also maintains so many private pensioners that it is difficult

to acquit him of some genuine kindness of heart, or at least of a vestigial Calvinistic conscience. If taxed with such a weakness, he will offset it by recounting some instance of uncharitable conduct on his part. Or he will tell a joke against himself—recalling, for instance, the case of an elderly Scottish woman, in poor circumstances, who came to him one day and gave him a Bible that had been used by his father before he emigrated to Canada. In the emotion of the moment, and thinking to ease the remaining year or two of her life, he gave her an annuity of £2,000 a year. 'Hah!' he snorts, in mock-disgust. 'She lived to ninety-eight!'

If the weather is hot, he may walk in the garden at Cherkley. Near the windows of the house he grows stramonium: from this flower is extracted a drug supposed to relieve asthma. There are many blue and purple flowers: bees, he has observed, prefer these; they will get honey from catsnip and lavender, but 'never, never', he insists, 'from the honeysuckle vine—never at all'. A guest was tactless enough one day to discover what looked like a honey-bee actively exploring the honeysuckle. 'It must be a bumble bee,' said Beaverbrook, slightly put out, 'a small bumble bee.'

In recent years he has spent only three months or so a year in London, Surrey, and Somerset. Several years ago he said: 'I am never going to spend another winter in England'— adding with great emphasis a pentameter quoted, perhaps unintentionally, from *King Lear*: 'Never, never, never, never, never'. He likes warmth—the heat of the sub-tropical sun, big fires as well as central heating indoors. He also, however, has a fear of fire. There is a strong guard over the fire in the drawing-room at Cherkley; but, if he comes down before dinner and finds his granddaughter Jean standing near it in a fluffy dress, he will upbraid her anxiously. This fear may derive from a semi-conscious memory of an incident in his childhood: he was five years old when a house he was staying in—his mother's old home in Ontario—caught fire. The

14

incident is thus described by a Canadian journalist, Donald Leno:

As it was in the winter, it was necessary to have many stoves to heat the big house. On one extremely cold morning, one of the family went downstairs early to light the fire before the others got up. It was necessary to cut some firewood in the shed adjoining the house. While splitting kindling, a splinter flew against an oil lamp which was sitting nearby on the floor. The lamp exploded, igniting the shed; the fire spread to the house and the occupants fled in their night attire.

The fire gutted the house badly before it could be brought under control. However, the stout brick walls were left standing. After the fire, the interior was rebuilt.

Beaverbrook remembers that he was wrapped in a blanket and carried to a house across the street.

Partly because of the climate, he spends little time now in Canada. He visits New Brunswick for a few weeks in the autumn. He is often irked, when in Canada, by delay and inaudibility on the transatlantic telephone service. 'I like to get to New York,' he says. 'You've only got to pick up the telephone and you're talking to your London office.' When he is in the south of France, he is connected with the *Express* office in Fleet Street by a direct private telephone line. A call is booked for 12.30 p.m. daily. This is the climax of Beaverbrook's Riviera day. To talk to London at this time he will refuse attractive invitations to lunch in Monte Carlo or at other rich men's villas; he prefers them to come to lunch with him. He may occasionally use this telephone engagement as an excuse for such refusals. He really does not care much for going out socially; here as elsewhere, he spends much of his time telephoning or standing at his high desk dictating to a secretary or into a machine, whose discs are flown to London each day. Otherwise he seems, for half an hour or so, almost happy in the exquisite garden of the villa, planning to bring it even nearer to perfection, beheading full-blown roses and

15

storming at anyone who inadvertently treads on the mauve-blue verbena, imported by him from North Africa and now spreading all over the lawns. When the sea is really warm, he will bathe from his rocky private beach. Only in Nassau, which he finds in other respects an ideal winter resort, does he sometimes feel really cut off from his newspaper empire and the world of politics, and, consequently, bored. Not all his editors have shared his view of the desirability of close and constant contact.

He is less interested than most millionaires in the standard millionaire pleasures. He had a yacht (named, whimsically, *John Calvin*); but he owns no racehorses. For a time he did go in for racing and had a house at Newmarket (called Calvin House); but he soon fell out with the moguls of the Jockey Club. He was annoyed by what seemed to him the hypocrisy of rules, such as the rule against pulling horses, which were constantly broken with impunity. He found the company of racing people tedious. 'They know nothing about politics,' he grumbled, 'and nothing about newspapers. They know nothing about anything but racing.' So he took to arriving at race meetings after the first race and leaving before the last; and, pretty soon, he sold out. He had won a few races—none of them big races. The experience had cost him some £200,000. Since then the leading figures of the turf, such as Lord Rosebery, have not been among his closer friends. His newspapers have also campaigned consistently against the exclusion of divorcees from the Royal Enclosure at Ascot.

He no longer bothers to maintain a private aircraft: it is simpler to hire or borrow one, or even, sometimes, to fly by the ordinary public service. (From flying he got the idea of the safety seat-belt, which he has fitted in his cars.)

The toys of wealth may, indeed, seem less worth bothering about when literally everything can be bought that money can buy. Nobody, not even he, can compute precisely Beaverbrook's wealth; but he is certainly one of the richest men in the world. He has always, moreover, retained his Canadian domicile, and thus has ample dollar as well as sterling resources. In February, 1953, it was estimated by a Canadian magazine that he owned British and Canadian properties worth seventy million dollars. His personal dividend from London Express Newspaper, Ltd, for the financial year that ended on June 30th, 1953, was some £85,000.

One of the axioms by which Beaverbrook's life has been guided is that money plus brains equals power. He has, it will be agreed, enough money; he has enough of the sort of brains that ought to be needed to secure the sort of power in which alone he is interested. Why, then, is the prevailing impression derived from a few hours or days spent in his company an impression of driving restlessness, of an absolute want of serenity, of a machine that must continue to operate after its function is exhausted? Partly this may be because, after a boyhood little of which was devoted to formal education, the single-minded pursuit of worldly power has left him no time to turn aside and develop wider intellectual resources and cultural interests. Therefore, if he stopped doing the only things he knows how to do, his life and his mind would be a vacuum. (By contrast, his friend Churchill, though his academic performance in boyhood was undistinguished, read widely and deeply in early manhood and has in later life cultivated the art of painting.) A main cause of this chronic restlessness, however, may be that the axiom itself has proved fallacious. He has the money, he has the brains: where is the power? It has escaped him. He has achieved high office, but not the highest. Most men have their price, but not every man. He has failed signally to influence public opinion, among those high in the state or among ordinary citizens. The former mostly regard him as a menace; the latter buy his newspapers in millions for their entertainment value, consistently disregard their editorial advice, and think of him politically, not without the bantering affection proper to a national insti-

17   c

tution, as a comic 'character'. It is hard to find anyone who has had much to do with Beaverbrook, who will praise him without qualification. Many, especially among Conservatives of the more feudal sort, regard him with remarkably intense disapproval. To the public he is 'The Beaver'—a zoological symbol of tireless industry. Some Roman Catholic intellectuals of the school of Belloc and Chesterton lampooned him as 'Caliban'; this did not increase his affection for Roman Catholic intellectuals generally—though Mr Stanley Morison, who might be so described, is a good friend of his and Mr J. B. Morton, Belloc's devoted biographer, has been employed by him for many years as 'Beachcomber'. The late Hugh Kingsmill, more wittily, called him 'Robin Badfellow'—a malign cousin of the good goblin of ancient folklore. One of his closest friends has said: 'Everything that everyone says about Max is true—the best things and the worst things'.

His story, then, begins to take shape as a story of ultimate failure. Yet, superficially, it is a 'success story' in the grand old tradition of rugged individualism. What is behind the enigma? How did such a life begin?

CHAPTER TWO

THE TRUANT OF THE MANSE

One would be in less danger
From the wiles of the stranger
If one's own kin and kith
Were more fun to be with.

OGDEN NASH

NEW BRUNSWICK is one of the Maritime Provinces of eastern Canada. It is a land of unspoiled natural beauty, of rivers and lakes; four-fifths of it is forest. The way of life of most of its people is hard, sturdy, and simple. The shop-windows of the hilly seaport town of Saint John testify to the nearness of the United States with their neon-lit super-hamburgers and 'P-nut brittle'; but they also offer hunting licences and Grand Manan Island dulse (an edible seaweed). Save for private parties and clubs, Saint John is 'dry': when there is a dance at the Admiral Beatty Hotel, the men's wash-room is a shambles of empty hip-flask-size liquor-bottles. A local radio disc-jockey is not ashamed to announce that he cannot play a popular record that has been asked for, 'because the record is broken'. The trim white wooden churches are as demure as those of New England.

In the mighty rivers abound Atlantic silver salmon. There are speckled trout and the militant black bass, pickerel, shad and gaspereaux. The forests, rich with game, grow close about the settled areas. They are at their most flamboyant in the fall of the year, when the maple-leaves glow and the birch is yellow against the dark-green mass of spruce—or, as a native poet, Sir Charles Roberts, put it:

> When the nut-fed chipmunks romp
> Through the maples' crimson pomp,
>   And the slim viburnum flushes
> In the darkness of the swamp,

When the blueberries are dead,
When the rowan clusters red,
    And the shy bear, summer-sleekened,
In the bracken makes his bed...

There is more spruce than any other tree because it grows fast, maturing in twenty years; and timber is the primary industry of New Brunswick. Timber has one by-product of special importance: in all the main timber centres, factories have been built by the big Canadian pulp and paper-making companies.

The place-names and surnames of the United States of America emphasize the pan-European cosmopolitanism of the American melting-pot: San Francisco and Roosevelt, Los Angeles and Eisenhower, New Orleans and LaGuardia. The place-names of Canada in general and New Brunswick in particular derive, first, as do many in the United States also, from the indigenous Indian languages (Winnipeg, Toronto); secondly, from the French colonization of the sixteenth and seventeenth centuries (Montreal, Sault Ste Marie); lastly, and predominantly, from the British connexion. The rivers had their Indian names long before the settlements grew into towns, so the rivers are still called Miramichi and Mamagekel and Upsalquitch. Two of the quaintest of these names occur in some light verses by Professor De Mille:

Sweet maiden of Passamaquoddy,
    Shall we seek for communion of souls
Where the deep Mississippi meanders
    Or the distant Saskatchewan rolls?

Ah, no! In New Brunswick we'll find it—
    A sweetly sequestered nook—
Where the smooth-gliding Skookawaskooksis
Unites with the Skoodawabskook.

But it was men from England and Scotland who called the towns and villages of New Brunswick by such names as

Newcastle, Chatham, and Woodstock, Campbellton and Dalhousie. Some of the first of them were traders from New England. Then, in 1783–4, towards the end of the American War of Independence, some twelve thousand defeated Loyalists came here as refugees: this influx was decisive in the development of the character and traditions of New Brunswick. 'Just as the first British Empire in America had fallen,' writes Professor W. Stewart MacNutt, 'a second rose on its ruins. Symbolic of this was the appearance on the walls of the new Trinity Church at Saint John of the Royal Coat of Arms: it had been removed from its former place in the council chamber of the old colony of Massachusetts at Boston.' Until then, what is now New Brunswick had been part of Nova Scotia. A new province was formed; it was called after the German home of the British royal family. The seal granted to the province showed a ship sailing up a river on whose banks a settlement rose beneath pine-trees. The motto on the seal was *Spem reduxit*.

The first great timber boom in New Brunswick was a result of the Napoleonic wars, which cut the British Navy off from its usual sources of supply of pine masts in the Baltic countries. During these wars, eighty-five per cent of the people of New Brunswick lived from the timber trade; and Britain was their only market. When peace came, the British Government continued to encourage this trade by imposing prohibitive duties on timber from the Baltic. In 1831 there was an attempt in the British Parliament to restore free trade in timber. The attempt was defeated. There were great rejoicings in New Brunswick: oxen were roasted in the streets of Fredericton, effigies were burned of the English noblemen who had sought to help the Baltic foreigners at the expense of their kinsmen in New Brunswick.

Trade prospered; the population grew. Gangs of Irishmen came to fell millions of trees: the gang bosses, and the traders who controlled them, were mostly Scots.

A bronze model of a full-rigged sailing-ship stands on a shaft of sandstone in a park in the town of Newcastle, by the Miramichi[1] river. It is a memorial to the early settlers, and the names inscribed on it indicate clearly enough their original homelands. The inscription runs:

MIRAMICHI

From Doon and Shannon
from Clyde and Dee
they spread their poverty
over the rich acres
they sowed their children
broadcast upon the
untested soil
Davidson
Peabody
Rankin
Cunard
Harkins
Bishop Rogers
Mitchell
Snowball
Burchill
Hutchison
Sinclair
Tweedie
O'Brien.

These names are English and Scottish and Irish: there is not a Latin or Scandinavian or German or Polish name among them.

Newcastle is a small town, straggling up a hill, one of those towns where everybody knows everybody and men stand in the streets to gossip, eyeing strangers curiously. It is a quiet place: its great lumbering days are over. Yet it is not stagnant. Its business men have the North American *élan*. In 1943 there

[1] Pronounced Mirrami-*shee*.

were 797 telephones in Newcastle: in 1953 there were 2213. It maintains a lively local newspaper, the *North Shore Leader*, in which national and provincial advertisers find it worth while to buy space.

An earlier Newcastle newspaper bore a similar name. On November 23rd, 1893, appeared the first issue of *The Leader*, with the proud slogan: 'We Lead, Let Those Follow Who Can'. Its first editorial was commendably frank. '*The Leader*,' it said, 'is not as good as may be expected.' However, it ran a prize essay competition. The essays were to be on New-castle's industries; the prizes were (1) 'a pair of genuine Acme skates', (2) 'a beautiful pearl handle pocket-knife'. The feature called Miscellany contained this series of similitudes: 'A good collector must be patient as a post, cheerful as a duck, sociable as a flea, bold as a lion, cunning as a fox, weather-proof as rubber, and as watchful as a sparrow hawk'. There was also an item which might have qualified, at a later date, for inclusion in the *New Yorker*'s most-fascinating-news-story-of-the-week department. It read, *in toto*: 'A thief of the worst type stole a hat the other night'. The last item in the paper showed even sharper outspokenness: 'There is in Grade 8 a little cur who cannot take a hint. He is becoming a nuisance to one and all.'

In the second issue of *The Leader*, dated November 30th, 1893, the serial story ('Climbing the Heights', by G. T. Marquis), which had begun in the first issue, was continued (in mid-sentence). The editor regretted the spoliation by seventeenth-century Calvinists of St Andrew's Cathedral in Scotland. A cold winter was foretold, because the husks on the corn were thicker than usual, 'the hog's melt runs jagged instead of smooth', squirrel and chipmunk were accumulating 'prodigious stores' of nuts, and green frogs were changing skin and seeking winter quarters.

The third issue of *The Leader*, dated December 9th, 1893, was notable for an editorial severely deploring newspaper exploitation of murders and other crimes of violence: 'We hardly like to see columns filled with accounts of infamy at police courts'. It is clear also that the controversial nature of some personal comments in the earlier issues had led to recriminations of a kind still familiar to journalists the world over. For the editor printed this bitter reflection: 'Newspaper editing is a very funny business. If you give a man a puff he never sees it; but let one line against him appear and he sees it before the paper is off the press; and while he would not have time to stop on the street and say "thank you", he has time to run all over town to denigrate the editor who seeks to print all the news.'

Alas for enterprise! This third issue of *The Leader* was also its last. The reasons given for its suspension are unusual ones; but they were evidently cogent. The sad event was thus announced: 'Owing to the large number of Christmas advertisments [*sic*] and the Supplement to the Advocate, the publication of this paper will be discontinued for a time'.

In fact, that paper never again went to press; and twenty-two years passed before its publisher and editor risked his money in the newspaper business again. He signed this notice of suspension as the paper's 'manager'. His signature was W. Max Aitken.

The child is father of the man. It may amuse present-day colleagues of Lord Beaverbrook to detect in embryonic form in this journalistic venture, undertaken when he was fourteen years old, some of the qualities characteristic of the immense enterprises of his maturity. In the weather forecast there is the exact observation of detail now found in the best of the reporting published under his aegis. In the condemnation of sensationalism there is the still-perceptible streak of puritanism: it would indeed be something of an exaggeration to say that the *Express* newspapers had ever begrudged space to a really juicy murder, but at least they pride themselves, with justification, on excluding the pornography fashionable in

24

other mass-circulation newspapers. There is, above all, the brashness, the boastfulness, the quick resentment, the direct personal attacks on doubtless identifiable citizens. Those who know Beaverbrook will be able almost to hear his very accents in that paragraph on the 'very funny business' of newspaper editing: they will see him raise his hand and beat time to the slow, emphatic monosyllables, '*but—let—one—line . . .*' It must have been a distinct relief to some of the public men and some of the schoolboys of Newcastle when *The Leader* went out of publication; just as the demise of the *Express* newspapers of today—an unthinkable event—would be an occasion of joy to the victims of their satire.

Newcastle was Beaverbrook's boyhood home from the age of eleven months: he often tells people there how sorry he is that he was not actually born there. He was born (on May 25th, 1879) at Maple, Ontario. He still occasionally visits his birthplace and the graveyard there in which many of his folk are buried; but he does so almost by stealth, and does not care to be involved in local affairs or acquaintanceships: his filial *pietas*, his nostalgia, his active beneficence are all concentrated in New Brunswick. Sometimes, if friends from England are staying with him in Toronto, he will invite them to come driving with him. It is not until they are nearly at Maple that he tells them where he is taking them. It is a sunny morning. He sets off in high good humour, singing, maybe, one of the songs of his boyhood:

> Down at the Wongan
> Just across the street
> From Gifford's Ferry,
> The factory boys meet,
> Waiting for Johnnie
> To come down and pay—
> Down comes old Matthew:
> 'No pay to-day!'

He roars the last line at the top of his voice, chuckling and repeating it with a relish that seems almost malicious. A few minutes later, his mood of bonhomie is beginning to evaporate. The sky is overclouded. His chronic restlessness is at him again. Perhaps, if an *Angst* so profound could be expressed in words, he would cry, like the narrator in Mr Eliot's savage parody of Marvell:

> But at my back in a cold blast I hear
> The rattle of the bones, and chuckle spread from ear to ear...

One of the saddest remarks that Beaverbrook has ever been known to make was on such an occasion. 'I enjoy the first five minutes of a journey,' he confessed. 'Then I start to get bored.' He does not suffer boredom passively: the choice by the chauffeur of an unexpected route may excite prolonged and apocalyptic remonstrances. Here as elsewhere, there are letters and clippings to be dealt with, and a secretary to take down enigmatic memoranda to editors. His spirit lightens again as the car reaches the open country. These rich, rolling, civilized Ontario farmlands are very different from the primitive wildness of New Brunswick. 'The countryside here,' he will say, 'is the heart of Canada and the explanation of Canada . . . Look at those barns! Aren't they huge? In splendid order, too. That's the way to tell a country, by its barns . . .' But it is New Brunswick whose spell is laid on him for ever—the whole province and, in particular, the town of Newcastle and the great Miramichi river. 'The river has me in bondage,' he says, with deep emotion—adding, 'I was born by it.' It is one of those historically inaccurate statements which are yet, poetically, true.[1]

[1] It was also made legally true, in 1954, by a legislative process surely unique in the history of the parliaments of the Commonwealth: no doubt to ease the embarrassment caused by the resignation referred to on pp. 59–60, the New Brunswick Legislative Assembly passed a special Act to Appoint Lord Beaverbrook Honorary Chancellor of the University of New Brunswick; and the second clause of the preamble to the Bill (which was not amended) contained the words, 'AND WHEREAS the said Lord Beaverbrook is a distinguished citizen of Canada [and] *a native son of New Brunswick* . . .' As is constitutionally proper, the Royal Assent to this unusual measure was given without a flicker of surprise or murmur of dissent.

Though Beaverbrook is often spoken of, and has spoken of himself, as a man of 'humble origins', and this is, in a sense, correct, the course of his life has not taken him, as it were, from log cabin to White House. It has taken him, rather, from something a good deal better than a log cabin to just short of the White House. His background was not proletarian. Indeed, in the modest society of Newcastle, New Brunswick, his parents were leading figures. His father—who had emigrated from Scotland in 1864—was a Presbyterian minister; the ornate Victorian Manse in which the young Max Aitken was brought up is still one of the most imposing houses in the town, and must have seemed even more so to the simple lumbermen of the last century.

The Revd William Aitken was a formidable man of God. He died in 1913, but the older people in Newcastle still recall vividly his patriarchal demeanour: he had a long white beard and, during service, wore a full-sleeved gown and black gloves (which he took off ceremoniously after the second hymn). Prayer recited by him is described as 'a very dignified conversation with the Lord'. He was a strong preacher on the eternal damnation of sinners; and sometimes also delivered anti-Catholic sermons (once, perhaps deliberately, when one of his daughters was in church with a Roman Catholic boy friend, the back of whose neck grew redder as the majestic denunciations rolled on).

When he was called to Newcastle from Ontario in 1880, he was forty-six years old and had five children, of whom Max was the youngest. Five more were born at Newcastle; one of these died in infancy. So it was in the rough-and-tumble democracy of a large family that Max Aitken grew up—a process popularly supposed to 'knock the nonsense out of' any children too lavishly endowed with original sin or anti-social appetites. So far as can be judged from the fragmentary reminiscences of surviving members and friends of the family —and hindsight is apt, in such cases, to bring to memory mainly those details which fit into an accepted portrait—the process was not successful in this case: Max was not a model citizen of the nursery. He is remembered as a rebel, a quarrelsome individualist, a lone wolf. He would sometimes go off by himself for long periods of brooding or planning. Privacy is not easily come by in a household with nine children: Max would go to the woods or the river. He found his closest companions, too, outside his own family; he seldom confided in his brothers and sisters. They may, indeed, have sometimes found him as trying a companion as the denizens of the Carlton Club and the Conservative Central Office were to find him half a century later.

A curious minor flash is that, in church, Max would often refuse to sit in the privileged gentility of the Manse family pew. Christians who were not of the Presbyterian elect, such as Baptists, were not expected to sit in the main body of the church. They were relegated to the gallery. Here, too, was often to be found Max—to the embarrassment and annoyance of his elders, it may be surmised—his round, wide-mouthed face peering down, gargoyle-wise, over the varnished pine guard-rail, or (more disconcertingly still to parents with a position to keep up) vanishing altogether for a few moments if some nefarious plot were hatching; though he went in too much awe of his father ever to attempt in church any tricks with the patent, improved pin-trap with which he used, in school, to torture the more studious boys and those disinclined to join conspiracies against the teachers. He would often sit up in the gallery with a coloured boy who was among his closer cronies.

At home, Mr Aitken seems to have been almost as numinous as in the pulpit. He was at heart a kindly man, but he seemed to his children as remote from their everyday pleasures and tragedies as the Old Testament deity on whose behalf he thundered each sabbath-day. When school-friends were visiting them, a hush would fall if the study-door opened

28

and the tall, bearded figure were seen pacing past. If, on such an occasion, he caught sight of his daughters and their friends, he would say 'Ha ha, little girls' in a preoccupied manner, and proceed without further comment on his stately way. Some of his rare hours of relaxation with them were at the chess-table: one at least of his sons—Traven Aitken—was expected to play chess with him from the age of seven.

As happened in such Victorian families, this heavy father may well have been, after his austere and unobtrusive fashion, more observant and affectionate than his children realized at the time. Some years later he wrote a letter which shows that he had formed a shrewd assessment of his troublesome son's tastes and gifts. A friend had suggested that Max, then eighteen, should be sent to college. Mr Aitken replied that, after consideration, he had formed the conclusion that Max would not make a satisfactory student: 'His nature . . . is too eager to grasp the practical. And now he has got a taste of business and a liking for the business intercourse of the world, I believe that he could no more set himself down to a course of theoretical study than he could take (or rather, think of taking) a journey to the Moon. He would be no good at College now; in fact, he would be sure to learn indolent habits and suffer harm.'

At Newcastle the standard of academic learning was not advanced. Such as it was, Max Aitken hardly took full advantage of it. He was sent when he was five years old to the wooden public school, grandly called Harkins Academy, and there became remarkable chiefly for his ingenuity in mischief and his prowess as a fighter. He was a bold rather than a good fighter. Some said he was a dirty fighter. 'You had to be,' he explains. 'They formed a ring round the fight: if you had the crowd rooting against you, you began to take liberties.' Such episodes would be followed by solemn remonstrances in the study at the Manse. He was also a frequent, if seasonal, truant. 'In winter I attended school,' he has written, 'because it was warm inside. In summer I spent my time in the woods, because it was warm outside.' The then Principal of Harkins Academy, Dr Philip Cox, many years later remembered Max, at eight or nine years old, as 'a fair-haired, bright, interesting lad, of a quick, nervous turn of mind, a little different from any of his fellow-pupils'. He added: 'Simply because of his inability to concentrate, I never believed that he would make any great success of his life'. Few would now be found to question the success, by the world's standards, of Beaverbrook's life; yet, curiously, the 'inability to concentrate' is still present in the form of that chronic restlessness already noted. It is perhaps part of the recipe for success in popular journalism, that volatile medium.

A few illustrative anecdotes of school-days survive. On their way home from school one day, Max and two other boys were arguing about the omnipotence of God. Max insisted that God could do anything. One of the other boys silenced him, for once, by retorting: 'He couldn't make your mouth any bigger without removing your ears!'

On another occasion a woman friend of the Aitkens found him and another boy just about to fight. Max had put down his skates and was squaring up. She asked what was wrong. 'He called me moccasin-mouth,' said Max. He may have been sensitive to such comments on his physical appearance. It is possible, however, that the insult was less a cause of thin-skinned resentment than a welcome pretext for the fight.

If 'theoretical study' was never much in his line, in the Manse at least there was little chance of his acquiring those 'indolent habits' which his father feared. Even though there was usually a maid to help, there was plenty of work for the children and their harassed mother to do in so crowded a household, living on a minister's stipend of some £300. 'There were too many of us,' Beaverbrook recalls. 'There was not enough money to go round.' There was the cow to milk, potatoes to be hoed in the glebe, wood to be sawn, water to be hoisted from the well. For there were, of course, no public systems of water and sewerage in Newcastle, New Brunswick, in the eighties. There was no WC, even in the grandest houses in the place: by day or by night 'you had to trail through the snow to the backhouse over yonder'. On the children's bath-nights, water for the tin tub would be heated on a wood-burning stove. Sometimes the boy, sick of household chores, would hide in the barn-loft under the hay, reading the novels of Sir Walter Scott or Robert Louis Stevenson or Captain Mayne Reid. (He still has a copy of Reid's *Afloat in the Forest; or, A Voyage*, inscribed in a spidery copperplate hand 'Christmas, 1893. W. Max Aitken, the Manse'.) Sometimes, in the winter, he would go off with the neighbours (not with his brothers) to the local skating-rink, where there was a band-night once a week; the subscription was a dollar a season. In the summer he swam often in the river. Sometimes he would go for long walks with a kindly, patient Roman Catholic priest, Father Dixon. (There was a convent next door to the Manse, and Max was once spanked publicly by his mother for throwing stones at one of the nuns.) The Revd William Aitken, who was himself on fairly good terms with the priest, may or may not have approved of this friendship.

In any case, like another Victorian father, the Revd Theobald Pontifex in *The Way of All Flesh*, Mr Aitken seems to have failed signally to instil a sense of sin into his son Max. Beaverbrook is apt to speak with pride of his knowledge of the Bible, especially the Old Testament; and it is held in awe by his employees. He deserves, in fact, little credit for it: he got to know the Bible in childhood as a parrot might have, through the incessant, repetitive recital of it, in his home and at the services that he was obliged to attend. (His only escape from it, in church, was when he had to pump the organ: here, during the long stretches of sonorous prose, when no psalm was being sung, he could enjoy, unseen by the severe eye of his father, his favourite novels of romantic adventure.)

31

Never was the sense of sin less present in his heart than when he roamed the banks of the great river. He learned to become a good fisherman—of course by poaching, as heinous an offence to the respectable citizens of New Brunswick as to their property-revering ancestors in Scotland. More than a generation earlier, another Presbyterian minister, the Revd W. Christopher Atkinson, had written[1] of a New Brunswick town: 'There is a sort of *non-chalance* pervading the labouring classes of society in this place that is quite novel and unpleasant to those who have enjoyed the benefit of the conventional regulations that abound in the Mother Country'. It is to be feared that the Revd William Aitken's disappointing son—dishevelled of hair, in worn-and-torn clothes—was already keeping disreputable company, perhaps even with men of 'the labouring classes'. It is certain that, from whatever example, he was acquiring nonchalance—a hard-shell, rough-edged nonchalance that was never to leave him. So he went on his poaching exploits, and was not perturbed when keepers threw stones and shouted angrily at him or, if they could get near enough unseen, sent him home with a slap in the face or a kick on the behind. But it was home that a boy of eleven or twelve still had to go to each night—home, and the domestic chores, and the brooding shadow of Jehovah's vice-regent shut in his study.

According to some modern schools of psychology, abnormally intense activity in adult life—activity of any kind, in the pursuit of gain or the collection of antiques, in social frivolity, in public business—is a compensation for childhood deprivation. Beaverbrook's career might seem, in the light of this theory, a classic case of over-compensation. But the Freudian analyst would not be able to diagnose an Oedipus complex, for an element considered essential to the formation of such a complex is absent from this case-history: the formidable father

[1] In his *Historical and Statistical Account of New Brunswick, British North America, with Advice to Emigrants*, 3rd Edition, 1844.

1a The Old Manse, Newcastle: boyhood home

1b 'The truant'

2 Winter in Newcastle: the young Max Aitken (second from the left)

is there, indeed, but where is the too-doting mother to whose apron-strings the wayward son is tied? The evidence indicates, on the contrary, that, of the two parents, Mrs Aitken was the stricter disciplinarian. It was she, not her husband, who used to beat Max after his frequent scrapes. A neighbour, Mrs Charles Sargeant, who was still living in Newcastle recently, stated some time ago that she remembered seeing Max 'quite often with his hand in front of his face, sobbing after being punished by his mother'.

Such treatment was harsh, by present-day standards, and a modern child-welfare expert might find in it an explanation of the later development of the boy so treated, and might further surmise that 'but for the grace of God', or a series of strokes of luck, or a powerful endowment of native cunning, or a mixture of all three, such a boy might easily have become what is now called a juvenile delinquent and so have embarked on a rake's progress to the usual felon's doom. Yet it is fair to Mrs Aitken to recall that 'a good thrashing' was the conventional nineteenth-century prescription for 'bad boys'; and there are many who testify that she had not only a strong but, in some ways, an agreeable character. She had 'great dignity and self-possession'. She was also less puritanical than most Presbyterians of that time. Card-playing, indeed, was not allowed at the Manse, though the Aitken children were allowed to play cards at other people's houses. (Characteristically, Max devised a game with home-made cards that looked innocent but differed little in practice from the forbidden whist.) But on occasion the Minister would serve whisky to friends visiting him, and it was Mrs Aitken herself who would often encourage her children and their friends to roll back the rug and spend a few hours dancing; and when the church trustees complained of this unseemly indulgence, she immediately sent out formal invitations to a much larger dance.

Possibly this independence of character, this refusal to be

intimidated by the sanctimonious bureaucrats on whom, after all, her husband depended for his stipend, is attributable in part to the fact that Mrs Aitken, who came of a well-to-do Ontario farming family, had some modest means of her own. Independence of mind was allied in her with organizing ability. She is spoken of as having been 'a wonderful manager'. So she must indeed have been in the home; but it is to her work for the church, and in the leadership of the community generally, that this tribute is especially paid. Mr Aitken is already seen in the character of an unworldly, scholarly recluse: his wife had outstanding executive skill, and the incidental activities of the church would not have flourished as they did if it had not been for her. She 'held the congregation together'; there would be large garden-parties on the lawn in front of the Manse, and high teas for smaller groups of the faithful. She baked her own bread. She liked flowers and flowering shrubs, and planted many about the Manse. One of her daughters once told a neighbour: 'We are all terrified of mother'. A significant fragment of conversation survives from a time, many years later, when her son Max had become rich and famous and had just been elected a Member of Parliament in London. A friend said to her: 'You must be proud of your son'. With her usual unruffled coolness, Mrs Aitken replied: 'Which son? I have several'. Her grandchildren, however, have gentler recollections of her: once, when two of them had borrowed a boat without leave, and lost the oars, she gave them a few dollars to buy new oars.

It would be fascinating to try to trace in the life and character of Beaverbrook—financial genius, newspaper impresario, tyrannical yet capriciously generous employer, maker and destroyer of Prime Ministers, political misfit, perennial poacher, dynamic producer of aircraft—elements derived from his childhood in the Manse at Newcastle. Conflicting elements can be merged in such a character: resentment against restrictive authority can provide the driving force, yet from that same authority can be inherited or learned the techniques of organization and of power. Superficially regarded, even if money was short, this could have been a happy childhood. Many such childhoods, in big, turbulent, hard-up, parsonage families, have been happy. In his old age there are no golden memories of the Manse for the boy who escaped from it whenever he could, and for good as soon as he could. Perhaps, somehow, in that teeming, busy household, governed by the aloof patriarch of pulpit and study and the dominant mother with the talent for organizing and the ready stick, love was crowded out. Perhaps the boy's whole subsequent career could be interpreted as a pursuit of the love of which he was deprived in those infant years when love is most needed—a quest for free, unmotivated, trustful love, a quest that becomes ever more frantic as the certainty grows that it will fail because such love cannot be got by force or by purchase. Power, particularly power over people, remains elusive. It is galling to the lords of this world to apprehend that, at the last, the still small voice will win.

> Never seek to tell thy love
>   Love that never told can be,
> For the gentle wind doth move
>   Silently, invisibly.
>
> I told my love, I told my love,
>   I told her all my heart:
> Trembling, cold, in ghastly fear,
>   Ah! she did depart.
>
> Soon as she was gone from me
>   A traveller came by
> Silently, invisibly—
>   He took her with a sigh.

Such reflections are necessarily so speculative as to be unprofitable. All that can and need be said with certainty, in plain words, is that Beaverbrook was convinced of the importance of money by the shortage of it at home, and that the circumstances of life at the Manse instilled in him a strong impulse to get out and earn as much of it as he could. This he undoubtedly did.

CHAPTER THREE

DEDICATION TO MAMMON

How pleasant it is to have money, Heigh-ho,
How pleasant it is to have money . . .
ARTHUR HUGH CLOUGH

HE STARTED early. He was only a small boy, twelve years of age, when he first sold newspapers on the streets. It is not a very striking coincidence that his later life also should have been devoted to the selling of newspapers: thousands of other schoolboys on both sides of the Atlantic have done this sort of job out of school hours. Few of them, however, can have applied themselves to it so scientifically as Max Aitken. He was always, alertly, on the make. Instead of selling all the papers himself, he employed other boys to act as sub-agents, and thus disposed of the papers more quickly and distributed them more widely through the town. (Later, when he produced his own *Leader*, he and one other boy, Jim Whalen, distributed the first issue between them. A customer on Jim's route, admiring their enterprise, gave Jim twenty-five cents. When the second issue came out, Max switched the routes.)

He was at school until he was fourteen years old; but when he was twelve, besides supervising the newspaper rounds, he started work in a drug-store (E. D. Street's). The worst part of this job, especially in the harsh Canadian winter, was that he had to be up in the mornings to collect the shop-key from the head clerk's house in time to open the shop at seven o'clock. Then he would sweep the floor, wash medicine-bottles, and go off to school (or on one of his truant jaunts). After school he would go back to the shop and work behind the counter, selling goods till ten or eleven o'clock at night. In those days, as now, the drug-store in North America was a far more diverse emporium, and far more of a social institution, than an English chemist's shop: to a quick-witted boy of twelve, the conversation of the loafers who hung around the store was of absorbing interest. He was acquiring knowledge and experience nightly—and, no doubt, a lot of backwoodsmen's prejudices, too, as well as their folklore and their songs. He did not mind the late hours—or the fact that, at first, his pay for all this work was only a dollar a week.

For both his out-of-school jobs, he badly needed a bicycle. His father either could not afford to buy him one or thought it an unnecessary luxury. A firm of soap-makers was offering bicycles 'free' in exchange for wrappers from the soap-tablets. Somehow, Max borrowed enough money to buy several cases of soap wholesale. He then hawked the soap from door to door at cost price—undercutting the local retailers—on condition that the buyers gave him the wrappers. Soon he had sold enough soap, and collected enough wrappers, to repay his debt and get the bicycle.

A curious accident, that might have been fatal, occurred when he was fourteen. He fell and was run over by a mowing-machine: the wheel went over his head. He says, with a chuckle, 'I was much cleverer after that'.

Soon after he left school—at about the time of the production of the short-lived *Leader*—his parents sent him to be examined for a job at the local bank. One of his elder brothers was already employed there as a clerk: such employment was eminently respectable; even, in Newcastle, fashionable. Had Max Aitken secured the job, he might well have risen to be a bank-manager. Fortunately or unfortunately for the world, he knew instinctively that a bank was no place for one of his temperament: he would have been stifled by the prim correctness of the atmosphere, the narrow routine of the work. He therefore did the most sensible thing possible: he pleased his parents by agreeing to undergo the examination—and then took good care not to pass it. Perhaps the rebel was already learning tactics.

Meanwhile, newspapers still provided the source of such income as he had. He was the sole vendor in Newcastle of two Saint John newspapers, the *Sun* and the *Telegraph*; he delivered them from shop to shop. He also became the *Sun*'s local correspondent, paid exiguously on a lineage basis. The rate was a dollar a column: the correspondent pasted his stories on a column-sized strip of paper; when it was full, he collected his dollar. 'You always pasted with great care,' he has recalled.

Whether because he was precociously intelligent (though not in an academic sense), or because, as has been suggested, he was at odds with many of his schoolfellows and not particularly intimate with his brothers, a noticeable fact in Beaverbrook's early life is that he was accustomed to the company of men older than himself. There was the kindly priest, Father Dixon. There were the customers in the drug-store. His great hero was a lumberman, Edward Sinclair by name, with whom he loved to go camping and from whom he learned much of the lore of the forest. Sinclair's name is kept alive at Newcastle: the skating-rink that Beaverbrook gave to the town in 1951 is called the Sinclair Rink. This rink, with an ice surface 190 feet by 85 feet, lit by a hundred and five 500-watt lamps, would suit a town far bigger than Newcastle; it may even be uneconomically large. The reason for this is typical: the rink was originally intended, and designed, for another place; there was a dispute about the site; Beaverbrook could not get quick agreement; the rink went to Newcastle.

Beaverbrook has cause to be grateful to the memory of Edward Sinclair: as much as any man, he helped to give him a definite start in his career. It was in 1896, when Max Aitken was seventeen years old, that he first took a regular office job, as student-clerk in a law office at Chatham, just across the river from Newcastle; and Sinclair paid four dollars a month towards the cost of this apprenticeship.

39

He was no better-liked by most of the other lads of his age in Chatham than he had been at school. What was probably defensiveness manifested itself as an aggressive pushfulness. He wanted to join a club, the Cypress Club; a majority of the members blackballed him. Then a friend of his, Albert McLennan, became president of the club. He urged the members to let Max in. They were still against it, saying that 'he would want to run the whole show'. McLennan promised that he would keep Max under control: they agreed, reluctantly, not to blackball him again. Within a few weeks of joining the club, Max decided that a rack for newspapers was needed in the reading-room. Without consulting anyone, he ordered a rack from Saint John—and then presented a bill for it, for six dollars, at a club meeting. This *gaucherie* excited universal antagonism: his few friends were as furious with him as his many enemies. He showed no dismay: he would pay the bill himself, he said. The vote of censure was changed to a vote of thanks: Max Aitken enjoyed his first taste of the pleasure of being a public benefactor—and, it may be, a faint intimation of the mysterious effect of money on human attitudes and relations. Albert McLennan was never able to find out where he got the six dollars from. 'The poor little beggar hadn't a damn cent,' he said afterwards.

Though he tried hard and did fairly well in his law preliminaries, the law was not to provide a permanent career for Max, any more than a bank could have; but his office job in Chatham brought him under one of the formative influences of his life. The law firm was that of Messrs Tweedie and Bennett; and a partner in it was Richard Bedford Bennett, then a young ex-school-teacher—only eight years older than his new clerk —but destined to become Prime Minister of Canada.

A year or two later Bennett left New Brunswick and went to Calgary, Alberta; and Max, after a lonely and undistinguished year in law school at Saint John—a year in which, however, he 'began to feel conscious of an inner strength'—

followed Bennett to Calgary. At Calgary he lived cheaply in one room. He scraped a living by selling insurance. He and another youth, Jack Maclean, borrowed the money to set up a bowling-alley. They charged the customers twenty-five cents—but themselves challenged them to bowl, and made them pay only if they lost. The partners became so proficient that the customers always paid. In due course the alley was sold: Max moved to Edmonton, and there engaged in his first small, but real, business venture—collecting and delivering cargoes of meat, whose destination was the romantically named Crow's Nest Pass.

It is clearly Bennett who first turned Max Aitken's thoughts towards politics—and not only his thoughts, for, as has been indicated, the boy was no theorist. His first practical experience of politics was in Bennett's first election campaign, in 1898, which he helped to run. Bennett was standing for the Legislative Assembly of the North-West Territories, as a somewhat independent Conservative. He had, on the whole, the support of the drink trade: it was Max Aitken's special job to mobilize that support effectively. John Donahue, the leading man in the drink trade, was himself a teetotaller. 'He came along nicely under my arguments,' recalls Beaverbrook.

From Alberta, after this glimpse of public life in the raw, he went east again, as an insurance company's inspector in the Maritime Provinces. He was now twenty years old, and had already learned much of the pleasures and evils of the world, much that had not been within the experience of the children of the Manse. He was developing a good head for business; he was as alert and spry as ever, and more nearly popular, probably, than he had ever been before; but his life was neither orderly nor diligent. He stayed up late at night, drank fairly heavily, gambled away much of what little he earned.

Hangover remorse rarely hardens into real amendment of life. In this case, extraordinarily, it did. On his twenty-first

41

birthday, after a late and rough coming-of-age celebration on the previous night, Max Aitken went out fishing in the lake at Truro, Nova Scotia. He was alone, and he felt far from well; and the fish would not bite. He seems at this moment to have experienced a conversion which (though somewhat different in kind) was as sudden, as blindingly intense, and as lasting in its effect on him as those of Saul of Tarsus and John Wesley. Such comparisons may seem far-fetched. Beaverbrook himself has resorted to them. 'Like Saint Paul,' he has recalled, 'I said, "Hell, I've got enough of this."' His life was 'the expense of spirit in a waste of shame'. He saw that there was no future in it. He took, then and there, a decision to work hard and to save money. He may have resolved at the same time, or perhaps a little later, that he would actually be a millionaire: even in the fabulous climax of the gold rush, few such resolutions can have been fulfilled more quickly.

This was the psychological and practical turning-point in Max Aitken's life. From now on he concentrated with de-monic energy on the pursuit of material success. He managed to attach himself to John F. Stairs, of Halifax, the leading industrialist and financier in eastern Canada. The former ne'er-do-well became a sober young business man, selling stocks and bonds in the steel company of which Stairs was president, making money quickly and saving it, attracting attention wherever he went. It became evident that his special gift was persuasiveness: staid, older business men found his enthusiasm infectious and his fiery, imaginative sales-patter irresistible. His chief notion was the simple but, at that time, immensely profitable one of promoting mergers; his special fancy was for the amalgamation of banks. In 1902, when he was twenty-two years old, he formed a finance company, the better to pursue these ideals: his fellow-shareholders in it were the four principal older capitalists of Halifax. They had plenty of money: he had the flair, the knowledge of 'values'.

In telling the story of this venture, he says 'I was the boss'. There is no immodesty in the claim; it is true. There is an almost religious conviction, too, in his advice to young men engaged in making their first fifty thousand dollars: 'You have to feel those early deals right down to the pit of the stomach if you're going to be a great man of business'.

His first serious crisis faced him only three years after the start of this enterprise. His principal associate and patron, Stairs, died of a heart attack. Aitken and his partners were left holding large blocks of shares in a bank; the position was less sound than they had thought. A powerful rival said to Aitken: 'You're finished now'. They went to the Bank of Montreal, and saw the General Manager, Sir Edward Clouston. There was a long and inconclusive conversation: no doubt Clouston was as cautious as serious bankers are apt to be with up-and-coming speculators. They left his office anxiously: nothing had been arranged. Then Clouston rang for his secretary and said: 'Send me back the little fellow with the big head'. The 'little fellow' went back. A lot of money was made by all concerned.

Next year Aitken was twenty-six years old. The Montreal newspapers were beginning to write of him as a 'financial wizard'. So, on the principle that 'if you want to make money, you must go where the money is', he moved to Montreal. As also happens, he was being spoken of as an 'eligible bachelor'. A wise friend told him: 'You'll never really get confidence in yourself until you're anchored'. He married Miss Gladys Drury, the eighteen-year-old daughter of a well-known New Brunswick military family, members of the 'aristocracy of the East'. He bought many properties, including house property; but he and his bride lived in a rented house.

By this time he was approaching dollar-millionaire status. He reached it soon after his wedding—five years after the spiritual crisis during the fishing expedition on his twenty-first birthday. ('I always said I was going for a million,' he has boasted. 'When I got it I raised my sights and went for five millions.') His fortune amounted to some seven hundred thousand dollars, made as a promoter by the selling of bonds. He did not hesitate to spend more than half of it—four hundred and fifty thousand dollars—in buying control of the solid, substantial, old-fashioned Montreal Trust Company. His delight in this coup (which brought him a net profit of three hundred thousand dollars and so just increased his wealth to the required million) was intensified by the recollection of his first approach to the directors of the company: they had been foolish enough to refer him, in a rather offhand way, to a junior manager.

He stayed in Montreal for three years. In that time he created every big trust that was created then in Canada. All those that he created still exist: not one of them has failed. When he is in one of his impish moods, this arch-propagandist of free, competitive enterprise will refer to them, with a nasal cackle of mirth, as 'monuments to the iniquity of trustification'. Banking, transport, steel, hydro-electric power, coal—all the great basic industries now considered, not only by Socialists, apt for public ownership—were involved in these remarkable feats of organization. It was through the formation of the Steel Company of Canada that he actually made most money (and found himself most acutely in conflict with the powerful Canadian Pacific Railway); but the most celebrated, or notorious, of all these deals was the amalgamation of thirteen separate cement companies into one gigantic monopoly, the Canada Cement Company. He bought these companies for sixteen-and-a-half million dollars. He sold them for twenty-nine million dollars. As a result of this merger, according to the *Grain Growers' Guide*, 'the price of cement at factories instantly jumped . . . from $1 to $1.50 per barrel'. Aitken's personal profit on this deal is believed to have been little more than five million dollars; but even in a continent already accustomed to get-rich-quick millionaires and their sensational utilization of the market, this transaction caused an uproar. Sir Sandford Fleming, the honorary president or figurehead of Aitken's purchasing company, resigned and himself demanded a government inquiry. When a question was asked in the Dominion Parliament, urging such an investigation, the Prime Minister, Sir Wilfrid Laurier, gravely advised those aggrieved to seek their remedy in the courts. The newspapers attacked Aitken violently as a young upstart who had been guilty of deals very near to the edge of illegality. He learned then—as so many controversial figures in public life have learned since then, in their turn, from his newspapers—what it feels like to be pilloried day after day in front-page news-stories and in editorials.

A Canadian journalist, Frank Rasky, writing in *New Liberty* in February, 1953, reports the following exchange of question and answer in an interview with Beaverbrook:

'How valid were the criticisms aimed at you?' I asked the Beaver.

'Well,' he said amusedly, 'the newspapers contended I'd done three bad things. One, put a cartel control over cement. Two, raised the price of cement. Three, that I'd made too much money.'

'And were those allegations accurate?'

'No. 1 was right—we did control cement. No. 2 was wrong—the price of cement went down. And about No. 3 . . . I did not make an excessive profit.'

As thus summarized by Beaverbrook, only one of the three charges, the second, is factually in dispute. Evidence of an immediate sharp increase in the price of cement has been quoted already; no doubt there were fluctuations later. On the third charge, the level at which profits become excessive is a matter of opinion, not of fact: there was no excess profits tax in Canada half-a-century ago. On the first charge, the fact is admitted: the commercial morality and social desirability of the transaction is, again, a matter of opinion. Responsible

opinion in Canada at the time, and for many years afterwards, was emphatic in its condemnation. A year or two later,
when Aitken had left Canada, his name was included in
King George V's Coronation honours list: he was awarded a
knighthood.[1] On July 4th, 1911, the *Toronto Globe* used this
event as the occasion of a severe retrospective survey of the
epidemic of mergers. Its editorial is worth quoting at length:

> The inclusion in the list of Canadians recently honoured by
> the King of the most active and daring of the promoters who
> during the past three years have made Canada familiar with
> trusts and mergers has raised in a quite striking form the whole
> question of the relations of the State to these vast consolidations
> of industrial enterprise. Everywhere people are asking what
> Sir Max Aitken has done or what hidden and mysterious power
> he wields that he should be selected for the honour of Knight-
> hood, while dozens of Canadians who have become eminent in
> the service of the people and the Sovereign are passed by. The
> Press, in seeking an answer to that question, has been led to a
> general discussion of the entire subject of 'high finance' that has
> been most illuminating. There is a general demand for inquiry
> into the circumstances under which mergers have been launched
> in Canada during the past three years with capital to the amount
> of not less than two hundred millions of dollars, much of which
> is quite frankly water.
>
> The Knighting of Sir Max Aitken was probably not inspired
> by anyone in Canada. We should be greatly surprised to learn
> that the Government of Sir Wilfrid Laurier had anything to do
> with it... But no matter how he entered, his presence has raised
> in Canada an issue of the first magnitude. What Sir Sandford
> Fleming's letter demanding inquiry by Parliament into the
> circumstances attending the promotion of the Cement Merger

[1] He had just been offered this honour, greatly to his delight, when F. E.
Smith, walking with him on Constitution Hill, began to dilate on the social
splendours available to Conservative politicians. 'We have dukes and mar-
quises and earls', he said, 'and the duchesses and marchionesses and countesses
entertain us in their magnificent houses ... What has the Liberal Party to
offer in comparison? A mere pack of knights' ladies!' Nevertheless, the knighthood was accepted.

failed to do has now been accomplished. Public attention has been centred on the trust and its methods.

A list of the chief industrial combinations launched during the past two or three years, compiled by Mr Fred W. Field of *The Monetary Times*, shows one feature in common—the issue or authorization of an excessive amount of stock, in some cases fourfold that of the companies gathered into the merger. This will be seen clearly by the following instances:—Amalgamated Asbestos: Former capital of the five companies included, $3,550,000; one private interest uncapitalized; capital of the merger $25,000,000, of which $15,000,000 is in the form of bonds. Canadian Car & Foundry: Capital of the three companies joining in the merger, $11,000,000; capital of the merger $20,000,000, of which $7,500,000 consists of bonds . . . Carriage Factories, Limited: Capital of the four companies included in the merger, $900,000; capital of the merger $5,000,000, of which $1,000,000 consists of bonds.

It must not be supposed that in all these instances the great increase of capital was entirely due to the watering of the stock. The expansion of business actually called in many cases for the enlargement of plants and for greater working capital, and this was provided out of the issue of the new securities. Speaking generally, however, there are many millions of common stock, and in some cases even of preferred, that represented nothing more substantial than the hope that the public would be forced to pay higher prices for the merger's products, or that expansion of business would enable dividends to be earned upon this fictitious capital.

Heretofore the people have viewed with indifference the formation of these Canadian trusts, feeling confident that if their extractions became burdensome redress would be secured by the reduction or removal of their tariff protection. Of late, however, there have been developments that make the value of the tariff as a trust-regulator less certain. The trust-forming contagion is spreading in directions over which the tariff has no control, such as the making of bread, inland navigation, and the manufacture of patented articles; while even in the case of industries sheltered under the tariff, it becomes evident that two

47

powerful forces would be set in motion against drastic tariff reductions were the public interest to require that they be made. The first and most effective is that of the minor industries not absorbed by the trusts. The creators of mergers have been clever enough, even in their most extended operations, not to include all the industries of any particular sort. They have shrewdly seen that if all the cement, or the paint, or the carriages were made by one concern the tariff would be removed very quickly. And so they have left 'independents' in most cases who say 'the removal of the tariff might cripple the trust, but it would destroy us, for even under a protective tariff our profits are not excessive'.

It is stated on behalf of such minor industries that the undoubted economies in production and in distribution made possible by the consolidation of several concerns manufacturing the same articles would enable the large industries to live without tariff protection, even though dividends might have to be suspended, while the smaller industries would go to the wall.

The second force making for the safeguarding of the trust from radical tariff reduction is that of the 'innocent' investor at home and abroad. During the past two years thousands of people to whom formerly 'industrials' were an unknown region of finance have become shareholders in Canadian mergers. It may be said that they did so with their eyes open, and that in consideration of the high rate of dividends paid or promised they were willing to take their risks. They could hardly be ignorant, it has been urged, of the fact that they were in many cases buying watered stock that would be rendered worthless by the removal or reduction of the tariff, by the organization of a rival merger, or by a falling off in the volume of immigration. We very much doubt whether the small investors in merger stocks either at home or abroad gave serious consideration to the dangers they incurred. It is quite certain that as usual they bought largely because the names of men prominent in finance and business appeared on the prospectus. The game of follow-my-leader is as popular in finance as it is when first learned on the school playground. That should be remembered by the bankers and industrial captains who lend their names, and often, it is to be feared, little else than their names, to the formation of mergers.

48

3a 'The little fellow with the big head'

3b Official eye-witness (1916)

4a With Lady Beaverbrook: Deauville (1923)

4b With Bonar Law (*right*) and his son Richard Law: Aix-les-Bains (1923)

A substantial block of bonus stock is not to be put in the balance against the loss to individuals and the harm to Canada's national credit that would follow the collapse of any considerable number of the consolidations of the past few years.

The *Globe* can see no way of preventing by law such consolidations. They have features of undoubted benefit. In not a few cases they will be able to effect marked economies in both production and distribution. The organization of modern business on a colossal scale is as inevitable as the organization of the nations of the world into a few great powers . . . Government, however, have a duty toward the people who are asked to put their money into these great consolidations. It should be required that the fullest details as to the actual value of the assets put in and their relation to the capital to be issued must be supplied when mergers are effected . . .

The present unrest and apprehension would speedily be allayed by the appointment of a carefully selected Royal Commission to examine into and report upon the circumstances under which the mergers of the last three years have been formed, and especially as to the disposal of bonus stock and other securities that have not found their way into the possession of the public. With the facts fully disclosed, Parliament would be in a position to frame laws that would effectively prevent the trusts from pouring out vast quantities of fictitious capital and spreading it so widely among the investing public as to make the consumers themselves effective supporters of a fiscal system of which they are the victims . . .

This editorial is of the first importance as a summary of the 'sound' or 'orthodox' business reaction to the spectacular success of Max Aitken. Despite the lofty tone of its prose, the distaste and chagrin excited by the news of his knighthood are expressed so sharply that the disinterested modern reader may well diagnose a good deal of personal envy and jealousy behind the criticism. 'How the hell did that little —— make it?' must have been the recurrent plaint, in the more exalted clubs of Toronto and Ottawa, of the upright citizens not mentioned in the honours list. On the other hand, the analysis of the trustifiers' shrewd tactics in leaving untouched some independent minor industries, and of their apparent reasons for doing so, seems valid and is still of interest—particularly to readers of Beaverbrook's newspapers who may have been puzzled by their tender concern for the 'small man' in British industry and commerce.

In recent years friends of Beaverbrook have said that the righteousness of Sir Sandford Fleming and those who supported him in his protest against the cement merger was as the righteousness of the scribes and pharisees. It is alleged that Fleming was acting privily for Aitken's competitors, and that Fleming was piqued because Aitken refused to include in the merger a cement company in which Fleming was interested personally. If this is so, the whole affair is removed still further from the area in which rational moral judgements can be formed.

In any case, the riproaring, unashamedly capitalist Canada of fifty years ago seems almost as remote from the Britain of 1955, or indeed from post-Keynesian capitalism, with its semi-controlled Welfare State economy, as the Regency or the Restoration or the Wars of the Roses. The whole tone and atmosphere of society have changed; other values prevail. To a mid-century Socialist, there would seem to have been no difference in principle between Aitken's mergers and a thousand other operations performed within the capitalist system, at certain stages of its development, with no loud outcry from those already occupying the seats of power. The difference was one of degree; nor was it a quantitative difference so vast as to become one of quality also. There was, however, one novel feature of the mergers, which may or may not have contributed significantly to their unpopularity with the mighty: they were engineered not by a conspiracy of the more venerable tycoons of Canadian business, but by a big-headed, big-mouthed, bumptious youngster from the backwoods.

This youngster was by now selling something like thirty or forty million dollars'-worth of bonds every year. His coming-of-age ambition was securely fulfilled. He already had all the money that he and his family could possibly need for the rest of their lives. It may have been about this time that his formula for power began to take shape in his mind. It may be, too, that, despite his brazen front, he was disconcerted by the first hints of a life-long discovery that riches alone were not a key to men's esteem. He was a rising figure in the world; yet— just as he had often felt in his childhood, and in the Cypress Club at Chatham—he began to feel (he told his friends) 'something of an Ishmaelite'. There was also in his mind an almost superstitious sense that he had been *too* lucky so far: if he went on as he had been going, he began to be sure that he would make a mistake and have a bad fall.

This is a bad mood for a business man to be in. Aitken took the wise way out of it: he cut and ran. On July 30th, 1910, he sold practically all that he had (for substantially more than a million, pounds not dollars), left Montreal, and drove off with his wife towards New York in one of the new automobile cars—a car, he recalls, 'as big as a house'. They spent a night on the way. The young financier's fame had preceded him: wherever they stopped they were 'besieged by favour-seekers'. At Saratoga he decided to go away for a long time. They took a Cunarder to England; at Fishguard they were met by a Daimler which Aitken had bought through his London office; and so they came, driving in leisurely stages, to London.

* * *

Time heals the resentment caused by the activities of new men the more surely because those chiefly aggrieved, in the natural course, die soonest. No echo is to be heard in Canada now—certainly not in New Brunswick—of that storm of anger and hatred aroused by Beaverbrook's early financial escapades. He is a *deus ex machina*, a universal provider, the

Nuffield or Carnegie of New Brunswick; and the people and newspapers of the Province heap slightly anxious praise upon him—'slightly anxious' because, as the incident of the skating-rink showed, he is by no means one of those aloof, benign deities who are content to pour out their bounty and leave its disposal and use to the free will of the beneficiaries. As a Calvinist, he has never thought too highly of the doctrine of free will: predestination is a concept more congenial to the jealous tribal God of his Old Testament upbringing and to himself as the supreme dispenser of material blessings to the children and grandchildren of those among whom his youth was spent.

There are three main centres of Beaverbrook's benefactions in New Brunswick: Newcastle, Saint John, and Fredericton.

Modest Newcastle is being enriched yearly by him with more and more public buildings and amenities. Besides the rink and the memorial to the early settlers (which is, incidentally, in excellent taste, having been designed and made in England by the Birmingham Guild of Craftsmen), he has preserved and enclosed a park in which many of the early settlers were buried[1] and has reconstructed a memorial playing-field; his latest gift—opened on November 2nd, 1954—is an imposing, fire-resistant, neo-classic building containing town offices, theatre, and community centre; while the focus of his own closest interest and attention is, naturally enough, the public library which he has founded in his own old home, the Manse.

The Old Manse Library is admirably decorated and furnished, in a quiet, chaste style, and has the most modern technical library equipment. When it was opened to the

[1] A plaque in this enclosure bears the lines (taken from a poem by T. H. Huxley on the death of Tennyson):—

> Not thine to kneel beside the grassy mound
> While dies the western glow; and all around
> Is silence; and the shadows closer creep
> And whisper softly: All must fall asleep.

public in August, 1953, Beaverbrook had stocked it with some six thousand books, each bearing his armorial bookplate. Many of these came from his own library at Cherkley: there, for more than a year before, a great sorting of books had been in progress, and visitors saw thousands of them, destined for Newcastle, stacked on the floor—books of all sorts, Carlyle, the *Imitation of Christ*, Frank Harris on Shaw, Henley's poems, Loti's *Pêcheur d'Islande*, Lord David Cecil's *Stricken Deer*, Hickey's *Memoirs*, Walter Pater, and the *Book of Mormon*. This is the second time in recent years that Beaverbrook has ransacked his own library; on the first occasion he sent most of his valuable first editions to the library of the University of New Brunswick.

It is evident, even from a cursory glance, that Newcastle now owns a notable and diverse library. It cannot, however, be called a comprehensive library: its scope and character are strictly determined—predestined, perhaps—by the prejudices and caprice of the benefactor. He did not, for instance, send the works by Freud that he had at Cherkley: they would have been 'unsuitable'. Each autumn, when Beaverbrook pays his annual visit to New Brunswick—'visitation', in the archidiaconal sense, might be more appropriate—he confers with those whom he has appointed custodians of the Old Manse Library: the conference, an unevenly matched contest of wits, somewhat resembles the presenting of petitions by suppliants at an oriental court. Lists of books, which it is felt should be in the library, are submitted; the lists are censored rigorously by the benefactor: 'Why d'you want that feller? Terrible! He's anti-British ... We can't have Louis Bromfield in this library. He's anti-English, too. Let him go to hell ... *South Wind*? Yes, it's beautiful—but it's not suited to Newcastle. ... Strike out *Antic Hay* ...'

The librarian pleads for two small concessions—a subscription to some book-of-the-month society, and a petty-cash fund out of which a few books published locally could be bought. Both suggestions excite loud roars of 'No!' Why do they want a book-of-the-month subscription? 'They'll only send you pornography. We will have no pornography in this library.' Why do they want to buy books of their own choice locally? 'This is *my* collection, and I won't let anybody else decide on a single book. *I* am the sole book-buyer. Let me know what you want, and I will send it from England, if I approve.' A slight show of resistance by the lady in charge of the library—who has the privilege of old friendship, for she used to play at the Manse in childhood with the Aitken sisters—provokes the most ominous reply of all, in a low, tired voice, heavy with doom: '*We're not in touch, you and I* . . .'—then, after a pregnant pause: 'You'll have to get hold of my policy, Louise. This is to be a recreational library.'

A visitor from England, who happens to be sitting in on this thunder-charged conference, ventures to express disagreement, suggesting that it is unusual to censor books on the basis of the views or character of their authors. Instantly the atmosphere is transformed. Beaverbrook swings round. 'Unless', he cries, with an enormous wink and a grating chuckle, 'unless you're a self-willed old b——— like me, eh!'

Various technical problems are raised. They will soon be running out of shelf-room. A good deal of it is taken up by fine library editions—for instance, of Eden Phillpotts—which are not in great demand and are, in any case, rather too good to let out of the library. There is the problem of lighting the children's room in the basement. There is the slipperiness in winter of the new steps up to the front door. 'Coconut matting? Never in my time . . . Huh!' But it all passes off tranquilly enough now—which suggests an important respect in which Beaverbrook's character differs from those of other newspaper magnates with whom superficial observers have compared him, Hearst or Northcliffe or the late Lord Rothermere. Like them, he is arbitrary and *exigeant* and often despotic: unlike them, he appreciates reasoned resistance; he

54

does not like to be surrounded with stooges (whom he despises); he will often quote against himself some repartee with which a friend or subordinate has scored off him; he has, in short, at least a rudimentary capacity for self-criticism. It is impossible to imagine Rothermere or Hearst making, in the presence of several dependants, the self-revealing remark quoted in the preceding paragraph.

Another institution in which he is closely interested is the Law School at Saint John: this is now, thanks to him, newly housed in an old and stately mansion, at the top of a hill, in one of the most commanding positions in the town. Late in 1953, when he was expected shortly to give up direct control of the School by formally handing over the title-deeds to trustees, he visited Saint John; inspected the newly-redecorated premises; approved the notice forbidding smoking (a disciplinary matter that had lately been the subject of some controversy, in which he had joined to the full); and entertained the entire faculty of the School to dinner in a private room at his hotel. As it invariably is, his hospitality was generous. It is unusual, at dinner-parties in Saint John, to serve champagne throughout the meal as well as before it. The slight nervousness with which some members of the faculty may have approached the ordeal of dining with their benefactor was soon dispelled; by the end of dinner they were in a relaxed and quietly merry mood. It was evidently to be a purely social occasion.

Few occasions in which Beaverbrook plays the leading part are purely social. Coffee and cigars were served—and this was the moment at which he chose to launch what became almost a direct offensive, addressing to each senior member of the faculty in turn a series of blunt questions about his plans and visions for the future of the Law School. Those present at the dinner report that consternation was caused by this unexpected attack; some of them had come unprepared for a serious business conference, and fumbled their answers badly; several provoked the downright, and terrible, anger of their host by essaying what seemed to him too jejune and paltry a prospect of the School's future. 'Well . . . I suppose,' one would stammer, 'it will continue to provide a specialized education for law students from all over New Brunswick . . .?' 'Nonsense,' barked Beaverbrook, aghast at so unambitious a view. 'It is not to be merely a provincial Law School. Not at all! It is to serve the whole nation, the whole of Canada, from coast to coast. More and more, as the years go on, the brightest of all the young men in the whole wide Dominion will be drawn to this outstanding Law School at Saint John. Don't you want to build it up into that? Don't you? Because that's my idea, that's the inspiration I should like to leave with you. Do you agree? Do *you* agree, X . . .? Do *you*, Y?' There were shifty glances and diffident murmurs: one or two of the younger men had the sense to assent, with some show of enthusiasm ('Why, yes, your Lordship, I think that's a fine concept.'); but the response was, in general, inadequate, and there was a grimness in the air when the party, quite soon, broke up.

People close to Beaverbrook say that he was deeply affected by this incident. For several days after it he was in melancholy and fretful mood, growling like a wounded bear; he seemed to be suffering from a gastric as well as an emotional disturbance. Constantly he would hark back, in conversation with others, to the narrow, unimaginative parochialism of some of those in charge of the School. It is hardly necessary to add that the transfer of power was delayed.

It would be unfair, however, to picture him as, in general, a curmudgeonly and oppressive benefactor. It was within a day or two of the dinner-party at Saint John that he took part in a more formal academic function. St Thomas's University at Chatham—the small town in which, as an adolescent law-clerk, he had made his first, clumsy experiments in social advancement—was conferring on him a Doctorate of Laws, *honoris causa.* This is a Roman Catholic university, and the tough old Presbyterian was thickly hedged in by sloe-eyed seminarists and sleek reverend fathers: 'black beetles', his folk would have called them in the old, rude days. Despite his adherence to the Westminster Confession, Beaverbrook has often shown an unCalvinistic tenderness towards the Church of Rome. This may date from his boyhood friendship with Father Dixon; it has happened, too, that, throughout his life, many of his dearest friends, such as Tim Healy and Lord Castlerosse, have been Roman Catholics. In a mind dedicated to the pursuit of power, moreover, respect for any really formidable and vital organization of power is natural; in quite another context, Beaverbrook felt more instinctive sympathy, even affinity, with Stalin than the prim and humble Christian Socialist, Stafford Cripps, ever could have during his term as Ambassador in Moscow.

On this occasion, at any rate, no cloud marred the radiance of mutual esteem and eulogy. After an elaborate panegyric, the degree was conferred on 'this distinguished nobleman', as he was called; and he in turn, speaking without notes (and he is at his best extempore), assured the scarlet-gowned Convocation and the students who crowded the hall how lonely he often felt when he was away from New Brunswick—'lonely for the river and lonely for the maple-trees garnished with gold'. Then indeed, he said, 'my heart comes back to you'. He told them, too, of another honour that had come his way —the conferring on him by Stalin of the Order of Suvorov (first class). They rocked with laughter as he explained that this entitled him to the dubious privilege of riding free on the Moscow tramways, and to being taken home by car if he was found drunk in the streets. The laughter died to a polite buzz as he added that the Order entitled him also to sit on red plush seats; no doubt they thought at first that this meant in trams or trains. '*On red plush seats*', he repeated, twice, each time more loudly and significantly, until they got it. This was the only passage in this speech that he worried about, in advance and retrospectively. He had wanted to say what he meant more plainly: puritanical friends had advised against it, at such a function. A commentator once said of Beaverbrook that he was not a bad man but a bad boy. . . .

Beaverbrook's most numerous and diverse benefactions have been to the University of New Brunswick at Fredericton. Fredericton is a gracious and charming academic town, with wide, lawn-fringed streets, porticoed houses of the eighteenth and nineteenth centuries, and spreading elm-trees. The University dates from 1785; it is the oldest English-language university in Canada. Shortly before the Second World War, however, it was not doing too well: its students numbered only some four hundred. Fortunately, Beaverbrook had begun to take an interest in it; the improvements due to his beneficence combined with the post-war influx of ex-servicemen to ensure an expansion proportionately greater than that of almost any other Canadian university. The number of students is now stabilized at about eight hundred.

Altogether, Beaverbrook's benefactions to this University alone have cost him well over two million dollars. He gave a male students' residence in memory of his wife, and a superb and unashamedly twentieth-century gymnasium. He bought a house for conversion into a residence for women students; and has handed over as a residence for the President of the University a comely old house, overlooking the river, which at one time he contemplated occupying himself. (His visits to Fredericton are too brief to make this worth while; he now stays at the hotel named, by the wish of the citizens, the Lord Beaverbrook Hotel.)

Perhaps his most important gifts have been to the University library. This had been seriously neglected: ten years ago it had only one untrained librarian, and the books were not properly catalogued. Beaverbrook insisted on its complete and efficient reorganization: six trained librarians now look after its sixty-five thousand scrupulously catalogued volumes; some fifteen thousand of these books were given by Beaverbrook. One wing of the library, containing a restful reading-room, panelled in bird's-eye maple, is dedicated to the memory of Beaverbrook's great friend and hero, Bonar Law; and the library's historic possessions include the papers of such statesmen as Law and Bennett, all acquired for it by Beaverbrook. No comparable university, on either side of the Atlantic, can have a finer instrument for the collection, preservation, and use of books than this library at the University of New Brunswick.

A slight *contretemps* occurred on one of the benefactor's recent visits to this library. A new box of books had just arrived from England. The assistant unpacking them held some of them up, with pleasure, for Beaverbrook and those with him to see. This was a daring or a naïve gesture, and it provoked a peculiarly inscrutable grunt; for the inscription in the books showed plainly enough—all too plainly—that they were a gift to the library from the British Council; and the British Council, as is well known, shares with the Arts Council and the British Information Services the honour of exciting in Beaverbrook and (by infection or instruction) in his newspapers the sort of blind fury which used to make Marshal Göring reach for his revolver when he heard the word 'culture'.

It is not surprising that, some years ago, the University decided to honour this outstanding benefactor, this illustrious son of New Brunswick, by electing him to the Chancellorship of the University. Nor is it surprising that, with his intense pride in his 'adopted native' province, Beaverbrook should have chosen to attend the Coronation of Queen Elizabeth II in Westminster Abbey wearing his academic habit as Chancellor of the University of New Brunswick, rather than the robe of a peer of the realm of England. Some surprise was caused soon after this, however, by the news that he was relinquishing the Chancellorship—an event as convulsive in academic society in Fredericton as, say, one of Mr Bevan's resignations in the British Labour Party. A conventional explanation was given out: Lord Beaverbrook had to be away from New Brunswick for too much of the year, he could not attend adequately to his duties as Chancellor, and so on; but, since he had attended to them adequately for ten years without visiting New Brunswick too often, and since they were largely ceremonial anyway, nobody believed that this was the full story. It was widely held in Fredericton that there had been some difference of opinion between Beaverbrook and a majority of the governing body of the University, possibly on the question of the appointment of a new President; and general concern sharpened into active uneasiness—at least among those responsible for the University finances—when it was learned that Beaverbrook had been entertaining to dinner, in Fredericton itself, the notably energetic President of a rival university in another part of the Province. These apprehensions were unnecessary: Beaverbrook has confidence in the new, young President of the University of New Brunswick, Dr Colin B. Mackay; and it is, in any case, highly improbable that any permanent coolness would develop between him and an institution on which he has lavished so much of his wealth and so much affection.

One recent sunny evening Beaverbrook was walking up the steep hill towards the peaceful, tree-clad campus with the President of the University and another friend. Suddenly—for it was on the stroke of the hour—they heard the carillon start to chime from the bell-tower ahead. They stopped to listen. The day was warm: Beaverbrook's head was bare. He and the President stood with bowed heads, hats in hand, listening, as the pretty, tinkling, irregular tune rang out. Their companion, to whom the scene was new, was irresistibly, and rather touchingly, reminded of Millet's famous picture, *The Angelus*; but he could not identify the half-familiar tune that the bells were playing. When the little ceremony was over, he asked what the tune was—and, when told, remembered at once that this was, of all the songs of Beaverbrook's youth, his favourite: it is called *The Jones Boys*, and it tells of two unsuccessful New Brunswick brothers, who

worked all night and they worked all day
But they couldn't make that goddam saw-mill pay.

'They couldn't make it pay,' echoed Beaverbrook, with the ghost of a chuckle. He sighed and put on his black hat, and they went on walking up the hill.

CHAPTER FOUR

'THE LITTLE CANADIAN ADVENTURER'

He saw the world as it is . . . and found in success the
ultima ratio mundi. *'Vautrin is right, success is virtue!' he told himself.*

HONORÉ DE BALZAC

BEAVERBROOK'S career falls into several phases, overlapping rather than clearly distinct, and may be said to have progressed in a series of violent upward and lateral jerks. From poverty, he had become a millionaire in five years: within six years of settling in England—a crude outsider who could have, as it seemed, no real influence in the great affairs of state—he was to be mainly responsible for the overthrow of the Prime Minister of the day.

He was not seeing London for the first time when he drove into it in August, 1910, in his new Daimler, with his young bride. He had visited it at least twice before—once, hurriedly, four months earlier, to raise money. This had been just before the crisis of his struggle to create the steel merger. He needed money to buy rolling-mills in Montreal. He was warned by a friend—by that Edward Clouston who had once said 'Send me back the little fellow with the big head'—that his enemies on the board of the Canadian Pacific Railway were directors also of the Bank of Montreal. 'Better borrow the money in London', said Clouston. He was able to show ample security: the money—several million dollars—was forthcoming from Parr's Bank. At a crucial moment, when the CPR men confidently challenged his financial stability, Aitken produced a bank-book showing 'an enormous cash balance'. He still has an account with the Westminster Bank, into which Parr's was later absorbed.

During this brief earlier visit to London, King Edward VII had died. For many years afterwards Max Aitken recalled one of those tiny incidents which photograph themselves on the memory. He saw a man read the news of the King's death on the tape-machine at the Savoy Hotel; the man turned away from the machine in tears. Aitken asked someone if the man were a relative or close friend of the King. No: he was just a member of the public. This was astonishing to the young Canadian then, and a comparable demonstration would be almost as incomprehensible to him today: he accepts constitutional monarchy as a convenient and expedient arrangement, but any sentimental or mystical concept of kingship is alien to him. Naturally, he did not wait in London for the King's funeral. 'Hell, no,' he said—he was in a hurry to get back to his steel-war in Canada. He was, however, delayed in London for a day or two by a sharp attack of liver trouble: a Dr Horder was called in.

It was on an earlier visit, in 1908, that he had first met another son of a New Brunswick manse whose life was to be strangely interwoven with his: Andrew Bonar Law, then fifty-one years old and Conservative MP for Dulwich. Little seems to have been said on this occasion from which their later intimacy could have been forecast: Aitken managed to sell Law a few bonds, and had the impression that Law was buying them in order to get rid of him.

The war of 1914–1918 was the historic watershed—much more so, in most ways, than the Second World War—between the old order of English and European society and the new. In 1910, every outward appearance seemed to show that Britain was still in the golden heyday of Victorian and Edwardian prosperity. True, Mr Asquith's Liberal Government was attacking the power of the House of Lords, there were a few dozen Labour MPs in the Commons, and the suffragettes were beginning to be troublesome; but nobody seriously expected that Britain would soon be involved in a world war, or that in that war some of the world's most puissant dynasties would fall; and there were few signs yet of the loosening of ruling-class etiquette and hereditary caste tabus that was to be a social phenomenon of the inter-war years. Oddly enough, it was only in the immediate circle of King Edward himself that—as in the brief reign of a later Edward—a certain laxity was perceptible. This was due to the King's sporting and amorous tastes. He gambled and got into debt: to the moneylenders who obliged him, and to their wives, the most acceptable form of interest would be badges for the Royal Enclosure at Ascot and the presence of royalty at their daughters' coming-out balls. The country-house parties most congenial to the King were those at which his mistresses also were welcome guests.

For the most part, however, the old aristocratic and landed families were still socially dominant, and accepted few newcomers on equal terms. They wore 'an effortless consciousness of their own superiority'. Many of them had great fortunes, and had not yet learned that this was a matter for uneasiness of conscience. Money was vulgar only when it was new. *Punch*, aping for its middle-class readers the snobbery of their betters, published hundreds of cartoons satirizing the uncouth speech and table manners of the 'new rich'—of, in short, men like Max Aitken. In those early days in England he suffered personal rebuffs more wounding—because delivered either unintentionally or with more subtle *expertise*—than any that he had sustained in boyhood. He was blunt and raucous and short of stature: the insolent blank stare, through lorgnette or monocle, of these idle Olympians with their soft white hands, who looked and behaved like the most frivolous characters in Saki's stories, must have enraged him even more than the overt snub, the half-heard drawling sneer at him as a 'colonial' or a 'bounder'. It was particularly infuriating because in one important sense, after all, he was on their side. He was already an ardent imperialist: when the chance came to enter politics actively, he could hardly not choose the Conservative side; of the two great parties, this seemed by far the more firmly committed to the cause of Empire as Aitken understood it.

In the complex character of Beaverbrook, one of a number of pairs of apparently contradictory elements is this: he can take strong public criticism with equanimity and even relish (possibly because it is a kind of tribute); yet a comparatively trivial private slight, perhaps not deliberate at all, will be inflamed and aggravated in his mind until a grudge is formed that may last for years. Some of the leading men in the Conservative Party today might find Beaverbrook a less uncomfortable ally if they or their fathers had been sufficiently shrewd and far-seeing, forty years ago, to welcome the young Max Aitken more warmly into their close society. Some, indeed, did so, and for them his friendship has been unswerving; but no Hyde Park orator could pack more searing contempt into the delivery of the name 'Salisbury', for instance, than he can. It is, perhaps, a cause of mild amusement to him that so many of these families should have been dispossessed of their former grandeur; and also that his own (divorced) ex-son-in-law should now be the holder of an ancient Scottish dukedom. Individually, members of this class have often been the victims of fierce attack or embarrassing exposure in his newspapers; and these newspapers have campaigned against the hereditary principle in government more consistently than any of their Radical or Socialist contemporaries.[1]

Future feuds did not trouble the young Aitkens when they arrived in London in 1910. They 'decided that London was

[1] 'Hereditary titles are an anachronism in the modern world. Better far to sweep them away and have life titles.' (*Daily Express*, March 12th, 1950.) 'Why . . . should men of no ability be allowed into the Lords on hereditary grounds alone? The whole system serves the country ill . . .' (*Daily Express*, August 18th, 1950.) 'It is wrong and indefensible that, in a democracy, political power should be distributed on a basis of birth.' (*Daily Express*, February 24th, 1951.)

F

lovely'; and they took a top-floor flat in Cavendish Square. Like many another transatlantic visitor, they went to see the homes of their forbears. At Torphichen, near Edinburgh, whence his father had gone as a young minister to Canada nearly half-a-century before, the old verger saw Max poking about in the churchyard in search of Aitken graves, eyed him keenly, and said: 'Ye're either R. B. Angus's or William Aitken's son'. He looked up a number of relatives: 'they've looked me up ever since,' he says, in mock-chagrin.

Though he was soon to be at the heart of high politics, he first gravitated to the City. Bonar Law had City interests; and Aitken's friendship with Law rapidly grew more intimate. He was often at Law's house in Edwardes Square, Kensington. They played chess together—at home and, later, at the House of Commons. When Law's wife died, Aitken went with him on a golfing holiday. Beaverbrook has expressed in one of his graphic phrases the powerful attraction that Law exercised over him at this time. 'He pinned me down and kept me ever after,' he says. It is fair to stress the genuinely mutual character of this attraction, and in particular Law's liking for Aitken; for some of Law's older friends, both then and later, disapproved of the association and regarded Aitken as Law's evil genius and as a gate-crasher who had attached himself to Law and was exploiting him for his own ends. One who disapproved was Law's own sister Mary: she thought Max Aitken —twenty years younger than her brother—too ribald, insufficiently grave and decent in demeanour. She tackled her brother about this one day. He was lying on a sofa reading. He looked up at her, took off his glasses, and said quietly: 'Do let me like him'. She was a devoted and unselfish woman, and soon became resigned to Max Aitken's growing influence.[1] Others were less easily appeased: they whispered and

---

[1] The dedication of the first volume of Beaverbrook's *Politicians and the War* reads, touchingly: 'To Mary Law and the memory of the past'. She died in 1929; Beaverbrook was her executor, and she left him £3,600.

gossiped, with the malice endemic in politics; they hissed scandal about the cement merger. Only one answer silenced them: would a man of Law's universally acclaimed integrity have anything to do with Max Aitken if he had really been guilty of financial malpractices? Nor was it possible to say that Law was an innocent and that Aitken had beguiled him: Law had certainly heard what was said about the cement deal, he was himself a man of dour rectitude, and he was by no means so naïve as to become entangled with a dangerous trickster.

The friendship, then, was a true one: it was also undoubt-edly useful—and it is hard to say which of the two men found it more so. To the younger it was of enormous value to have a friend so solidly established, so experienced already in English politics, under whose respectable patronage he could advance his career; while he in turn supplied two elements which Law lacked—the confidence, the *élan*, the drive without which Law's somewhat plodding virtue would not have carried him to the highest office, and an equally ne essary capacity for intrigue.

Within a few months of Aitken s arrival in England, there was a snap General Election, the second within a year. Bonar Law gave up a safe seat to fight a much less safe one, North-West Manchester, and called on Aitken to come to Lancashire and help him. Aitken agreed—and caused wide-spread astonishment, not least among his old associates in Canada, by announcing that he also would contest a Lancashire seat: the Conservative candidature at Ashton-under-Lyne happened to be vacant, and Aitken secured it At this time he himself had not the right to vote in an English election.

Ashton, most of whose electors were spinners and weavers in the cotton-mills, had been for some years a Free Trade stronghold, and Aitken's opponent had been its Liberal MP. Despite official Conservative caution, Aitken stood uncom-promisingly for Tariff Reform and Imperial Preference. His campaign technique was as startling to the more conventional and timid Tories as his policies. Election contests, though often lively, were still fought in traditional 'sporting' style: Aitken introduced modern business method, reorganized the local party machine, insisted on the most thorough canvassing and the most scrupulous book-keeping, had all the voters card-indexed.

He was an unpractised speaker; but he preached his Empire cause in a rough and passionate way that carried conviction to many (often referring to dollars and cents when he should have referred to pounds, shillings, and pence), and he also pledged himself to fight the poverty and squalor in which so many working people lived. There was an element of demagogy in such a pledge; but it may not have been altogether insincere. The slums of industrial England must have been peculiarly shocking to one brought up in the clean forest air of New Brunswick. Research in Hansard for the years 1910–1914 does not, however, bring to light any sustained campaign on this subject by the Member for Ashton.

Demagogue or not, inexperienced in public speaking as he was, Aitken soon showed that his quick wit was equal to the task of dealing with hecklers and dodging awkward questions. Asked if his Canadian trusts helped British workmen, he replied, with more magniloquence than candour: 'I control no trusts. I am a shareholder in several consolidations'. Bonar Law left his own difficult campaign for one evening only, to speak for Aitken, and testified that the electors would find him 'one of the best men' they 'ever came across'. It was left to the more cynical F. E. Smith,[1] some hostile propaganda having been made of the fact that Aitken was a millionaire, daringly to invert the sense of a famous poem and to say of him that 'A man's a man for a' that'. Among the prominent Lancashire Conservatives who refused to speak for Aitken, though asked to do so by Bonar Law, was

[1] Later the Earl of Birkenhead.

Lord Derby. Derby's prestige was immense in Lancashire; no man could have helped Aitken more. It is not known whether the reasons for his refusal were political or personal, or both; it was not soon forgiven him.

On the eve of polling-day Aitken organized a huge procession through the streets, designed to impress those 'floating voters' who like to be on the winning side. His tactics were successful: he won by 196 votes—by 4,044 to the Liberal's 3,848. His victory seemed the more sensational because his friend Bonar Law was defeated in North-West Manchester.[1] Less successful was a celebration banquet which some of his new political colleagues gave Max Aitken in London: the older among them took offence at what they took to be his arrogant cocksureness. They had, of course, never heard of the Cypress Club in Chatham, New Brunswick.

So he entered politics; and, though he later became known to the public chiefly as a newspaper-owner, politics were to absorb his inner energies more intensely than any other activity for the rest of his life—newspapers being, as instruments of propaganda, only an element in politics. There is a woolly liberal *cliché* which condemns 'power politics': in a sense, all politics are power politics—an exercise in power, its transfer and its use. This is the only sense in which politics have been Beaverbrook's concern: the glories of the Englishman's constitutional heritage and the niceties of Parliamentary procedure are alike meaningless to him—irrelevant, picturesque perhaps, but boring—except in so far as they can be used to secure power for this or that group or person. (At this point his materialism overlaps with the dialectical materialism of the Marxists: both alike despise the 'humbug' of those who revere tradition for its own sake and suppose state pageantry to have a real content unconnected with a current struggle for power.) He applied to politics in Britain

---

[1] Law was re-elected to the House of Commons soon afterwards, as MP for Bootle.

the realism and ruthlessness that had revolutionized finance in Canada. He was the supreme exponent in politics, before and during the First World War, of the art more recently defined by Mr Stephen Potter as gamesmanship—'the art of winning games without actually cheating'.

His brain was young, his sleight-of-hand superb: he now juggled in politicians as he had once juggled in bonds. 'The quickness of the hand deceives the eye': these political manipulations were successful because, like the movements of the conjurer's hand, they were unseen by the audience. Beaverbrook has never been what would be called a bookish man; his reading has been wide but desultory. Quite early in his political career, however, some friend—perhaps F. E. Smith, perhaps Winston Churchill—innocently advised him to study Burke; and in Burke's *Appeal from the New to the Old Whigs* he found one passage that appealed to him so strongly that he copied it out, learned it by heart, and often quoted it: 'The world is governed by go-betweens. These go-betweens influence the persons with whom they carry on intercourse by stating their own sense to each of them as the sense of the other; and thus they reciprocally master both sides.'

It is essential that the go-between should be invisible, an *éminence grise*, the stage-manager rather than the star: it spoils the play, by destroying illusion, if his gesticulating hand protrudes from the wings. Aitken understood this perfectly and stayed out of the limelight during his most important political operations. It was some years before he published any record of them; and it is only in the eighth decade of his life—and especially since his unexpected and sensational success as a television performer—that he seems to have developed a real taste for personal publicity.

He did not give up business altogether. For a brief period, in 1912–13, he controlled the renowned firm of Rolls-Royce. When Mr C. S. Rolls was killed, Aitken bought enough of

his shares (thirty per cent) to secure voting control. He found
that output was being limited deliberately and that costs were
heavy. Aitken advocated the introduction of new techniques
of mass-production. There was obstinate resistance to his
proposals; but he was obstinate, too. Eventually the deadlock
was broken: the manager of the firm, Mr Claud Johnson,
persuaded Lord Northcliffe to intercede with Aitken;
Mr J. B. Duke, the tobacco magnate, offered him a good
profit for the shares; and he sold out. Two directors whom he
had nominated, Sir Edward Goulding[1] and Mr G. Rowe,
remained on the Board after he had gone.

For some years he was also a banker. Youthful business
excursions to the Caribbean area—in the course of which he
had promoted electric light, tramways, and many other
utilities, to his own substantial profit and incidentally, no
doubt, to the convenience of the inhabitants of various colonies—had shown him the immense possibilities for lucrative
and useful exploitation of such undeveloped territories as
these, with their teeming, illiterate populations and with, consequently, limitless supplies of cheap labour. On one such visit
he had become acquainted with an old-established English
chartered bank, doing much business in the West Indies—
the Colonial Bank. The idea of imperial economic development and unity was already forming in his mind: before
coming to London, he had bought control of this bank. He
made himself chairman of it, extended its operations into
West Africa, and began to make plans for similar expansion
throughout the British Empire. Then the politics of the United
Kingdom began to claim his closer attention. Much later, in
1917, on accepting government office, he was obliged to resign
from the board of the bank; and after the First World War he
sold it to Barclays Bank (for at least twice what he had paid
for it). Had he continued to concentrate primarily on business,
and merely dabbled incidentally in politics, he might have had,

[1] Later Lord Wargrave.

71

over the next twenty or thirty years, more practical success in the cause which he has failed so notably to promote through newspaper propaganda and political action: the history of English politics, and even of two world wars, would also have been different, to an extent beyond speculation.

There is, obviously, no fundamental inconsistency between Conservative political activity and City financial activity. An anecdote is told of a Balkan politician visiting London at the time of the victory of the Labour Party in 1945. Accustomed to the ferocity of politics in his own land, and unaware of the comparative mildness of the British political climate, he said to a British friend, 'I suppose the defeated Conservatives are taking to the hills?' 'Not at all,' replied the Briton. 'They are taking to the City.' When leading Conservatives, such as Sir Anthony Eden, are out of office, it is as a matter of course that they become directors of banks and other concerns. The two interests are complementary. Aitken, however, could not have been content merely to be a part-time financier and a moderately active Tory back-bencher. He had to go straight for the centre of power, and capture it. This meant that he must concentrate on politics almost exclusively.

It meant also that he had to get to know well all the important men in politics, not only in his own party, which was not then in power. He was, as he has himself put it, 'always pushing around with and pursuing the great men'. Some of them did not like it: to this period belong some of those aristocratic snubs. Another 'self-made' man, F. E. Smith, was more encouraging. One day Smith and he were walking on the terrace of the Houses of Parliament when a stocky, sandy-haired figure happened to pass them. Aitken cried: 'I'd give five pounds to dine with that fellow Churchill'. The remark was jocular: the terms in which it was spontaneously phrased are characteristic. Churchill was then a Liberal, and Home Secretary in Mr Asquith's Government. This encounter was the start of a chequered but deep and lasting friendship:

Churchill and Beaverbrook have sometimes quarrelled furiously, but Beaverbrook, even when his newspapers have criticized the politics of Churchill's ministers, has never, in public, attacked him personally. In moods of depression, Churchill still seeks the company of this old crony, who is so bitterly mistrusted by most of Churchill's other friends. The two old men have, after all, been through many battles together; they are indeed, in 1955, the only two survivors of the Government that won the First World War.[1] Their relations are happiest at such times, when Beaverbrook, with charming badinage and the finest of brandy, will coax his old comrade out of the *cafard* that besets him. Beaverbrook has recorded that it is in these moods that he finds Churchill 'most fascinating'; but he has also written[2]:

> Churchill 'up' is quite a different proposition. I remember once a terrible scene with him when he was in a position of uncontrolled power and authority in dealing with public affairs which closely concerned me. If any other man living had used such outrageous language to me as he did on that occasion I should never have forgiven him. Churchill on the top of the wave has in him the stuff of which tyrants are made.

Aitken and F. E. Smith may have been attracted to each other because both were, basically, materialists; both believed that the world offered—in Smith's famous phrase—'glittering prizes to those who have . . . sharp swords', and were apt to despise the idealist, the dreamer, and the drudge. Churchill is much more romantic in outlook than either of them: what he has in common with Beaverbrook is a buccaneering adventurousness of spirit.

Churchill's new friend was an awkward guest at his elegant table. Beaverbrook has always had a disturbing effect on

[1] *Cf.* Churchill's *Second World War*, vol. IV, pp. 66–7: 'People . . . often wondered why his influence with me stood so high. . . . All my other colleagues had been unknown figures . . . on the battlefields of those bygone but still living days.'

[2] In *Politicians and the War*, vol. ii, p. 82.

73

dinner-parties: if he cannot dominate them he is likely to be mischievously provocative or morosely silent. As a newcomer to London political society he was less sure of himself than he is now, and so even more uncouth. Nevertheless, the association flourished; and ever since then, at crucial moments, Churchill has called on Beaverbrook for advice or for action.

But it was at Bonar Law's house, Pembroke Lodge, that Max Aitken was to be found most often. It must have been at about that time, or a little later, that F. E. Smith composed a quatrain which quickly went round the clubs and the lobbies of the House:

> Round Pembroke Lodge in Edwardes Square
> Like rooks the claimants caw,
> While Aitken keeps, with gargoyle stare,
> His vigil over Law.

'Gargoyle' seems unkind; but Smith was a friend and Aitken was by now more indifferent than he had been as a boy to gibes at his personal appearance. An otherwise obsequious article in *Maclean's Magazine* for September, 1911, described him as having tousled thin hair 'the colour of wet sand', nervous hands, and 'a voice that sounded as though he was recovering from a cold'.

The claimants were indeed beginning to gather like rooks— or vultures—at Law's house, at Aitken's suite in the Hyde Park Hotel,[1] and at his new home, Cherkley. For Aitken, only six months after his election to Parliament, was already fully engaged in his first major political intrigue, the object of which was nothing less than the replacement of the leader of his own party, Mr A. J. Balfour, by his own friend and fellow-countryman, Bonar Law.

---

[1] One who sometimes called at the hotel was Ben Tillett, the dockers' leader—not indeed as a claimant but as one of the forthright opponents whom it has always amused Beaverbrook to make friends with. Tillett used to ask first if Law were in Aitken's suite: if he was, he would not go up.

His technique was largely that suggested in Burke's dictum on go-betweens. Throughout the summer of 1911 he went to and fro, quietly organizing the dissidents who are to be found in all parties—the impatient younger men, the disappointed older men, the men whose policies have been rejected by their party. 'Regretting the necessity,' it was written later, 'he had joined with those who felt that Mr Balfour must go, and he spent busy nights and days greasing the skids.' Only one semi-public manifestation was instigated, the passing from mouth to mouth of the three-letter slogan, 'BMG'—Balfour Must Go. A general uneasiness was skilfully created, and Balfour, with his *fainéant* aloofness, was not the man to deal with it. Indeed, he did not bother to hide the fact that he thought as poorly of some of his supporters as they thought of him: many had rebelled against his leadership during the constitutional crisis occasioned by Asquith's attack on the House of Lords, and had supported Lord Halsbury and the 'last-ditchers'. 'Balfour,' says Sir Harold Nicolson, 'left England for Bad Gastein in a mood of philosophic contempt.'[1]

By the time he returned, the damage to his leadership was irreparable. Prominent members of the Party—much more prominent than the carefully inconspicuous Aitken—were challenging him openly. On November 8th he announced his resignation at an emergency party executive meeting in his own constituency, the City of London. The announcement caused consternation and astonishment among those not in the inner circle of plotters; some of those ambitious to succeed Balfour were caught unprepared.

Aitken was not unprepared. Events were moving rapidly, but his head was cool. Five days after Balfour's resignation, his successor was to be chosen at a party meeting at the Carlton Club. There were two 'official' candidates, each strongly supported: Mr Walter Long and Mr Austen Chamberlain. They had agreed that, if neither of them could secure

---

[1] *King George the Fifth: His Life & Reign*, p. 164.

unanimous support at the Carlton Club meeting, they would both withdraw in favour of some third candidate. (It is a powerful myth among political organizers, very useful to dark horses, that a division on such an occasion is to be avoided at all costs.)

Who was the third candidate to be? Sir Edward Carson was approached. He refused to stand. (He had been among Aitken's dinner-companions in recent months.) In the moment of doubt, another compromise candidate was suggested by *The Times* newspaper, which still retained some of its old prestige, though now owned by Lord Northcliffe. (Northcliffe was among those whose friendship Aitken had been cultivating.) *The Times* suggested Bonar Law.

Three days before the party meeting Lord Balcarres, who was organizing it, informed Long and Chamberlain that their supporters were almost evenly divided, but that there was 'a residuum' in favour of Bonar Law; and that Law, though he might have fewer supporters than either, also had fewer implacable opponents, and was therefore more likely to attract unanimous support without a division. Both Long and Chamberlain sank their ambition in party loyalty: at the Carlton Club, Long proposed Law for the leadership, and Chamberlain seconded him. The motion was carried unanimously.[1]

Recalling this episode twelve years later, in a *Sunday Times* obituary of Bonar Law, Lord Birkenhead remarked that it was then that Beaverbrook had first given 'evidence of intuitive political genius', and that 'with as much boldness, subtlety, friendship, and success as Lucien Bonaparte showed on the 18th Brumaire', he had 'realized that a supreme opportunity lay in front of a third candidate'. Mr Robert Blake,

[1] For Chamberlain's account of this episode, see his *Politics from Inside*, pp. 380–400. For Long's account, see Sir Charles Petrie's *Walter Long and His Times*, pp. 170–2. Credit for suggesting their joint withdrawal is claimed for Chamberlain in his book, for Long in Petrie's.

in *The Unknown Prime Minister*, has indicated the tactics used by Beaverbrook to ensure the deadlock between Long and Chamberlain that would give Law his best chance: he 'urged the Bonar Law party to vote, during Balcarres' successive attempts at canvassing, not for Bonar Law, but for whichever of his two senior rivals seemed at the time to be losing'.

Quite often, both before and since then—most notably in the case of Mr Attlee—a comparatively colourless *tertius gaudens* has slipped into the leadership of a party between two apparently stronger candidates. The phenomenon is invariably puzzling to those not in the know. One of those not in the know in 1911 was King George himself: Sir Harold Nicolson records[1] that the King was surprised that Bonar Law, 'this almost unknown iron merchant from Glasgow', should have succeeded Balfour. 'He was at that date', adds Sir Harold, 'unacquainted with Mr Bonar Law's melancholy, austere, and combative nature, or with the slow precisions of his mind.' Lord Derby hastened to write to the King what would nowadays be called a 'profile' of Law:

> He is a curious mixture. Never very gay, he has become even less so since the death of his wife . . . But still he has a great sense of humour—a first-class debater . . . a great master of figures . . . He has all the qualities of a great leader except one— and that is he has no personal magnetism and can inspire no man to real enthusiasm.

By November 16th, 1911, when this letter was written, neither the King nor Lord Derby would have known (and they would not have relished if they had known) the full story of the stratagems which had led to Law's succession; and it is clear that Derby was overlooking an important fact about Law—the existence, close to him, of one man in whom he did inspire 'real enthusiasm', of a familiar spirit or Svengali who might be able, as it were vicariously, to compensate for his

[1] *King George the Fifth*, p. 165.

want of 'personal magnetism' and to drive him along the road of leadership.

This was indeed the task in which Aitken was now constantly employed in his relations with this irritatingly self-effacing leader. On the day of the Carlton Club meeting, Aitken said to Law: 'Remember, you are a great man now'. Law replied: 'If I am a great man, then a good many great men must have been frauds'. Austen Chamberlain, though deeply involved in this incident, was in a position to assess objectively the qualities of the others also involved: many years later he wrote[1]:

> With all his qualities, Bonar Law had not the power to stand alone, and in the day of battle needed someone to stay up his hands. My first criticism of Lord Beaverbrook's story [in *Politicians and the War*] is that he wholly underrates his own influence with Bonar Law and the part which he himself played in determining Law's action at this and other decisive moments of his career. It is characteristic of Lord Beaverbrook's whole attitude to Bonar Law to represent himself as merely the clarifying medium which enabled Bonar Law to precipitate his own thoughts ... No one who ever saw them together ... can accept that account of their relationship.

This estimate is not inconsistent with Beaverbrook's testimony to Law's modesty and diffidence. Few personalities can be summed up in a word or two, however: many men, inwardly ambitious, may lack the ability or confidence to act at crucial moments, or may fritter ambition away in daydreams, concealing it from even their closest friends. It is unusual that a man with no ambition at all should go into public life and rise to high office. Chamberlain was almost certainly right: Beaverbrook enabled Law not only to 'precipitate his own thoughts' but to crystallize his ambitions and to act so that they would be realized. He was goad as well as catalyst.

[1] In *Down the Years*, pp. 113–14.

Chamberlain himself wrote of Law as a man with ambition ('I sometimes think he was the most ambitious man whom I have known in politics . . . He knew that he was ambitious and could not understand why others did not perceive it.'); and one of the lesser actors in the drama also saw him in this character. Two days after Balfour's resignation, but three days before the Carlton Club meeting, Balfour's devoted private secretary, Mr Jack Sandars, wrote a letter which supplied him—too late—with fuller information on the events leading to his overthrow than was yet available to the King and Lord Derby:

> 4, Carlton Gardens,
> Pall Mall,
> S.W.
> November 10th, 1911

My dear Chief,

I have just heard that it has been settled that Bonar Law will be elected Leader of the Party in the House of Commons. Much intrigue has been at work. Walter, up to some few hours ago, appeared to be winning. Austen was so satisfied that Party detriment would result that he wrote a considered letter to Walter, pointing out that he, Austen, would withdraw, and that he and Walter together ought to concentrate upon the unanimous election of Bonar Law. It was rather a clever move on Austen's part, because he forced Walter's hand . . .

Bonar Law's own methods are open to much criticism. In the struggle I am told[1] he has been run by Max Aitken, the little Canadian adventurer who sits for Ashton-under-Lyne, introduced into that seat by him. Aitken practically owns the 'Daily Express', and the 'Daily Express' has run Bonar Law for the last two days for all it is worth. Bonar Law has been inflexible throughout in his intention to stand, no matter what harm to the Party of division there might be. The real Bonar Law appears to be a man of boundless ambition, untempered by [any]

---

[1] The words 'I am told' are written in ink above the typewritten line,

particularly nice feeling.[1] It is a revelation to me. He found Goulding[2] had committed himself to a hearty support of Austen. He went to Goulding and, reviving ancient memories and rash promises, he practically ordered his support, and this support and influence was then transferred by Goulding from Austen to Bonar Law. I have no time to write another word, but this is just a bird's-eye view for you.

Yours affectionately,
Jack

P.S.[3]

As I have another minute before post.

I have just seen Bal.[4] He confirms the main tenor of this report. But Austen, it appears, also had an interview with Walter, and in conference they confirmed the concordat I have mentioned. Walter's strength in the Lobby surprised Bal. The rally of the country gentlemen was greater than was expected and Austen suffered badly from being a Diehard. Bal says Walter and Austen have behaved well. The news being communicated to Bonar Law, he now is coquetting a little and quotes his inexperience. Bal retorted 'Was yours then a frivolous candidature?' But Bal has no doubt really that he will accept . . .

This exemplary letter is among the Balfour papers in the British Museum. At the top of it are scribbled the words 'very *Confidential Burn*'.

'The little Canadian adventurer' could indeed congratulate himself on the success of his first essay in the art of political prestidigitation. This was surely a taste of real power. Yet it was to be followed, almost at once, by blank, sour frustration. His devotion to Bonar Law was not only personal: he had

[1] The typed words are 'untempered by any nice feeling'. The writer crossed out 'any' and wrote above it 'not particularly', which does not make sense; he wrote in haste and under stress of great emotion.

[2] Sir Edward Goulding—one of the two directors nominated by Aitken to the Board of Rolls-Royce. He was made a peer in 1922, when Law was Prime Minister—perhaps one of the 'rash promises' referred to by Mr Sandars.

[3] The whole of this postscript was written by hand.

[4] Lord Balcarres.

seen in him the likeliest advocate of the 'United Empire' policy by which he was now obsessed.

This policy included the taxation of food imported from foreign countries; but such taxation—a 'stomach tax', as Northcliffe had nicknamed it—was not generally popular in the Conservative Party, for obvious electoral reasons. Moreover, powerful members of the party, such as Carson, insisted that the Liberal proposals for Irish Home Rule were a more important issue to fight on; and Law himself, though born in Canada, was of Northern Irish ancestry.

Aitken nagged as only he can nag; Law threatened resignation; Aitken almost despaired of his chosen leader, and thought seriously of returning to Canada. Law persuaded him to stay, but did not yield to his importunacy: the fight against Home Rule had first priority in the party programme, imported food taxes were shelved. This was the first of many grievous disappointments that Max Aitken was to suffer at the hands of those whom he sought both to be loved by and to dominate—a split ambition whose two halves can never jointly be fulfilled. He reacted to it in a way which will be recognized as characteristic by all who have known him well: he fell seriously ill. The illness might have been diagnosed, thirty years later, as psychosomatic.

An encouraging reception in his constituency (where he had been talking of resignation), and a holiday in Canada and in Switzerland, restored his health and his morale. He had, after all, plenty of time yet; he had grit, he had money, he had brains; he and his wife were now Sir Max and Lady Aitken; and he had completed one exercise in power with notable success.

Many a politician of the second rank would regard such an exercise—the organizing of a revolution in the highest leadership of a great party—as a sufficient achievement for one career. To Aitken, who was not content to stay in the second rank, it was merely a rehearsal for a still unforeseeable but even more extraordinary *coup*.

CHAPTER FIVE

'VAULTING AMBITION'

After such knowledge, what forgiveness? Think now
History has many cunning passages, contrived corridors
And issues, deceives with whispering ambitions,
Guides us by vanities . . . Gives too late
What's not believed in . . .

T. S. ELIOT

IN A country childhood the eye is never wearied by monotony: the life of the brightest flower is brief, the leafy boughs
soon reach their autumn, harvest is golden, the black skeleton
of the tree in winter is decked overnight in the soundless
grace of snow. These natural changes and contrasts are at
their most dramatic in the North American continent. When
the long winter sets in—winter which cracks the concrete of
the sidewalks—it is still the task of the boys in many a country
family to put up the double windows and to pack the sawmill
shavings tightly, for greater insulation, about the walls of the
house. Such a childhood may induce a chronic restlessness in
those whose later life is spent in cities, where the seasons
are told by quarterly rent-days or the financial year and the
weather is usually neither a menace nor a godsend but merely
a nuisance. Beaverbrook at least is one of those who never
stays long in one place. By 1914 he had established himself,
satisfactorily near the top, in London; the outbreak of war
provided him with the chance of a drastic change of scene and
work (and, incidentally, of rehabilitating himself in the eyes
of those in his homeland who still murmured against him).
He became Canadian Record Officer and, soon, 'eye-witness'
at the front.

It suited him better to represent Canada than to be an
observer or correspondent from the United Kingdom. He
was less hampered by red tape than he would have been

in a directly subordinate position at Sir John French's head-quarters. Moreover, Lord Kitchener, the Secretary of State for War, was doing his utmost to suppress irregular corre-spondents (some of whom had managed to get to Belgium and France in the first days of the war), to delay the arrival at the front of the accredited correspondents, and to feed the public with rosy official communiqués. It is possible to feel some sympathy with Kitchener, harassed as he was by the real news of disastrous reverses, prolonged retreats, and heavy casualties; but the policy was certainly wrong. It was wrong for two reasons: in a grave emergency, as Winston Churchill was to prove in a later war, the British people are braced, not enfeebled, by the truth; and in any case they were learning the truth, piecemeal and more alarmingly and inaccurately, from wounded soldiers flocking home with tales of unpre-cedentedly terrible conditions of warfare and ammunition shortages.

Aitken's semi-independent position as a Dominion eye-witness—and as an MP with influence in high quarters—made it easier for him to break down official reticence. Again and again he fought and beat the censors, arguing that this war was the affair of the mass of the people as no previous war had been, and that without knowledge public morale could not be sustained. He managed to get past the censorship the first photograph ever published of a hitherto secret weapon, the tank; the *Daily Mirror* paid £5,000 to charity for this picture. He also started the first newspaper ever produced exclusively for the troops—the *Canadian Daily Record*. It lasted until July 31st, 1919. As many as a quarter of a million copies of each issue were distributed free. This newspaper was officially in trouble at least once; it was criticized for taking sides in a Canadian election. The charge was true—but by the time the inquest took place, the election was over.

He was commissioned with the rank of lieutenant-colonel, and sailed to France with the Canadian troops. The first

BEAVERBROOK

major battle in which they were engaged—at Ypres—was the
first that it was his duty to describe; he did so without dis-
guising the cost and the suffering, and since his story was
released officially to the press from Canadian headquarters,
this was also the first battle of which the British public had
read an unvarnished account. The grimness was there; but
so was the gallantry:

> The battle . . . was bloody, even as men appraise battles in this
> callous and life-engulfing war . . . The Canadians wrested from
> the trenches, over the bodies of the dead and maimed, the right
> to stand side by side with the superb troops who, in the first
> battle of Ypres, broke and drove before them the flower of the
> Prussian Guards.
>
> Looked at from any point, the performance would be remark-
> able. It is amazing to soldiers, when the genesis and composition
> of the Canadian Division are considered . . . It consisted in the
> main of men who . . . at the outbreak of war were neither disci-
> plined nor trained . . .
>
> The Canadian Division, enormously outnumbered . . . with a
> gap in their lines, and with dispositions made hurriedly . . .
> fought through the day and through the night, and then through
> another day and night; fought under their officers until . . . these
> perished gloriously, and then fought . . . because they came
> from fighting stock.
>
> They suffered terrible casualties. For a short time every other
> man seemed to fall . . . The 4th Canadian Battalion at one
> moment came under a particularly withering fire. For a moment
> —not more—it wavered. Its most gallant Commanding Officer,
> Lieutenant-Colonel Birchall, carrying, after an old fashion, a
> light cane, coolly and cheerfully rallied his men, and at the very
> moment when his example had infected them, fell dead . . . With
> a hoarse cry of anger they sprang forward (for, indeed, they
> loved him) as if to avenge his death . . . After a hand-to-hand
> struggle, the last German who resisted was bayoneted, and the
> trench was won . . .

Few correspondents in any war have written more vividly
than this. Some indeed refused to believe that the Max Aitken

they knew had written the despatch; they whispered that it had been 'ghosted'. In this they were less than just. Before going to France Aitken had made a deliberate effort to train himself in the writing of straightforward descriptive prose. He had one of the best of tutors—his friend Rudyard Kipling. Kipling taught him many tricks of the trade, and told him: 'Model your stuff on Kinglake'.

This single, moving story did more than any other action in his life to endear Max Aitken to his countrymen; the successful financier who had accepted an English title was forgotten in the patriotic eye-witness. His work was recognized: he was appointed Canadian Government representative at the front. He now, therefore, had free access to GHQ, with authority and with, still, some independence.

He did not fail to exploit such an opportunity: GHQ was quarrelling with the War Office on the question of the supply of shells, and Aitken, from France, kept in close touch with Lloyd George and other politicians at home, and provided them with data for their campaign on the same subject against Kitchener. After furious dissensions in the Cabinet, with both Lloyd George and Kitchener threatening to resign, Lloyd George—then Chancellor of the Exchequer—was victorious. In April, 1915, Asquith appointed him chairman of a special Munitions of War Committee; five weeks later, when the first Coalition Government was formed, he became Minister of Munitions. This Government was formed three days after the most sensational development in the munitions crisis—the publication in Northcliffe's *Daily Mail* of an article headlined:

THE TRAGEDY OF THE SHELLS
LORD KITCHENER'S GRAVE ERROR

The most extraordinary feature of this attack—which in itself may well have been justified in the national interest—is that it was actually instigated by the Commander-in-Chief, Sir John French, who sent a secretary and an aide-de-camp

to London to contact Northcliffe and various Opposition
MPs. Commanders in the field do not always agree with their
political chiefs in Whitehall; but they have rarely intrigued
against them so daringly as this.[1] Aitken thought little of
French: the battle of Neuve Chapelle, which French had
represented to the public as a victory, he called 'a horribly
costly failure'. But it is hard to believe that he was not privy
to French's plot against Kitchener; he would have been aware
of the despatch of the emissaries from GHQ. Possibly he
realized that French, by taking such action, would be over-
reaching himself, and saw no need to restrain him. If so, his
intuition was sound. The King observed to the Duke of Con-
naught that French was 'behaving in a very bad way'.
French's own Chief of Staff, Sir William Robertson, was
seriously concerned by his inadequacy. By the end of the
year, French had been replaced as Commander-in-Chief by
Sir Douglas Haig; he was (of course) 'kicked upstairs' to the
House of Lords, with warm tributes to his distinguished
services, and was given command of the Home Forces.

Aitken soon decided that he must come back to London to
organize the supreme political manœuvre that was now beginning to seem necessary to him and to others—the removal
of Asquith from the premiership. Temperamentally, Aitken
found Asquith uncongenial: he was 'a scholar and a gentleman' in the old sense of the phrase, incapable of a mean or an
impulsive action, with something of the philosophic detachment of his old opponent Balfour (who had replaced Churchill
at the Admiralty when the first Coalition was formed), and
therefore open all too easily to the charge of indecision.

[1] It was fortunate for the emissaries that they did not encounter the Prime
Minister's redoubtable wife. In her diary at this time Mrs Asquith wrote:
'Henry is as indifferent to the Press as St Paul's Cathedral is to midges, but I
confess that I am not! and I only hope the man responsible for giving information to Lord Northcliffe will be heavily punished: God may forgive him; I
never can'. A month or two later French, an old friend, came to see her. She
found the interview 'painful': he 'denied all knowledge of the shell affair'
but was 'dejected and confused'.

Moreover, Aitken could argue plausibly that Asquith's new government, even with Lloyd George in charge of munitions, was unlikely to have any lasting stability: for one thing, Asquith had been foolish enough, as it seemed, deliberately to slight his Conservative colleagues (no doubt under pressure from his own supporters) by keeping them out of the main posts. Bonar Law, their leader, was Secretary of State for the Colonies. He could have had higher office if he had insisted on it: Aitken noted, almost impatiently, that Law's 'simple patriotism' had enabled the Liberals to keep all the best jobs for themselves.

Even within the Liberal section of the Government, however, harmony was not complete. Asquith himself later described an interview in the Cabinet Room at which he was endeavouring to patch up a quarrel between Lloyd George and his successor as Chancellor of the Exchequer, Mr Reginald McKenna. When it seemed that his mediation was going to fail, Asquith said (not perhaps without a touch of pomposity, or of what actors call 'ham'): 'In another week I shall have sat in this chair for seven years. If I have the slightest reason to think that there is any one among you who has the faintest suspicion about me, I will gladly abandon it.' According to Asquith, these words thawed the anger of the irreconcilables and they both exclaimed: 'The day you leave that chair the rest of us disappear, never to return'. The anecdote may be accepted with a certain reserve: if these selfless words were indeed exclaimed simultaneously by both parties—which seems improbable—one at least of them, Lloyd George, must be convicted either of the most cynical insincerity or of having a conveniently short memory; for within a few months he was in the thick of the intrigue to remove the occupant of 'that chair', and in the following year he was to sit in it himself.

Though Bonar Law was ultimately to play a crucial part in this intrigue, his concern for the appearance of national

unity made him reluctant to disturb the existing set-up.
He shared with Asquith a cautiousness in examining new
proposals quite unlike Lloyd George's approach, which was
more like that of a messianic grasshopper. One Sunday,
however, Law and Lloyd George met, at Aitken's house at
Leatherhead, to discuss the succession to Kitchener at the
War Office. 'The position,' Aitken recorded, 'practically lay
between the two of them. Lloyd George was anxious, Bonar
Law was willing, to take it.' In the end, after a conversation
which began badly—for there were many issues on which
they disagreed—Law promised to back Lloyd George's claim
to the War Office. Law and Aitken went by road to Asquith's
house at Sutton Courtney in Berkshire; Aitken sat outside in
the car while Law went in and persuaded Asquith to send
Lloyd George to the War Office.

Looking back later on these events, Aitken saw in this
acceptance by Asquith of the joint will of his two most
powerful colleagues the first sign that his leadership was
doomed. At the end of the first volume of *Politicians and
the War*, he wrote: 'Asquith fell because he was by nature a
Conservative. But the beginning of his fall dates from the
struggle over the War Office.' Of the mercurial and dynamic
Welshman who succeeded Asquith, and of the plot that
effected the change, Aitken wrote in the same place: 'The
new school of reality . . . gathered not out of political principles, but out of sheer preservative instinct, round the new
man who strode on to a battlefield which suited his adaptive
genius.'

There was indeed much dissatisfaction, on both sides of the
House, with the conduct of the war. Lloyd George, though
serving under Asquith, had long been fretting for what he
euphemistically called 'reorganization'. The Conservative
critics were mostly grouped around Sir Edward Carson. In a
private interview at the War Office on November 13th, 1916,
Lloyd George admitted to Aitken that he and Carson had

been working underground together; Aitken promised Lloyd George his support, subject only to his overriding loyalty to his, and Carson's, leader, Bonar Law.

Appreciating the situation realistically, Aitken saw that Asquith and Law together were invincible. His task, therefore, must be to prise Law apart from Asquith and persuade him to combine with Carson and Lloyd George in demands which Asquith would then not be strong enough to resist. In order to do this, he had first to 'sell' Lloyd George to Law. This proved to be no easy task: with that dogged puritanism that must have been so infuriating to his less scrupulous friends, Law argued that Lloyd George was a self-seeker, out for his own advancement. Aitken pleaded that Lloyd George was sincere, but that such personal considerations were in any case irrelevant to the main issue—the more vigorous and efficient prosecution of the war. Law agreed about the main issue, but was still 'desperately "sticky"' about Lloyd George.

At last, after much coming and going, difficulties about dates and about who would or wouldn't dine with whom, Aitken managed to get Lloyd George, Law, and Carson together, on November 20th, in his suite at the Hyde Park Hotel. The atmosphere was 'strained'. Lloyd George, however, showed 'great skill and tact': the main reform that he had been advocating was the transfer of power from the cumbersomely large Cabinet and its War Committee to a small War Council of three or four ministers with quasi-dictatorial powers; on this occasion he deliberately under-stated his demands, emphasizing that, so long as he got his War Council, Asquith should remain Prime Minister. Law was still not convinced that Lloyd George's intentions were honourable.

Meeting after meeting followed, most of them in Aitken's rooms. Once Lloyd George nearly ruined the whole thing by saying frankly that Asquith must not be a member of the new War Council: a Prime Minister must dominate any body of which he was a member, and this Prime Minister would render useless any such body that he dominated. The quixotic Law was shocked, and, fond as he was of Aitken, rounded quite roughly on him, when they were alone, for having let him in for all this nefarious scheming. 'The lot of the negotiator,' wrote Aitken in his diary, 'is never quite happy.'

On November 25th, the four men met again, this time for luncheon at Law's house, Pembroke Lodge. (The food was, as usual, execrable.) At a certain stage in any negotiations—when people are beginning to tire of 'talking in circles'—some advantage will go to the man who has taken the trouble to prepare a written draft of a statement or memorandum: at least, it will provide a new basis for discussion; at best, all can sign it, no doubt in amended form. This Aitken had done that morning. He had not merely drafted a statement for Law, Lloyd George, and Carson to sign: he had drafted it in the first person singular ('in my opinion . . . I have decided . . . I have invited . . .'); and the 'I' who was to be required to sign and publish it, if the other three men agreed, was none other than the Prime Minister of the day, Mr Asquith.

Aitken's initiative was audacious; his psychological insight was sound. Law, while still anxious about the conduct of the war, was wearying of these long-drawn-out secret meetings; Carson was becoming desperately impatient; Lloyd George was—Lloyd George. With only a few minor amendments by Bonar Law, the draft was accepted by the three men. It announced almost precisely what Lloyd George had been demanding—a 'civilian general staff' of three Cabinet ministers without portfolio, to meet daily. There was one concession to Law's scruples: besides the three ministers, the new body was to be presided over by the Prime Minister. But this concession was surely offset by the fact that, while two names were modestly left blank, that of Lloyd George was included, with the words 'and he has consented to act as chairman and to preside at any meeting which, owing to the pressure of other duties, I find it impossible to attend'. It may be supposed that Lloyd George foresaw with some confidence that the Prime Minister's 'other duties' would be numerous and pressing.

In retrospect, it is hard to believe that the leader of a government—a wartime Coalition government with, on paper, overwhelming support—could have even considered signing a document so humiliatingly prefabricated and presented with such menacing implications. A Churchill or an Attlee would have dismissed it with withering contempt. Perhaps Asquith knew that his majority was on paper only, and would vanish quickly if men so variously potent as Lloyd George and Law were united against him. At any rate, Law—who was no doubt relieved that the conspiratorial phase of the operation was ending—agreed readily to show Asquith the memorandum; and Asquith actually said that he would sign if these terms represented Lloyd George's final aims and were not merely an instalment. This was on Saturday, November 25th; Asquith promised to give a definite answer on the Monday. Lloyd George and Aitken spent an uneasy Sunday; on the Monday Bonar Law received, and showed them, a letter in which Asquith turned down their proposal, with some sharp comments on Lloyd George: 'he does not inspire trust' and 'one construction, and one only, ... could be put on the new arrangement—that it has been engineered by him with the purpose ... of his displacing me.'

This was too near the truth to be comfortable. It was now almost open war: Law, indeed, tried for a time to act as mediator; but Carson induced the *Morning Post* (a newspaper of the extreme Right, hitherto hostile to Lloyd George) to say that Lloyd George alone could save the country; and that mysterious (and then unpolled) force, public opinion, was beginning to say this too.

Then Law met with strong opposition from his Conservative colleagues: Lord Robert Cecil complained that he was 'ruining the Conservative Party by dragging it at Lloyd George's coat-tails'. (In the event, it was the Liberal Party whose ruin may be said to have begun with Lloyd George's feud against Asquith and subsequent alliance with the Tories.) This Tory opposition to Law, though it was based on hostility to Lloyd George and, to some extent, on loyalty to Asquith, proved more useful to Lloyd George than to Asquith; for Law's character was such that, having been won gradually by his vehement friend to the view that Lloyd George must be supported, opposition merely tended to strengthen him in this view; and without him Asquith could certainly not have been unseated.

Beaverbrook has in his diary at this point[1] an eloquent passage deflating what he calls the myth of Asquith's indispensability. As it turned out, it was perfectly easy to form a new government: Asquith's Liberal ministers had vowed not to serve under another leader, and kept their vow; but there was a rush of back-benchers eager to replace them—no doubt, as Beaverbrook says (without, he says, irony), from motives of pure patriotism. All the same, Beaverbrook is probably entitled to dramatize, as he does, the apparent hopelessness of the enterprise, at this quite late stage, less than a week before Asquith's fall: 'I went home that night [November 30th] to the Hyde Park Hotel . . . A cold north-east wind blew in from the night and the single lamp was so shaded as to give hardly a glimmer . . . I thought how vastly greater were the forces ranged against Bonar Law than those ranged on his side . . . The external forces were arrayed in their entirety on Asquith's side . . . Count heads on either front bench, and opposition to him would appear to be ridiculous.'

This was so: but for Carson, Law was alone in his party, Lloyd George had only one doubtful supporter (Mr Edwin Montagu) in his. On December 1st Mr Arthur Henderson, the Labour Party leader, said that Asquith was 'indispensable'

---

[1] *Politicians and the War*, vol. ii, pp. 178–82.

for the winning of the war: within a week he was in office under
Lloyd George. There is indeed no myth that can be dissipated
so instantaneously as that of any one man's indispensability.

There was, however, one 'external force', not reckoned in
the balance at this point by Beaverbrook, which was to
contribute decisively to the issue: the force of press publicity
and comment. Lloyd George was now, though he remained
outwardly cool, phrenetically determined to bring matters to
an issue at once. He had an exchange of letters with Asquith
on December 1st, on the constitution and scope of the proposed War Council: the gist of Asquith's reply was that he,
the Prime Minister, could not be 'relegated to the position of
an arbiter in the background'. He added the perhaps needless
irritant of a phrase in Latin: the council 'should . . . sit *de die
in diem*'. Lloyd George and his friends moved in to the kill—
and they now enlisted the aid of a number of newspapers.

In such a *coup*, the timing of publicity must be calculated
with care (or with flair, which Aitken at least had): at a particular moment publicity which would have been fatal a week
earlier becomes urgently necessary. So Aitken 'leaked' the
story of the political crisis to the *Daily Express* (which he did
not then control) and the *Daily Chronicle*. 'To the man in the
street . . .', he boasted in his diary, 'their news contained the
hope of salvation'—adding, perhaps a shade too innocently,
that 'to the narrower sect of Liberals . . . the whole business
savoured of a conspiracy'. Meanwhile, Northcliffe was trying
to see Lloyd George.[1] A headline in his *Evening News* gave the
first hint of Lloyd George's ultimate tactical bluff: 'Lloyd
George Packing Up'. Next day, Sunday, December 3rd,
Reynolds News published a full and accurate account of the

---

[1] In fact, he did not see him: both Asquith's friends and his detractors,
including Mr J. A. Spender, Beaverbrook and Mr Tom Clarke (*My Northcliffe
Diary*), have been misled by the accident that Northcliffe was seen by Edwin
Montagu coming out of Lloyd George's room at the War Office. He had only
been in the anteroom; Lloyd George was unwilling, or too busy, to receive
him.

situation, saying that if Lloyd George's terms were not agreed to he would resign and appeal to public opinion against Asquith. It was, again, Aitken who had given this information to the proprietor of *Reynolds News*, Sir Henry (later Lord) Dalziel. In doing so, he was taking a risk: as he must surely have foreseen, the *Reynolds* article excited the Tory ministers' anger against Lloyd George, whom they supposed responsible for the 'leak'. Presumably it was felt by the conspirators, or at least by Aitken, that this reaction would be outweighed by the effect on public opinion and that, in any case, the publicity would all help to precipitate the now urgently desired 'show-down'.

Certainly the Tory ministers were in an obstreperously anti-Georgian mood when they arrived for a meeting at Bonar Law's house that Sunday morning, several of them brandishing the offensive rag. Aitken, too, was there—lurking, unseen by the others, in another room. He did not want them to know that he was there: 'they were ready enough as it was,' he wrote, 'to charge me with possessing too much influence over Law—a charge which was not true'.

Whether this charge was true or not, Law left the others at least once during the meeting to report to Aitken on its progress, and to consult with him. He was having a difficult time: he alone, the party leader, was firmly committed to Lloyd George; the others were solidly against him. This, at any rate, was the impression conveyed by Law to his backstage counsellor; but it would be hard to find—except perhaps in the newscolumns of, say, the *Daily Express* and the *Daily Worker*—two apparently factual accounts of one event more utterly contradictory of each other than the account of this meeting in Beaverbrook's book and the account of it in Sir Charles Petrie's *Life and Letters of the Rt Hon Sir Austen Chamberlain*. Chamberlain was a conscientious, unimaginative, systematic man; Petrie's book is largely based on his full and frequent letters to his stepmother. Beaverbrook's *Politicians and the War* is based on the diary that he kept at the time. Both accounts, therefore, are derived from contemporary observation.

According to Beaverbrook:

> It became rapidly apparent that Bonar Law stood absolutely alone. Opposed to him sat the whole array of the Tory leaders— Lord Curzon, Austen Chamberlain, Lord Robert Cecil, Walter Long, etc. The dominant note of the meeting was hostility to Lloyd George and to his plans for organizing a War Council . . . The only explanation . . . must be sought in the hypnotic influence which Asquith—using his position as Prime Minister—had very subtly acquired over their minds . . . They determined not only to support the Prime Minister against Lloyd George, but to compel the Prime Minister to advance far beyond his own intentions in a vigorous counter-offensive which was to turn Lloyd George out of the Cabinet . . .

According to Sir Charles Petrie:

> In the discussion . . . Austen played a prominent part. He took the line that a reconstruction of the Government was inevitable since Mr Lloyd George was in open rebellion and the Prime Minister had failed to assert his authority: . . . an administration under a Conservative Prime Minister was inadvisable if not impracticable, and it was therefore for the Liberals to decide which of their leaders they wished to see at the head of the Government. Austen's views found favour with the meeting, and there was a unanimous feeling that . . . the Conservative Ministers should hold themselves aloof from the personal quarrel between Mr Asquith and Mr Lloyd George.

It may be supposed that the progress of the meeting was a little less clear-cut than this. No doubt Chamberlain's description, as summarized by his biographer, is tidier than the reality. Even if the fullest allowance is made for tidying and condensation, this does not agree at essential points with the other account: Law–Beaverbrook and Chamberlain–Petrie cannot both be right.

These ministers were, no doubt, in a dilemma. They were suspicious of Lloyd George; yet they were anxious for a more vigorous direction of the war. Perhaps they half-realized that their dilemma was, in part, the result of their own innate preference for a Prime Minister who shared their social and ethical traditions and their English accent, and of their corresponding distaste for the 'bold bad men', the pushers, the vulgarians whose adventurousness was beginning to seem a necessary prerequisite of victory. Such introspection, however blurred, would tend to make them all the more angry; and a common defensive mechanism would have externalized this emotion automatically, against Lloyd George and, to a lesser extent, against Bonar Law.

It is not surprising that a group of men, meeting in a mood of such psychological confusion—and meeting on a Sunday morning, when Englishmen of the old ruling class most hate to meet for serious business—should have passed, eventually, a resolution which meant little or nothing without full explanation. The resolution—a typical example of committee drafting—reads as follows:

> We share the view expressed to you by Mr Bonar Law some time ago that the Government cannot continue as it is.
>
> It is evident that a change must be made, and, in our opinion, the publicity given to the intentions of Mr Lloyd George makes reconstruction from within no longer possible.
>
> We therefore urge the Prime Minister to tender the resignation of the Government.
>
> If he feels unable to take that step, we authorize Mr Bonar Law to tender our resignations.

Before agreeing to sign this resolution, Law—leaving the meeting on some pretext—discussed its general sense with Aitken, without showing him the text. Of the two men, Aitken was the more subtle: it may well have been he who put it into the mind of Law, troubled as he was by his colleagues' hostility to Lloyd George, that he could perfectly well assent to a general demand for resignation (since both he and the others were agreed on that, from different motives), because he, after all, as leader, would have the advantage of actually delivering the message to Asquith and would thus be able to give whatever emphasis he preferred to an ambiguous document. Whatever passed between Law and Aitken at this crucial moment—on which there is only the uncorroborated evidence of the latter, who has always been anxious, as has been seen already, to minimize his own influence on Law—it is certain that Law went back to his colleagues and agreed to sign the resolution and to convey it to Asquith at once.

It was noon. The Tory ministers went away. Aitken stayed to lunch with Law—who now showed him the actual text of the resolution. Aitken was startled by the second paragraph, with its open hostility to Lloyd George: he saw at once that this might endanger the whole operation. Asquith would guess that he could still count on solid Tory support; in extreme emergency he would be able to release to the country this damaging indictment of Lloyd George, signed not only by the Tory ministers hostile to Lloyd George but by Law himself. Again, only one account is extant of the exchanges between Law and Aitken, but the latter has admitted[1] that he was 'aghast at the results that must follow' the showing of the resolution to Asquith. His account adds that when Law set off to see Asquith, he went with him as far as the Colonial Office; they went into Law's room there, and Aitken lit the fire because the day was cold. He then waited there, communicating by telephone with Lloyd George, while Law went over to Downing Street.

Whatever was said during and after lunch, one thing that Bonar Law did—or rather, omitted to do—when he saw Asquith that afternoon, must be regarded as highly significant. *He did not show Asquith the text of the resolution.*[2] He merely

---

[1] *Politicians and the War*, vol. ii, pp. 217–18.
[2] *Memories and Reflections*, by the Earl of Oxford and Asquith, p. 131 *n*.

conveyed to him verbally what he considered an adequate summary of its sense. Asquith was later told that the written resolution 'was torn up on its way to 10 Downing Street'; but Law himself is quoted by Mr Robert Blake as stating that he had it in his pocket and 'forgot' to show it to Asquith.

Anybody experienced in politics will agree that this was surprising conduct in the leader of a party on so momentous an occasion. When a resolution has been drafted in conference by a number of persons, arguing it out phrase by phrase—and particularly, perhaps, when its obscurity of wording veils real differences of opinion—it is the duty of the man who goes as spokesman or delegate on behalf of all who have signed it to stick as closely as possible to the written text, and not to essay too many glosses on it. It has already been shown that Law agreed to sign the resolution only because its ambiguity seemed, to some extent, to cover his own attitude as well as his colleagues' quite different attitude. It would surely have simplified his mission merely to have shown the resolution to Asquith and to have said as little as possible by way of interpretation. A day or two later, some of the Tory ministers found that Asquith had not at all understood the purport of their resolution. The discovery was disconcerting: it was even suggested, says Beaverbrook, that Law 'had abused his position as an ambassador in order to misrepresent the views of his clients because he did not happen to agree with them personally'. Beaverbrook has defended his friend with some heat against such charges: 'One could hardly imagine a more terrible accusation against any public man'.

According to Beaverbrook, Law 'was the last person in the world to fail to give a lucid exposition of a political situation'. He explained the position to Asquith 'with the most complete frankness'. Asquith, on the other hand, was so 'frightened' by the single word 'resignation' that he 'did not at that moment grasp the importance of that part of the resolution which accused Lloyd George of trafficking in Fleet Street'.

According to Asquith's friends and biographers, such an account of the interview misrepresents fundamentally the respective qualities of the two men. They say that two of Asquith's outstanding characteristics were coolness of head and quickness of understanding: he was not the man to be flustered or bemused or thrown off his balance in such circumstances. His dignity of demeanour was the outward expression of a classically well-ordered mind. By contrast, some of them add, Bonar Law, though he had pertinacity and skill in debate—and was, indeed, not thought of as a man capable of dishonourable dealing—was yet notably taciturn in private conversation, allusive rather than lucid, and sometimes almost inarticulate.

Chamberlain was one of the Tory ministers who found that Asquith had misunderstood their message to him. Though he would not have accepted Beaverbrook's interpretation of the message, he equally would not have wished Asquith to think that it implied that the Tory ministers were deserting him *en bloc*—the impression apparently left with Asquith, intentionally or unintentionally, by Law. Chamberlain's testimony on this curious episode is contained in his book, *Down the Years* (pp. 119–20):

> Lord Beaverbrook is wrong in supposing that any one of us then or afterwards charged Bonar Law with bad faith or suspected him of it. We thought that he had blundered . . . we felt strongly that the actual words of our resolution should have been communicated to [Asquith] and a copy informally given to him. The sequel shows that we were right; for lack of this commonplace precaution, misunderstandings followed which could easily have been avoided.

Beaverbrook's own account, though it is much the fullest and most detailed account of these events that has ever appeared, neither states nor denies that Law omitted to show Asquith the document. In view of the controversy on this important point, Law's own omission is hardly more strange than Beaverbrook's omission to mention it.

The 'misunderstandings' referred to by Chamberlain may indeed have had some effect on the course of affairs; for on the Sunday evening, when Asquith saw Lloyd George (Lloyd George having been given by Aitken a full account of the Tory ministers' meeting and resolution, including the clause censuring Lloyd George's relations with the press), they nearly reached agreement. No doubt this was partly because Asquith was unaware of the actual balance of the Tory resolution, and thought that his position was weaker than it really was. At any rate, he agreed in principle to Lloyd George's proposals for a War Council, reserving only the question of its personnel; and issued that night an announcement not of resignation but of a mere 'reconstruction' of the Government.

Next morning, December 4th, Northcliffe's *Times* published a leading article attacking Asquith personally; the writer of it seemed to be aware of the confidential exchanges between Asquith and Lloyd George.[1] Both Tory and Liberal ministers were now furious, the latter partly, no doubt, because they had not been consulted about the 'reconstruction' suddenly announced on the previous night, which was interpreted as a victory for Lloyd George; their intransigence, and *The Times* article in particular, stiffened Asquith's attitude. On the previous night he had thought that he and Lloyd George were substantially in agreement: now he felt that he neither need nor could go so far to meet him as he had intended. He wanted once more to fight. He wrote to Lloyd George withdrawing from their tentative agreement: Lloyd George retorted decisively—by resigning office, coupling with his resignation the threat of a national campaign against the Government.

[1] The article was actually written by the editor of *The Times*, Mr Geoffrey Robinson (later Dawson). He had been spending the week-end at Cliveden, which was to become famous for its political house-parties at the time of Munich. His informant was not Lloyd George, but Carson; and the part of the article which dealt with the confidential exchanges was added when he returned to London on the Sunday night.

There is a fundamental divergence between the various accounts of this crisis. According to Beaverbrook, almost all the Tories—whose contact with Asquith after Sunday was through three of their number, Lord Curzon, Lord Robert Cecil, and Austen Chamberlain ('the three Cs')—were strongly pro-Asquithian; the intention of their resolution had been to egg Asquith on to resign *in order to call Lloyd George's bluff*, in the belief that Lloyd George, even with Bonar Law to help him, would be unable to form a government and that the King would therefore have to send for Asquith again; and Beaverbrook believes that this was Asquith's motive in resigning, as he eventually did at 7 p.m. on Tuesday, December 5th, 1916. According to Asquith's own official biographers, J. A. Spender and Cyril Asquith, on the other hand, 'the three Cs' told Asquith, 'to his great surprise', that they could no longer support him, because 'they saw no prospect of holding their party' if Law and Carson went into opposition with Lloyd George. As Dr Thomas Jones put it[1]: 'He asked them whether they would be prepared to go on with him whilst Lloyd George and Bonar Law resigned. They answered with a perfectly definite negative, and held themselves free to serve in a Lloyd George administration.' According to this version, therefore, Asquith's resignation was genuine, and he felt obliged to resign because the forces against him were now so strong.

This discrepancy is puzzling. On the one hand, all the evidence cited by Beaverbrook shows that Law and Carson were almost alone among the Tories in supporting Lloyd George; on the other hand, 'the three Cs' themselves accepted office under Lloyd George when he was invited by the King to form a government. At this stage in their careers, such men were not greedily clinging to office at all costs; nor is it sufficient to say that, as patriots, they were bound to serve under any man to whom the King extended such an invitation. If

[1] In *Lloyd George*, p. 85.

101

Beaverbrook's analysis is correct, and the Asquithian-Tory tactic was to demonstrate that Lloyd George was incapable of forming a government, would they not surely—of course, in the national interest as they saw it—have refused to serve?

Cecil has written[1]: 'We . . . went to see Mr Lloyd George and explained that we were not anxious to go on in office and if he preferred to do without us we would readily stand aside'. Chamberlain was certainly not eager to serve under Lloyd George. Some days later he wrote to his sister: 'I take no pleasure in a change which gives me a chief whom I profoundly distrust . . . who has tired out the patience of every man who has worked with him . . . who let his Unionist colleagues down about conscription at the critical moment and then took up the question again when he thought the audience more favourable and the limelight more concentrated on himself . . .' If this was what he really felt about Lloyd George, the incentive to have helped to save Asquith by such a manœuvre as Beaverbrook suggests must have been strong indeed; yet it was Chamberlain and a few other Tories —most notably Balfour—who, by going over to Lloyd George, made it possible for him to form a government. Why should they have done this if, as Beaverbrook insists, 'the plan of wholesale resignation . . . was only intended to make more certain the destruction of the common enemy', Lloyd George?

In this kind of argument, probability is not everything (because men behave so improbably in emergencies or under the stress of emotion or at the spur of ambition), but it is something; and the probability of the case seems to be against Beaverbrook's interpretation, intimate though his concern with these events was.

There is a further reason for doubting the soundness of Beaverbrook's theory of Asquith's resignation. On December 6th—a few hours before it became necessary for him to

---

[1] In *A Great Experiment*, by Viscount Cecil, p. 45.

send for Lloyd George—the King presided at an all-party
conference at Buckingham Palace; the purpose of the conference was to discuss the formation of a government in which,
it was still hoped by many, Asquith might be willing to serve
under Bonar Law. It was agreed that, if he would not, Lloyd
George should try to form a government. Those present
at the Palace conference were Asquith, Bonar Law, Lloyd
George, Balfour, and Arthur Henderson. Beaverbrook, who
presumably got his information about the proceedings at this
conference from either Law or Lloyd George, says that 'every
one present—with a single exception—was anxious, and
especially anxious on one point—the retention of Asquith's
services . . . in one capacity or another'. The one exception,
he says, was Asquith himself: 'He was neither worried, nor
anxious to serve . . . His manner . . . was fairly like that of a
schoolboy who has got an unexpected half-holiday. He was
jocular with everybody . . .' He did not absolutely refuse to
serve in a new government, but 'said he must first consult his
friends'.

Beaverbrook's explanation of this behaviour—unusual in
so dignified a statesman on so grave an occasion—is that
Asquith thought that his resignation bluff had worked: the
conference was 'an acknowledgement of weakness' by his
opponents, 'presaging [their] ultimate failure'. He 'decided
to play the game to the end', went away 'with his mind already
made up', and an hour or two later wrote to Law refusing to
serve, as confident as his Liberal and Tory friends that Lloyd
George would not be able to form a government and that he
would have a 'triumphant return'.

Lord Stamfordham, private secretary to the King, kept
an official record of the conference which gives a somewhat
different picture from Beaverbrook's necessarily second-hand
account. It is clear from this report that, so far from being
irresponsibly 'jocular', Asquith spoke with his customary
weightiness, reopening the whole argument about the War

Council (or War Committee, as it was now called), 'denouncing in serious terms the . . . daily vindictive, merciless attacks' on him in the press, and referring 'in touching terms' to the King's confidence in him. It was after this lengthy speech that the King, perhaps feeling that enough words had been spent in this inconclusive debate (and noticing, no doubt, that it was nearly tea-time), 'now called the attention of the Meeting to the fact that, although the matter had been fully discussed, no decision had been come to'.

It may well be that Beaverbrook reports correctly Asquith's demeanour before and after the conference (the sort of moment at which there usually is some trivial conversation), but only one sentence of Lord Stamfordham's report fits in with the general impression that he gives: 'He [Asquith] could honestly say that on waking this morning he was thankful to feel he was a free man'. There seems no reason to doubt the sincerity of such a sentiment—and, indeed, Beaverbrook's own account of Asquith's cheerfulness, so far as it is not exaggerated, is in keeping with it: an exhilaration, amounting almost to lightheadedness, is often felt by those who, after long mental conflict, have just resigned from burdensome office. But this phenomenon, whether Beaverbrook's or Stamfordham's emphasis is the truer, is itself, surely, the strongest argument against Beaverbrook's main theory. It tends to show that Asquith's resignation was sincere and irrevocable: this thankfulness, this sense of relief could hardly have been counterfeited, and would not have been felt by a man engaged in a momentous game of bluff whose outcome was still perilously in doubt.[1]

---

[1] Mr Frank Owen, author of *Tempestuous Journey*, the latest and most fully documented life of Lloyd George, accepts the genuineness of Asquith's resignation. In the main, however, he follows uncritically Beaverbrook's account of the whole episode, and thus underestimates the significance of Law's failure to communicate to Asquith the text of the Conservative ministers' resolution, which he slurs over by saying that Asquith 'misunderstood the clumsily drafted words'.

Those who accept Beaverbrook's view sometimes cite in support of it a passage in Winston Churchill's *Great Contemporaries*. Churchill (who always thought that Asquith should have appealed to the House of Commons in secret session for a vote of confidence) says of him that, throughout these days of crisis, 'he was certainly not the helpless victim which his enemies have believed and his biographer has depicted', and that 'when he resolved to put his rival to the test, of forming a government or being utterly discredited, ... he played the tremendous stake with iron composure'. But these statements are of little value as independent evidence: Churchill was far from the centre of power at this time, and even a cursory reading of his text shows that he merely accepted Beaverbrook's account *in toto* and paraphrased it in somewhat more sonorous language.

More difficult to explain, except on the supposition that Beaverbrook is correct, is one sentence in a letter written by Lord Crewe (one of Asquith's Liberal ministers) many years later (on October 1st, 1928): 'The prompt agreement of Curzon and one or two others to take part in the Government at the end of 1916 has always stood in need of some explanation *after what they had previously said to Asquith*'. The words italicized seem to bear out the theory that these Conservatives were conspiring with Asquith to put Lloyd George 'on the spot', and that they had assured him that they would not take office under Lloyd George.

Crewe was certainly very close to Asquith at this time. For instance, on Tuesday, December 5th—an hour or so after Asquith's resignation—he was dining with him at Downing Street when Asquith had to leave the table to see Bonar Law, who had called to ask if Asquith would serve under him. (Asquith was 'altogether discouraging'.)

It seems likely that Crewe, in his later letter, was not referring to all 'the three Cs' (or he would have named them) but to Curzon alone of them, and that his 'one or two others' included Balfour; in 1928 Crewe may not have known that Balfour, according to Mrs Dugdale,[1] 'had already made up his mind to back Lloyd George' by the Sunday afternoon, when he was informed by Cecil of the Tory ministers' resolution and that its 'effect . . . would be an open trial of strength between the Prime Minister and Mr Lloyd George'. (This communication from Cecil to Balfour would tell in favour of Beaverbrook's view only if Asquith had understood the resolution.)

Crewe himself, in his account of the crisis, provides one item of evidence that seems to tell strongly against Beaverbrook's view. On the Wednesday afternoon, immediately after the Palace conference, when Asquith was considering with the Liberal ex-ministers at Downing Street whether or not he should agree to serve in the new administration, whoever else might be going to lead it, Crewe reports him as saying that 'Mr Lloyd George would in all probability find no difficulty in getting the requisite support; and if a new system was to be tried, it had best be entrusted to colleagues of the same school of thought as the new Prime Minister'. Quite apart from the naturally partisan testimony of Asquith's friends, who say that a tactical bluff, of the kind that is suggested, would have been 'alien to his character', there would have been no need at all, at this moment and in this company, for an elaborate pretence that he was resigned to the prospect of a Lloyd George administration, if in fact he still believed that Lloyd George would fail to form one. Indeed, there would even be a certain danger in such a pose: some of those present might feel that if their leader regarded such a prospect so philosophically, there would be no great harm in making themselves available for service in the new Government—even though, two days before, they had undertaken not to do so. If Beaverbrook is right, Asquith should

[1] *Arthur James Balfour, 1906–30,* by His Niece Blanche E. C. Dugdale, 1936, p. 169.

have said at this point, in effect: 'The most powerful Tories are with us, save only Law and Carson'—for so Beaverbrook believes that he still supposed—'and if we stick firmly together, Lloyd George can do nothing: we shall be back in office tomorrow'. He said, as Crewe indicates, no such thing.

Chamberlain's own account of the interview between 'the three Cs' and Asquith may point towards a synthesis of the conflicting views. At different times in these closely-packed few days, the attitude of some at any rate of the Tory ministers seems to have varied. At first they may have been inclined to hope that Asquith would crush Lloyd George's rebellion; later they realized that matters had gone too far, and veered towards Lloyd George. Curzon's behaviour in particular was puzzlingly—even suspiciously—ambivalent: he seems to have been determined to make the best of both worlds. Both attitudes may have been telescoped into one interview between 'the three Cs' and Asquith. Chamberlain wrote (three days after the interview, in a letter to Lord Chelmsford, the Viceroy of India):

> [Asquith] told us the whole story from his point of view, and we explained to him the meaning of our resolution, which he had not previously understood . . . He asked whether we should be prepared to go on with him while Lloyd George and Bonar Law resigned. To this we replied that our only object was to secure a Government on such lines and with such a prospect of stability that it might reasonably be expected to be capable of carrying on the war; that in our opinion his Government, *weakened by the resignations of Lloyd George and Bonar Law* . . . offered no such prospect; and we answered this question therefore with a perfectly definite negative. This was evidently a great blow to him . . .

Chamberlain added that they had told Asquith that, though they 'were under no obligation to Lloyd George', they would be prepared to serve in any government that looked like being stable and successful in its conduct of the war: 'whether Lloyd George could form such a Government we did not know'.

The line italicized above[1] is of importance. Lloyd George had scored a tactical victory by getting his resignation in first. Had Asquith read the text and understood the full meaning of Sunday's resolution, he might have taken the advice offered to him therein and resigned forthwith: whether Beaverbrook's or Petrie's account of the discussion from which the resolution emerged is correct, Asquith would at least, on Sunday, have had a sporting chance of holding the allegiance of the Tory ministers. Nor would he then have been so conciliatory to Lloyd George on the Sunday evening—thus putting himself in the wrong subsequently, and giving Lloyd George his cue and final pretext for resignation, when Asquith went back on what he had agreed.

It follows, therefore, that Law's omission to convey to Asquith the text of the Tory resolution contributed substantially to Asquith's downfall and to the success of the plot to replace him by Lloyd George. It is said that men must be assumed to intend the natural consequences of their actions: in so complex and confused a situation as this, it could hardly have been foreseen with certainty that these consequences would follow Law's failure of communication; but it is a good general principle of political, as of military, warfare to keep your enemy in the dark. Whether the principle was followed on this occasion by accident or by design will never be known.

Even stranger than the clash of opinion already set forth is the fact that there is a conflict of evidence on the date of one of the most important incidents in the crisis—the interview between Asquith and 'the three Cs'. Chamberlain—who ought to have known, since he was there—says that it took place on the afternoon of Tuesday, December 5th. So do J. A. Spender and Cyril Asquith: they worked from Asquith's

[1] Not italicized in the original text.

own papers, and he also should have known. Lord Crewe, however, seems to date it on the Monday, and Asquith accepted his account of the whole episode, including it as a chapter in his *Memories and Reflections*. Beaverbrook, who was keeping a diary at the time, says that 'the three Cs' had two interviews with Asquith—one on the Monday morning, a second on the Tuesday afternoon. Chamberlain states with emphasis, of the Tuesday afternoon: 'This is the first and only time the three of us met Asquith during these fateful days'. He seems here slightly to be emphasizing the words 'the three of us'. Perhaps he knew that one of the three, Curzon, had seen Asquith on the Monday, had given him certain assurances, and had yet come to a separate accommodation with Lloyd George—later indeed, but not much later. Perhaps the confusion about the dates arises from Curzon's Monday visit to Asquith, which may have been taken by Crewe and Beaverbrook to be a visit of (or on behalf of) 'the three Cs'. This discrepancy is secondary and may seem trivial—except that, as Chamberlain remarks, with some perspicacity: 'Lord Beaverbrook's mistake about the date invalidates his account of what happened on the Monday'.

At any rate, the job was now done. The intrigue had been successful: historians may hold that its success was, ultimately, to the benefit of the nation, whatever the motives of all the conspirators may have been; no doubt their motives included what they themselves believed to be a real concern for the public interest. The 'noblest Roman' was out—'destroyed', to use the exultant word that Beaverbrook always prefers to use in speaking of a politician's enforced resignation: the Welsh attorney was in. The 'little Canadian adventurer' had brought off the biggest *coup* of his life. If he had been a man capable of rest, he might legitimately have taken things easily for a while: as it was, he felt a sense of anticlimax, but waited—at first, serenely enough—for the summons to high office which the new Prime Minister had given him cause to expect. (The Board of Trade had been mentioned in conversation.)

Beaverbrook is not, however, a patient man. The leaden hours wore on; Lloyd George, he knew, must be busily going to and fro, offering, soliciting, scribbling notes in green pencil, piecing together the jigsaw puzzle of his Cabinet. But 'a quietude like death settled on the Hyde Park Hotel ... No special messengers arrived with notes. Even the telephone bell ceased to ring.' Serenity turned to boredom, boredom to positive anxiety; as night fell, and no word came, he grew desperate and went out in search of news. He walked as far as the War Office, where Lloyd George would still be working: he did not dare to go in, but walked round and round the bleak, pretentious block. After some time, he met a senior civil servant whom he knew: this man told him, 'in the most casual manner', that the new President of the Board of Trade was to be Mr Albert Stanley.[1]

If Max Aitken had been guilty of hubris, this was nemesis indeed: the biggest *coup* was followed by the most severe shock; nor was he ever to recover the ground lost on that winter day in 1916. This was a decisive moment in his career; and at this moment it was settled irrevocably—by his own egregious folly, by a single prematurely boastful word—that his career in politics was to be limited, that he could never reach the highest office. It was not merely that his vanity was wounded by his exclusion from the new Cabinet. That he could have got over; that could even have been a salutary lesson. He was indeed offered a minor job—the Post Office or something faintly ludicrous like that. He refused it, either out of pride or because, as he said, he was 'not content to be a passenger'; he wanted something directly related to the active conduct of the war. The Board of Trade would have been suitable in this respect, because it was responsible for

[1] Later Lord Ashfield

110

troop movements by rail in France, which needed drastic reorganization. The really serious difficulty that he was in was this: he had already told the chairman of his constituency Conservative Association that he was to be President of the Board of Trade, and had warned him to be ready for the by-election which at that time was necessary on the acceptance by an MP of a ministerial 'office of profit under the Crown'. His wife had actually gone to Ashton-under-Lyne, and was preparing to play her part in the campaign.

It seems likely that he told Lloyd George of this acute local embarrassment. At any rate, as soon as they had had their first interview after the change of government, when the minor post was offered and refused, Lloyd George wrote inviting him to accept a peerage, so that he could answer in the House of Lords for 'two or three important business departments'. No doubt Lloyd George felt: 'I suppose I must do something for Max'. No doubt, also, Bonar Law—to whom Aitken had mentioned the promise of the Board of Trade—had in turn mentioned it to some of those Conservative colleagues by whom Aitken was so heartily mistrusted and disliked. During the complex and delicate process of coaxing the more influential Tories into his Cabinet, Lloyd George may have found it impossible to 'sell' them Max Aitken as well as himself; he was not the man to allow mere personal loyalty to a useful friend to block the fulfilment of his main purpose.

The peerage was not particularly attractive to Aitken, but it was, in a sense, better than nothing: it would at least impress the snobbish Tories at Ashton, and would let him out of that situation. It seems that at this stage—six years after his arrival from Canada—he was still so imperfectly accustomed to the climate of English democracy that he did not fully realize that the acceptance of a peerage by an ambitious young man in public life was a form of political suicide, a self-relegation to limbo: not since 1902 had a Prime

111

Minister sat in the House of Lords, and it was almost certain that there would never be another there.[1] At any rate, he did not sufficiently consider this aspect of the problem: it was outweighed in his mind by the difficulty at Ashton, which was really of secondary importance and would have been forgotten quite soon if he had tackled it briskly, even humorously. Almost certainly, he should have accepted the minor office; he would have been promoted within a year or two. Instead, in this crisis of his own affairs he failed notably to exercise that judgement which, in his gnomic writings, he was to commend as one of the three qualities essential to success.

For one night, indeed, it seemed that even the peerage was to be snatched from him, and that he would be left naked before the ridicule of his constituents. Lord Derby—the Lancashire potentate who had refused to help him win his Lancashire seat—told Bonar Law that there were other Lancashire MPs with better claims to peerages than Aitken. On Law's advice, Aitken wrote to Lloyd George refusing the peerage.

Next day, the tantalizing affair took yet another turn. To Aitken's astonishment, Law now told him that everything had been arranged and that he must apply at once for the Chiltern Hundreds. Aitken was half-relieved but still half-doubtful about the wisdom of going to the Lords. He asked why Law had changed his mind again. The explanation provided the final touch of irony: he was to go to the Lords because his seat at Ashton was wanted for the new President of the Board of Trade, Stanley! This time he did not delay. He hastily accepted what looked like the easiest way out of his dilemma. The choice of a title was a less serious problem: Newcastle, unfortunately, was not available—an English duke had it—

---

[1] It is true that, in 1923, both Curzon and Baldwin were considered as possible successors to Bonar Law; but the fact of Curzon's peerage told decisively against him, or was at least made the excuse for not offering him the succession.

but the simple, alliterative, and nostalgic name of the Beaver Brook, in which he had fished and bathed as a boy, suited him well.

Sir Harold Nicolson's record[1] of an interesting clash between the King and Lloyd George is worth quoting in full at this point:

Far more complicated and distressing were the constant difficulties that arose over the bestowal of political honours. Ministers were inclined to make promises to individuals before His Majesty's pleasure had been obtained. A flagrant case of such disregard occurred in 1916. Mr Lloyd George and Mr Bonar Law, desiring to obtain a seat in the House of Commons for one of the new Ministers, offered a peerage to a Conservative Member representing a safe constituency. The King, when asked for his consent, replied that he did not 'see his way' to approve of this honour, since he did not consider that the 'public services' of the individual in question 'called for such special recognition'. Mr Lloyd George replied that any refusal would 'place him in a position of great embarrassment' and begged Lord Stamfordham to discuss the matter with Mr Bonar Law. The latter divulged that, not only had the individual himself been informed of his intended elevation, but that the Conservative Association in his constituency had been told that their Member was about to move to a higher place and that a by-election would be held immediately:

'I cannot conceal from you', wrote Lord Stamfordham to Mr Lloyd George, 'that His Majesty was surprised and hurt that this honour should have been offered without first obtaining his consent . . . The King recognizes (in view of the promises made and information given) that it is impossible for him now to withhold his approval. But, in thus signifying his acquiescence, His Majesty commands me to say that he feels that the Sovereign's Prerogative should not be disregarded; and he trusts that in future no honours whatever will be offered by any Minister until his approval has been informally

[1] *King George V*, pp. 511–12.

obtained. His Majesty further asks that this be made clear to your Colleagues.'

Mr Lloyd George returned no reply to this protest. Lord Stamfordham therefore embodied it in a formal memorandum which he sent to the Prime Minister on January 9th, 1917. In this memorandum Lord Stamfordham pointed out that 'the Crown is the fountain of honour, and grants and honours can only be made by the King, acting with the advice of his Ministers'. It was only right therefore that the King should be informally consulted before an honour was actually promised to an individual or that promise was divulged. Mr Lloyd George still refused to put his views in writing, but promised the King, in private audience, that he would not fail to communicate His Majesty's views verbally to the members of the Cabinet.

The name of the individual to whose elevation the King objected so strongly is not given by Sir Harold. He was, in fact, Max Aitken. Ashton-under-Lyne, with a Conservative majority of 196, was a 'safe' seat only in so far as every seat would at that time be safe for a nominee of Lloyd George. Probably it was chosen rather as the seat whose Member was (rightly) thought most susceptible to persuasion by Bonar Law. It is not known whether Law ever told Beaverbrook of the King's disapproval. If he did, the incident can hardly have tended to strengthen Beaverbrook's lukewarm attachment to the Royal House. Yet, had the King been able to persist in his refusal to consent to the peerage, he might have been saving Aitken, and Aitken's future career, from the consequences of Aitken's own misjudgement.

In a newspaper article[1] on the occasion of Beaverbrook's seventy-fifth birthday, Mr Randolph Churchill expressed the view that the 'one big mistake' of Beaverbrook's life was his illusion (caught from Northcliffe) that power could be exercised through the press, and his decision to concentrate on newspaper ownership rather than on the indirect political

[1] *Evening Standard*, May 28th, 1954.

action for which he had shown such marked talent. It may be
that the part played by the newspapers in bringing about
Asquith's downfall seemed to him more vital than it really
was: it was important, but it was secondary. Asquith might
have been dislodged without the publicity: he could not have
been dislodged without the Hyde Park Hotel conspiracy. But,
after all, had Beaverbrook continued to concentrate mainly on
politics, he would not have been content always to remain
merely an unseen influence, powerful only through others.
Like other ambitious men, he hoped for the highest advancement; and from this he had debarred himself. He may have
been in error in becoming a full-time newspaper proprietor,
but this error was, in a sense, consequential on his previous
action: the acceptance of the peerage was the cardinal blunder
of his life, and a classic minor example of the phenomenon
of self-destruction through pride—of Macbeth's

> Vaulting ambition, which o'erleaps itself
> And falls on the other.

CHAPTER SIX

PROPAGANDA UNDER FIRE

*What you say is important: how you say it is
more important still.*

CICERO

IN PEACETIME Beaverbrook has vociferously opposed any
kind of Government supervision of newspapers and their
source of news, or of the functioning of industry. It is strange
that, in two world wars, he should have been outstandingly
successful (in the first) as Minister of Information and (in
the second) as Minister of Aircraft Production; perhaps it is
true that poachers make the best gamekeepers.

After his traumatic elevation to the Lords, he seems to
have sulked in his tent for some time, seeking no doubt a
clear way forward. His restiveness was not soothed by the
newspaper-cuttings sent to him from Canada, many of them
commenting in harsh or sardonic terms on his peerage, which
all supposed to be an eagerly sought reward. 'This engrafting
on Canada of the effete system of hereditary titles,' said the
Stratford Beacon, 'is most reprehensible.' The *Toronto Globe*
pontificated: 'Honors bartered in the political market are a
source of weakness to the Empire. The house-cleaners after
the war would be well-advised to put an end to this traffic in
titles . . .'

This onslaught from his native land, in which his despatches
from the front had done so much to retrieve his reputation,
was particularly galling to Beaverbrook, not so much because
it happened to be unjust and unrelated to the facts—it is
usually possible to bear completely grotesque accusations
equably—as because he too, in his heart, agreed with much
that his calumniators said about hereditary titles, but could
not himself then say so.

The Prime Minister whom he had hoisted into power made further tentative offers of office, but still of minor office in some department in which his special gifts would hardly be exercised—for instance, in the Ministry of Food. At this time Lloyd George must have had greater problems on his mind than Beaverbrook's temperamental frustration or even than inter-party relations within the Coalition. None the less, it was important that these should be reasonably smooth; and here Lloyd Geroge—who was often insensitive to the sensitiveness of others—did not scruple once more to make use of Beaverbrook as a private go-between and salesman.

The article to be sold was a discredited Liberal politician who was, if anything, even more thoroughly mistrusted by orthodox Conservatives than Beaverbrook himself: Winston Churchill. Lloyd George was anxious to make Churchill Minister of Munitions, and Beaverbrook was constantly urging him to do so. Towards the middle of 1917, Lloyd George said to him, in effect: 'All right—I agree that he's the best man for the job. But you must first square your Tory friends.'

In 1955, fifteen years after Britain's, and Churchill's, 'finest hour', it is hard to realize the intensity of the feeling against him almost universal in the Conservative Party in that earlier war. Apart from the fact that he was then a Liberal—not, in itself, an insuperable obstacle—he had been associated in the public mind, to some extent unfairly, with a series of disastrous adventures: indeed, his exclusion from office had been insisted on by the Conservatives as a condition of their joining the first Coalition, under Asquith; and when Asquith fell, according to Churchill himself,[1] 'four prominent Conservatives, judged indispensable to the new combination, signed or made a statement stipulating as a condition of taking office' that neither he nor Northcliffe should be a

[1] In his *World Crisis, 1916-18*, Part I, p. 251. The four were 'the three Cs' and Walter Long.

minister. None the less, rumours that Lloyd George had him in mind began to be current. In June, 1917, at a meeting of the National Unionist Council, an emergency resolution was moved from the floor: it declared that the inclusion of Churchill in the Government would be 'an insult to the Navy and the Army'. Three hundred delegates from all over England and Wales carried it with only two dissentients. The *Sunday Times* said that Churchill's return to office 'would constitute a grave danger to the Administration and to the Empire as a whole'.

Despite such demonstrations of hostility, on July 17th Lloyd George sent for Beaverbrook and asked him if he was still in favour of giving Churchill office, and if his soundings showed that the Coalition would stand so sharp a strain. Beaverbrook said 'Yes'. Lloyd George asked him to go and see Bonar Law, and to inform him that he had just told the Press that Churchill was to be Minister of Munitions. Law was angry: Beaverbrook had often canvassed him informally about such an appointment, but he felt that, as leader of the second party in the Coalition, he should have been consulted officially by Lloyd George before a decision was taken and announced. It may well be that Lloyd George and Beaverbrook had foreseen that such preliminary consultation would have led to a sharp internal tussle, long delay, and menacing Tory demands for compensatory concessions: a *fait accompli* was a lesser risk. They were right; the Coalition survived; but there was a fearful uproar behind the scenes and in the Tory newspapers—the *Morning Post*, controlled by the redoubtable Lady Bathurst and sharpest-tongued of all, going so far as to describe Churchill as 'a floating kidney in the body politic'. The metaphor was varied by more impartial observers who called him 'the weakest link in the Coalition chain'.

He was soon to be succeeded in this invidious position. There were many complaints that Britain's war propaganda was being incompetently handled. These were not irresponsible newspaper complaints: the Select Committee on National Expenditure was sharply critical, 'especially with regard to the lack of financial control and wasteful expenditure'. The administrative head of the Department of Information, as it was called, was Colonel John Buchan,[1] the popular novelist; Parliamentary responsibility for it was borne—somewhat indifferently—by Sir Edward Carson. In one case, the Select Committee reported, 'a gentleman was entertained at the private house of one of the officials of the Department to meet some Members of the Cabinet, and a charge was made for the dinners, not only of the guests but also of the host himself'.

In February, 1918, Lloyd George appointed Beaverbrook Minister of Information: the sinecure office covering this unprecedented appointment was—despite one or two growls from the King—that of Chancellor of the Duchy of Lancaster. There was, of course, furious opposition to the appointment, mainly from the Asquithian Liberals and from such Conservatives as Lord Salisbury.

However justified these opponents may have felt in their political and personal disapproval of Beaverbrook, the appointment looks, in retrospect, reasonable. Beaverbrook had not at that time, indeed, his present record as a successful newspaper-proprietor; but he was known to have intimate contacts in Fleet Street, and the impact of his Canadian war despatches had been such that, it was said, many newspaper-readers in the United States believed that Canada was fighting the war alone. He had organizing ability, vigour, a flair for dramatizing himself or others, and skill in the art of cajolery —all qualities useful in a propaganda chief. It is difficult not to think that his enemies were blinded by prejudice to his potential value in this post.

At any rate, Lloyd George's intuition was once more proved shrewd: as in the case of Churchill, he knew just how far he

---

[1] Later Lord Tweedsmuir.

could go without breaking up the Coalition. The Tories would simply not have taken Beaverbrook as President of the Board of Trade: they could just stomach him, not without some queasiness, as Minister of Information. But now it was he who became 'the weakest link': when Austen Chamberlain, for instance, attacked him, it was thought by some that his underlying motive was to damage Lloyd George's prestige by forcing him to get rid of Beaverbrook.

Chamberlain—who was at this time out of office—opened his public attack almost immediately after Beaverbrook's appointment, in a debate on the Army Estimates on February 19th. He spoke in general terms: 'The functions of the Press are not the functions of the Government and the functions of the Government are not the functions of the Press, and it is not possible, without misconception and misunderstanding, that they should be combined in the same person ... Three great newspaper-owners[1] are members of, or are intimately associated with, the Administration ... [It would be] impossible for the Government to dissociate itself from articles which appeared in the Press owned by a member of the Government.'

A back-bench Member, Colonel Archer-Shee, was more direct, personal, and bitter. 'Lord Beaverbrook,' he said, 'was responsible for making the statement that the British troops had deserted the Canadians at the second battle of Ypres ... that statement was circulated in Canada by Lord Beaverbrook. I say that to make a man capable of making a statement like that, which ... was a gross libel on our troops and absolutely inaccurate, director of propaganda, ... on top of having been smothered with honours before, ... does not inspire one with trust in the Government.'

If such an attack were made in the House of Commons on any minister today, an alert Parliamentary Private Secretary would hurry from his seat immediately behind the Treasury

[1] Beaverbrook, Rothermere, Northcliffe.

120

Bench to engage in whispered consultation with the civil servants 'in the box' near Mr Speaker's chair; within five minutes, after a bout of telephoning, the PPS would be back with some sort of reply to whisper to the Minister in charge of the debate; and that Minister, in his speech, would deny the accusation with vigour, or at least, if informed that it was probably all too true, would say—with rather more heat and a touch of unction—that he did not propose to deal with so 'utterly unworthy' and 'irresponsible' a suggestion, and that he felt sure that his honourable and gallant friend would, on reflection, regret that he had stooped to make it. There would be a low susurrus of sympathetic indignation from the benches behind the Minister, a few cynical noises and cries of 'Claptrap!' from the malcontents opposite, and the incident would be over. Possibly ministers and their parliamentary private secretaries were less quick in the uptake thirty-seven years ago; possibly they were not specially anxious to 'stick their necks out' by defending unpopular colleagues; possibly, even, they may have agreed privately with the critics. At any rate, the Minister replying to this debate—Mr Ian Macpherson, Under-Secretary for War—made no reference at all to Colonel Archer-Shee's speech; and three weeks passed before, on March 11th, Lloyd George himself notified Chamberlain that he was ready to make a statement on the Government's relations with the Press. The delay is the more puzzling because Beaverbrook had not, in fact, said the things attributed to him by Colonel Archer-Shee.

Chamberlain, accordingly, asked a question by private notice, and Lloyd George explained that, of the three newspaper-owners in question, Northcliffe held 'no ministerial office', while Beaverbrook and Rothermere 'gave up all direction of their papers' on taking office. It is difficult now to understand why it should have taken the Government three weeks to produce this simple explanation, especially since—as these experts in publicity must have reminded

Lloyd George—the attack was the more damaging the longer it was left unanswered. No doubt their enemies within the Government were still fighting a rearguard action against the appointments. ('You see how impossible it is, Prime Minister, for us to defend men like these. After all, Austen carries a lot of weight, you know.') Some arrangements for disengagement from business may not have been impenetrably tied up. Or Lloyd George may simply have been too busy with the war. The contrast between the obviousness of such an explanation today, and the delay in making it then, is some indication of the novelty in 1918 of a phenomenon that has since become familiar—the actual interlocking of Fleet Street with the executive government.

A debate took place on the same afternoon as Lloyd George's statement. Chamberlain reiterated his criticism, in somewhat ponderous terms. 'It would not be right or tolerable,' he said, 'that any Prime Minister ... should seek to buy the support of a section of the Press by introducing people connected with that Press into Ministerial positions.' At this point he was nettled by laughter and ironical cheers from Labour and Asquithian Liberal MPs; he hastily disclaimed having 'the same motives or ... the same objects' as theirs. However, he went on: 'There has been too much coincidence. I take it as pure coincidence that certain papers have attacked particular servants of the Government, and that shortly afterwards the Government have found it impossible to continue those servants in the offices that they held.'

He then made a direct personal attack—without mentioning his name—on Northcliffe:

> One of these gentlemen addresses to the Prime Minister a public letter which I should have thought [it] was contrary certainly to practice and perhaps to the honourable traditions of confidence which prevail in public life to have published at all, in which, with an insolent and offensive patronage of my right honourable Friend, he combines an equally insolent and

offensive criticism of my right honourable Friend's colleagues. As I have said, the Government find it impossible thereafter to retain in their offices the officials who are specially attacked, and the people who have been specially associated with those attacks and with this letter are shortly after found, in each case on their individual merits and that alone, to be indispensable to the Government in particular offices. That is coincidence, but it is very unfortunate coincidence, and for no one is it more unfortunate than for my right honourable Friend and his Government, because coincidences of that kind will breed suspicion.

Some of the real difficulties of the Government-Press nexus began to emerge in this debate. Chamberlain thought that newspaper-owners would be in 'a very invidious position' if, as ministers, they had access to confidential information. Mr Pringle affected to assume that the newspapers concerned would now be 'official papers', that the editors would 'send their runners along to No. 10 Downing Street . . . to find out what ought to be said and who ought to be attacked', that they were 'become, therefore, a kind of kept press, a sort of *maison tolérée*; they are the same thing—they are inspected.' [Mr Outhwaite: 'Not clean!'] Lord Hugh Cecil suggested a curious form of censorship: 'Could not [the Government] make a definite rule under the Defence of the Realm Act that the name of no one, except a Minister responsible to Parliament, should be mentioned by way of criticism in the Press at all?' The eccentric Mr Pemberton Billing denounced 'the hollow mockery of the capitalist press', and cried down Lloyd George's assurances that the newspaper-owners had severed their Fleet Street connections. 'How would any editor,' he said, 'have the audacity to criticize a government of which his own proprietor was a member, without having previously taken the views of the proprietor . . .? When all is said and done, the journalist has his living and his obligations to consider . . . he has got to say what the old man wants.'

The press lords were not without one or two back-bench defenders. Colonel Lowther—generalizing the attack—asked: 'Since when has journalism become a synonym for criminality?' Lloyd George himself paid a stout tribute to Beaverbrook (saying whimsically that he 'managed to excite a good deal of prejudice'). He had been appointed solely because he was the best man for the job. 'There is no doubt at all about the success of his Canadian propaganda . . . He was the first man who broke down the War Office rule that you are not to single out particular units in the field for public recognition of their valour . . . We suffered in America from the success of the Canadian propaganda, and are suffering to this day.' He challenged members to name anyone who would make a better Minister of Information. No one took the challenge up.

Despite these Parliamentary pin-pricks, it may be imagined that Beaverbrook set about his new task with considerable energy: though it was not the post he had hoped for, it was intrinsically interesting to him, and it helped to cure his fifteen-month-old distemper. He had to improvise extensively, to expand and reorganize the existing propaganda machine, and at the same time (in view of Parliamentary criticisms) to economize drastically. To secure economy as quickly as possible, he asked the celebrated firm of chartered accountants, Messrs Deloitte, Griffiths, to advise him: they suggested a new system of checks on expenditure, which he adopted. Soon he was able to inform Parliament that the Estimates for his department for that year, originally more than £1,800,000, had been reduced to £1,200,000, though more work was being done for the smaller sum. This initial economy, which might have been placed by the thoughtless to Beaverbrook's credit, formed the basis of a solemn remonstrance to him: to initiate departmental economies is a function of the Treasury, and of nobody else. 'If the assistance of a firm of Chartered Accountants were necessary, as may well have been the case,' said the

Select Committee, 'Treasury concurrence ... should have been requested.'

The headquarters of the new Ministry were set up at the Howard Hotel, in Arundel Street. The staff were spurred into coming to work far earlier in the morning than was customary in Whitehall; and talent was found in quarters from which the Civil Service is not normally recruited. Lord Northcliffe—working from a different office and to some extent independently of Beaverbrook—had been put in charge of propaganda to enemy countries; Arnold Bennett looked after propaganda in France. (There was trouble about this appointment with Lloyd George himself, whom Bennett criticized in a newspaper article.) Beaverbrook also encouraged such official war artists as C. R. W. Nevinson and Eric Kennington.

His principal achievements were two. As he has since put it, he 'seized on the cinema', which was then becoming the only medium of mass-entertainment. (Broadcasting was in its infancy.) He introduced propaganda through news-reels; he persuaded producers and distributors to let him tag slogans on to the end of feature films; he used public money to finance, among others, D. W. Griffith's classic *Broken Blossoms*.

Secondly, he instituted a new technique—now widely familiar—of spreading propaganda overseas. Instead of spending a lot of money on distributing printed pamphlets and newspaper hand-outs all over the world, he spent, probably, rather less on the far more effective and hospitable method of inviting editors (and others in 'key' professions, such as doctors and clergymen) from America, from the Dominions and from other countries, to come to see Britain's war effort, at home and at the front, for themselves. Their reports were invariably more convincing to their own people than official propaganda literature had ever been.

As escort to American visitors he appointed a young Irish officer of charm and wit, who had been severely wounded in the arm. His name was Lord Castlerosse. He was to become, after the war, one of Beaverbrook's closest personal friends and a successful regular contributor to the *Sunday Express*.

Despite what must have been much useful work, the rumblings of criticism continued; they exploded in another debate in the House of Commons on August 5th, just before the summer recess, when MPs are especially apt to betray the asperity of fatigue. One of the main grounds for complaint was that Beaverbrook had packed his ministry with his cronies from the world of big business. One Member, Mr Swift MacNeill, called the ministry 'a sty of guinea-pigs'. Moreover, the Minister himself—as a contribution to the economy campaign already frowned on for its heterodoxy—was not accepting the salary attached to the Chancellorship of the Duchy. Mr Leif Jones, who led the attack, made a valid constitutional point when he said: 'I prefer ministers with salaries. Ministers with salaries are answerable to the country which pays them ... We may have an unpaid minister saying to us, if we complain: "We do your work for nothing, and we decline to be talked to by paid Members of Parliament."'

Mr Leif Jones painted a lurid picture of the machine for centralizing and censoring information that Beaverbrook was supposed to be creating: this machine would control the political intelligence departments, the wireless, the newspapers ... 'Wrong opinions will be suppressed. The Empire is to be advertised—' Another Member interposed: 'All this for nothing?' Mr Leif Jones went on: 'All that for nothing! I ask my honourable friend opposite, are they to do all that for nothing? What does he think? He is familiar with business. Does he think that this is all being done for nothing? [An honourable Member: 'No!'] I regard the whole thing with suspicion. I admit I am prejudiced, but I think the whole thing is detestably vulgar.'

There was a revealing phrase in one back-bench speech expressing the contrary view, by Mr McCurdy. '... *Even though the Minister be Lord Beaverbrook,*' he said, 'there ought to be some sense of fair play . . .'

The Government spokesman was Mr Stanley Baldwin, then a Joint Financial Secretary to the Treasury. In view of the enmity that arose in later years between him and Beaverbrook, it is interesting to note that he made a strong defence of him on this occasion, while neatly intimating to the House that there was no personal intimacy between them—and that therefore, as he pointed out, he could 'speak with perfect freedom'. After some characteristic animadversions on the English dislike of self-advertisement, he remarked that Beaverbrook was 'a man of very strong personality', and that in such men 'the magnetism which comes with that personality either attracts or repels'. He added : 'Lord Beaverbrook has taken on a most difficult, delicate, and thankless task . . . Give him a fair chance, and judge him by results. Do let us, in time of war, pull ourselves together to this extent, that we do not allow the personality of an individual to warp our judgement as to the value of the work he is doing or the means he employs in doing it.'

Effective though this plea was, it could not bring the debate to a close, for the business before the House was the second reading of the Consolidated Fund Bill, on which debate can range widely and there is no time-limit. When Baldwin sat down, other members got up. The attack on the business men around Beaverbrook was renewed. The impression made by Baldwin's speech began to fade. Then, quite suddenly, the debate took an unexpected turn. Beaverbrook himself has given the best description of how this came about, in a tribute which he paid nine years later to his friend Tim Healy, the Irish MP :

> He knew not only every form of the House and every trick in the game, but he also knew humanity, and he could play on the House as a musician would on the organ, just putting in or taking out the stops while the instrument responded . . .

I don't think he ever deliberately prepared anything—even a speech—in advance. His were the tactics of the sally and the surprise, the assault from the flank, the method of the 'Red Herring'. He realized . . . that the House of Commons is an unruly pack of hounds, with strong primitive instincts. The party whips may arrange a certain hunt, but once anyone comes along with the red herring and drags it across the trail, the hounds will follow his way and let the predestined fox go home quietly.

Beaverbrook went on to explain that he had learned in advance that Leif Jones and others were to attack him in this debate: he 'rather resented the injustice', because he had already been attacked twice in the House and did not want the job of Minister of Information, anyway; but he was worried about the way the debate might go. Bonar Law would not reply, because he and Beaverbrook were known to be close friends: Beaverbrook had (wrongly, as he later admitted) little confidence in Baldwin, a comparatively obscure junior minister.

So he wired to Tim Healy to come over from Dublin to help him. Beaverbrook's account continues:

He reached my country house on Sunday, August 4th, having kept me in suspense by wiring that he would arrive 'shortly after Mass'—a phrase which meant nothing to me.

When at last he came, he gave me small comfort. I wanted to show him all the documents I had accumulated for my defence. Healy would not look at them, but continued to discuss my gardens and my children.

I pressed him hard to discuss the matter seriously, and asked what line he intended to take.

He brushed my defence aside.

'Whatever line I take tomorrow', he said, 'will have nothing to do with a prepared case. I shall watch the House and decide.'

He laughed at my anxiety.

'Leif Jones', he said, 'is a teetotaller and can't hurt a fly! He's one of those who tried to stop the tot of rum to the soldiers in the trenches. I killed that move, and I'll checkmate him tomorrow.'

'But how?' I enquired.

'Well', he said, 'Neil Primrose once was angry with Lord Loreburn, the Lord Chancellor, and felt sure he would force him to resign over the non-appointment of Liberal magistrates. As Lloyd George was behind Neil, Loreburn telegraphed for me as you have done, and laid all his cards on the table at breakfast before the debate came on, and though Neil had a good case, and many Liberals were strongly with him, I beat them, for Loreburn had stood by Ireland in the old days.'

I got little satisfaction out of this and had to wait for the next day.

Leif Jones made his attack on the expected lines, and was followed with some pretty wild accusations by Mr Pringle and Mr Swift MacNeill.

As a matter of fact, most of what they tried to lay at my door had happened when Lord Carson from the War Cabinet had general control of propaganda.

Tim would occasionally interject, 'That was done in Carson's time', which seemed to disconcert the assailant. Otherwise he did nothing.

Both Mr McCurdy and Mr Baldwin made good speeches for me, but as the debate was going it was likely to do me harm, because if a whole debate turns on one man, more charges are made than can possibly be answered, and a kind of general bad atmosphere is created.

. . . Then Healy struck—and utterly side-tracked the debate.

He wanted to know what all this nonsense was about—£5 being spent on cigars and £20 on drinks on a mission to Dublin. Such a point was frivolous, and it was a waste of time in war. Anyhow, this was done by an emissary of Carson's, and if that was all Carson had done it would not have mattered much.

But Carson had made his department an organ for anti-Irish propaganda and filled it with his nominees from Trinity College, Dublin. The result had been the absolute ruin of Irish recruiting.

Immediately on this the vials of inter-Irish wrath were poured forth. Mr Ronald McNeill intervened to defend Carson. Mr

Shortt [Chief Secretary for Ireland] was brought up to make a lengthy reply . . .

The debate was abruptly switched off from the discussion of my supposed iniquities, and a regular Irish debate ensued. By the time Mr Devlin had summed up for the Nationalists all the earlier speeches had been completely forgotten, and the question of the Ministry of Information and its chief had faded out of the picture.

Healy's performance was a perfect exhibition of parliamentary tactics.

Hansard shows that Beaverbrook's account is not exaggerated. Even today (as Mr Geoffrey Bing has proved) Ireland provides the best material for inflammatory diversions; and on this occasion the Irish members threw in everything—the murder of Sheehy-Skeffington, the exclusion from Ireland of his widow, the fate of ninety men detained without trial at Belfast, who were alleged to have had to kneel at 'God's altar' manacled and filthy. 'Lastly,' said Healy, 'I remember in 1870, when O'Donovan Rossa was in gaol . . .'—and the House must have known that this was going to be a fairly protracted peroration. At one point Mr Speaker said, as Speakers have said from time immemorial: 'One interruption leads to another . . . and we get carried out of the course of the debate'. But—no doubt because he knew from experience that it would only cause further delay—he did not venture to rebuke Healy for his constant unparliamentary use of the word 'you': you, Healy told the House, have murdered, you have detained, you have persecuted; and 'that'—said Mr Devlin to the Chief Secretary, who had dared to answer him back—'is thoroughly characteristic of your insolence'.

Not another word was said about the Minister of Information. When the Irish were at last exhausted, the House went on to discuss cellulose acetate—and Tim Healy went off to have supper with the Minister of Information at the Hyde

Park Hotel, saying as he entered the suite: 'Get me some pea-soup and a steak, and I will tell you all the fun'.

*   *   *

So three men—Healy, Baldwin, and Lloyd George—between them saved Beaverbrook from the wrath of Parliament.

Healy was bound to him by ties of personal friendship; and there burned in him, as in so many Irishmen, a patriotism more ardent than any concern that he might feel for the conduct of the British Government's war against Germany. Beaverbrook's record of his conversation just before his sortie of rescue shows him recalling an incident from the past—his support of another minister in difficulties, Loreburn, because 'Loreburn had stood by Ireland in the old days'. Beaverbrook had already, before the war, quarrelled with his closest friend, Bonar Law, on the electoral aspect at least of the Irish issue. Just as the wartime services of a spokesman of another ancient and oppressed people—Dr Weizmann—had already secured for them, in the Balfour Declaration of 1917, the promise of a national home, so it must have occurred to Healy that it would do no harm to put under some obligation a man, influential (as it seemed) in British politics, whose mind was not closed to the cause of Irish freedom.

Baldwin was no friend of Beaverbrook; the terms in which he had chosen to defend him made that clear. He was simply doing a ministerial job, and doing it ably. Baldwin already regarded Beaverbrook with distaste and suspicion: it is less certain that Beaverbrook saw in Baldwin, from the start, a natural antagonist. The man resolved on enmity first has an advantage, in political conflict, over the man not yet sure that he has got to fight: this may in part explain why in later years, when the hostility between them was open, the apparently mild and lethargic Baldwin was to seize the initiative repeatedly against Beaverbrook, and in almost every case to seize it decisively and with success.

131

Lloyd George had been, indeed, among the closest of Beaverbrook's cronies, and it might have been thought that his part in Lloyd George's ascent to power would have earned Beaverbrook the most enduring rewards that friendship could offer. But Lloyd George himself had once told Beaverbrook that there were no friendships in politics at the highest level; and his calculating ruthlessness had already been illustrated in his disregard of Beaverbrook's expectation of the Presidency of the Board of Trade.

In the last few months of the war, such friendship as there was between them grew rapidly cooler. Beaverbrook gave an explanation of this seven years later, in a little book called *Politicians and the Press*: as Minister of Information, he said, he was constantly asking Lloyd George to receive editors from overseas; 'no editor . . . was satisfied to leave England unless he could say that he had seen Mr Lloyd George'; and Lloyd George 'felt he was being pressed too hard and began to decline . . .' (Beaverbrook adds that he secured the interviews, all the same, by making Northcliffe his intermediary: to have had to use this device probably aggravated his sense of grievance, for a strong element in his character has always been the common human failing of jealousy.)

This explanation is unconvincing. Lloyd George was shrewd enough to know how useful such interviews could be: they used time tiresomely, but did not waste it. Nor would any dispute on so relatively trivial a point of administration account for the fact that the two men no longer met socially all the time, that Beaverbrook was now 'not a frequent visitor at Downing Street'. The cause of the estrangement must have lain deeper: can it have been that Lloyd George felt that he had treated Beaverbrook shabbily in the matter of office? Such uneasiness—'sense of guilt' is, in this case, too strong a phrase—can grow, almost imperceptibly, into resentment against the person to whom the injustice has been done: it is akin to the resentment often displayed, by one to whom a

good turn has been done, against the benefactor convention-
ally entitled to gratitude—and perhaps this emotion, too, was
involved with it in Lloyd George's heart.

Interesting evidence of the bitterness that he felt against
Beaverbrook, from whatever cause, is provided by the records
of an incident that occurred at the end of August, 1918, a few
weeks after the Commons debate which had passed off so
satisfactorily. Although the war was not yet over, there was
talk of a general election. Lloyd George was in difficulties
with the die-hard Conservatives in his Government; some
were threatening to resign. On August 29th the *Daily Express*
published an editorial written with some show of objectivity,
but disparaging certain intentions that were believed to be
forming in the mind of Lloyd George:

> . . . We do not want a new khaki election. We cannot vote in
> the dark. If the Prime Minister seeks re-election as the head of a
> Coalition Government which is to endure, he must satisfy those
> who are to vote for him that his views and theirs are the same.
> The Conservative voter is expected to support him; and would
> support him on the war; but before he will support him on a
> post-war policy he will want to know what that policy is.
>
> What, for instance, is the Prime Minister's programme on
> TARIFF REFORM and IMPERIAL PREFERENCE? No
> mere holy formula will satisfy the electorate. It is essential to
> know whether we are to have a real Imperial Preference or a
> sham one. On the Tariff issue the Conservative party is deeply
> committed through the strength of its convictions. Nothing
> short of a tariff on foreign manufactured goods will serve.
>
> What would be the IRISH POLICY of the Government
> which hopes to be returned?
>
> Is the WELSH CHURCH to be sacrificed simply because the
> party of spoilers just tottering to its fall over the Irish crisis of
> 1914 was saved for a moment by the outbreak of the great war?

These were embarrassing questions. Perhaps they were
meant to be; perhaps the editorial would never have been
published if Lloyd George had made Beaverbrook President

133

of the Board of Trade or if they had dined together more often in recent months. However, such an editorial in a popular newspaper today—even if the newspaper happened to be owned by a member of the Government in power—would not unduly disturb a prime minister. It would be an irritating pin-prick. The influence of the mass-circulation press may have been greater in the days before the BBC, ABCA, and other instruments of rudimentary political education (and the *Daily Express* already boasted 'the second largest circulation in London'); or the editorial may have provided the personal *casus belli* which Lloyd George had been groping for sub-consciously. At any rate, he flew into what might otherwise have seemed a disproportionately violent rage, and wrote at once to Bonar Law:

My dear Bonar,

Have you seen the leader in to-day's Express? That is Max. Having regard to the risks I ran for him and the way I stood up for him when he was attacked by his own party, I regard this as a mean piece of treachery. It explains why no man in any party trusts Max.

The reference to the Welsh Church is deliberately introduced to make it impossible for me to arrange matters with the Unionist leaders.

I am sorry, for I have sincerely tried to work with him.

Ever Yours,
D. L. G.

This is strong language from one colleague to another, of a third—particularly as both the sender and the receiver of the letter happened to owe to that third party the greatest political advancement that had yet come to them. Any gratitude that Lloyd George may have felt had indeed been swallowed up by now in resentment. The process which psychologists call rationalization had been at work: the supreme achievement, the overthrow of the old Prime Minister, was forgotten, and a few quite secondary incidents in the House of Commons had become 'the risks I ran for him'. An editorial (whose inspiration by the newspaper proprietor was likely but had not yet been verified) was seen as a 'mean piece of treachery'. At this moment the ill-used Prime Minister may almost have found it in him to sympathize with Asquith ...

Nor was he content merely to complain informally to Beaverbrook's party leader. Winston Churchill was sent to see Beaverbrook personally, and to ask him if he admitted responsibility for the article. 'If he admits it, he's out,' fumed Lloyd George. Possibly he thought that Beaverbrook would repudiate responsibility, claim that he had been too busy at the Ministry to attend to his newspaper, and regret that the editor had been so indiscreet. (This has indeed been Beaverbrook's practice on various awkward occasions during the past thirty-nine years.) Such a repudiation, in this case, would have been an admission of weakness on Beaverbrook's part and would have inhibited him from publishing further editorials of the same kind, since the indiscreet editors would obviously have had to be severely disciplined. So he did not deny his guilt: he took full responsibility for the article—and he was not, after all, 'out'. Why Lloyd George thought better of this threat is not known: presumably Beaverbrook at large 'like a roaring lion, seeking whom he [might] devour', seemed an even more disquieting risk than Beaverbrook caged at least some of the time.

He was, however, fairly soon 'out', not by dismissal but by resignation on account of ill health. He had been working at the Ministry early and late: one of his staff has noted that 'a kind of lemon hue on his countenance sometimes showed the terrific strain'. Though he was not yet forty years old, lines were beginning to be graven in his round face. It was now that actinomycosis took him by the throat. He resigned in October, a few weeks before the Armistice. Despite the now somewhat surprising enthusiasm of Mr (later Sir Charles)

Higham,[1] he had no successor: he would have been a difficult minister to follow, and the job was as good as done. There were valedictory tributes from all sides in a House of Commons debate. Mr Baldwin spoke of his 'rare vision' and 'ability to master details'; Sir Hamar Greenwood said that his propaganda had 'actually rescued from the Germans the neutral countries and America'; Mr T. P. O'Connor praised him as 'a strong partisan'.

Four days after this debate, the Armistice was signed.

[1] 'We have in the Ministry of Information the nucleus of what will one day become an ideal Department of State. Its great function is enlightenment; it will enlighten not only opinion at home, but opinion abroad . . . It will be spokesman for most other Departments of State . . . I cannot conceive this Ministry being dissolved . . . it will become a peacetime necessity.' (C. Higham, article in *The World's Work*, May 1918.) Except that they are not directly or formally the agents or spokesmen of the Government in domestic matters, the BBC, the Central Office of Information, and the British Council have performed most of the functions here forecast for the Ministry of Information.

CHAPTER SEVEN

MORDECAI AT THE GATE

*In this sacred grove there grew a certain tree round
which at any time of the day, and probably far into the
night, a grim figure might be seen to prowl. In his
hand he carried a drawn sword, and he kept peering
warily about him as if at every instant he expected to
be set upon by an enemy. He was a priest and a
murderer; and the man for whom he looked was sooner
or later to murder him and hold the priesthood in his
stead. Such was the rule of the sanctuary. A candidate
for the priesthood could only succeed to office by
slaying the priest and, having slain him, he retained
office till he was himself slain by a stronger or a craftier.*

SIR JAMES FRAZER

SOON Winston Churchill was to approach Beaverbrook
again on Lloyd George's behalf, but on a more specific
mission. The war was over, the election pending; Lloyd
George was anxious to 'fix' the press, or as much of it as
could be fixed, in support of his Coalition project. Churchill
invited Beaverbrook to dine with him and Lloyd George, to
discuss the possibilities. There were only the three of them at
dinner; Beaverbrook was still recovering from an operation,
and his head and neck were swathed in bandages.

The fact that the Prime Minister felt unable to send an
invitation direct, and had to use Churchill as an intermediary,
shows how far he and Beaverbrook had drifted apart since
the great conspiratorial days of 1916: the fact that the invitation could be issued at all, less than three months after his
denunciation of Beaverbrook's 'mean piece of treachery',
shows that Lloyd George, like any other politician with a
keen sense of priorities and an election in the air, could sink

137

personal differences and compound with treachery itself if votes might thereby be gained.

A *concordat* was soon arrived at. Beaverbrook found Lloyd George's arguments for rushing the election 'reasonable and honourable'. He agreed to support Lloyd George in the *Daily Express*, and to approach Lord Rothermere and Sir Edward Hulton—but not, ironically enough, Lord Northcliffe, who had so recently helped him by persuading Lloyd George to meet the visiting editors. Lloyd George and Northcliffe had once more fallen out: towards the end of the war, Northcliffe had pressingly demanded for himself the high office of Lord President of the Council, and had been piqued by Lloyd George's refusal to let him have it. Lloyd George now said firmly that it was 'hopeless to attempt to deal with Northcliffe'.[1] In this he showed some courage—for Northcliffe could be an ugly enemy—and a sounder judgement than either Beaverbrook or Lord Reading had shown; for they had both allowed themselves to be used by Northcliffe to communicate and commend his ambition to the Prime Minister. Neither had known at the time that Northcliffe was so using the other; some years passed before they discovered that he had not considered either alone a sufficiently reliable or persuasive messenger. Four years after their unsuccessful efforts on his behalf, Northcliffe died, mad.

Despite Northcliffe's enmity, the support of Beaverbrook and other press magnates, and the general atmosphere of Armistice hysteria, sufficed to win Lloyd George an overwhelming majority in this 'coupon' election, as it was called. Churchill himself, who had helped to bring this about, later wrote that the election had 'woefully cheapened Britain'.

---

[1] One week before polling day he even telegraphed, in reply to one of Northcliffe's attempts to dictate to him: 'You are quite wrong . . . Don't be always making mischief.' None the less, Mr Frank Owen has shown, in *Tempestuous Journey* (p. 502), that it was partly fear of Northcliffe's opposition that restrained Lloyd George from inviting Asquith to join both the Government and the British delegation to the Peace Conference.

It was as a newspaper-owner rather than as a political colleague that Beaverbrook was now thought of, and dealt with,
by Lloyd George. In *Politicians and the Press*, published in
1925, he thus described his acquisition of the *Daily Express*:

> I had for a number of years a considerable connection with the
> *Daily Express* of an indefinite character, but it never interested
> me much. Towards the end of the war that newspaper wanted
> money very urgently to keep up its supply of newsprint. None of
> its shareholders would put up any money. Finally the editor
> came to me and suggested that I could purchase the controlling
> shares in the newspaper for £17,500. Of course such a purchase
> implied not merely finding the necessary sum for the purchase
> of newsprint, but the financial responsibility for the newspaper
> as a whole.
>
> I hesitated. But a merciful delay was given me by the fact that
> I was placed in quarantine as a 'carrier' of spino-meningitis
> germs. When I was released I went on a black Saturday winter's
> evening to consult Lord Rothermere on the venture. His sum-
> ming up amounted to this: To buy the shares of this concern at
> the price offered implied a good deal of courage. To do so meant
> the supply not only of a considerable amount of money in
> addition to the price of purchase, but also in the long run the
> expenditure of a good deal of time and energy in looking after
> the business. I asked him whether he would take a share in the
> enterprise, but he explained that he could not do this as it
> would involve competing with his brother, Lord Northcliffe, as
> owner of the *Daily Mail*. None the less he advised me to accept
> the offer—and I did.

He also consulted Northcliffe. Northcliffe asked him: 'How
much are you worth?' 'Over five million dollars,' said Beaverbrook. 'You will lose it all in Fleet Street,' said Northcliffe.

Rothermere's advice—and perhaps his assessment of
Beaverbrook's capacity—was better than his brother's. The
net circulation of the *Daily Express* was then 229,344[1]: in

---

[1] A circulation of 285,962 was claimed, but this was found to be the gross
sale, not the audited net sale.

December, 1954, it was well over four million. The property then purchased for £17,500 had, at the end of 1954, a market value of some £7,275,180.

The amount that had to be paid at once was considerably larger than £17,500; the paper had lost about £40,000 in the previous year. The sum required for newsprint supplies, used or needed, was £40,000. The controlling shareholder who had been unable or unwilling to find this sum was Mr George Lawson Johnston (later Lord Luke), owner also of Bovril. The editor who suggested the deal was Mr R. D. Blumenfeld, a gentle, shrewd, and much-loved journalist of American origin.

There seems to be, in the account of this transaction in *Politicians and the Press*, a certain telescoping of events; and it is vague about dates. The date of the transfer of the con-trolling shares is concealed by such phrases as 'towards the end of the war'. In fact, it was not towards the end of the war but little more than half-way through the war: December 2nd, 1916. The political significance of this date is obvious: it was the Saturday before Asquith's resignation. The deal may well have been discussed at the very interview at which the inside story of the crisis in the Government was 'leaked' to the *Express*.

More than thirty years later, Beaverbrook was to tell the Royal Commission on the Press, with notable candour: 'I run the paper purely for the purpose of making propaganda, and with no other motive'. In 1916 he was beginning to be fascinated by the idea of controlling newspapers, not primarily as money-making concerns (for at that time this seemed likely to be an expensive hobby), but as weapons in the battle for power. Like the political hopes that he still cherished—the beguilement of office, the promises or hints of party leaders—this idea was a mirage; but it was a mirage which, as it faded, left behind it a solid pot of gold. He hoped that newspaper-ownership would win him political power by enabling him to impose his views on political leaders, and he was prepared to lose a good deal of money in the process: in the event, he amassed an even greater fortune than before, but gained no real power at all.

At the very outset of his ownership of the *Express* he learned how costly it could be to own a newspaper. This was not the first time that he had had dealings with Blumenfeld. Back in 1911, he had secured the support of the *Express* and its editor for Bonar Law.[1] No doubt the policy was presented rationally and accepted on merit. Its adoption, however, happened to coincide with two private arrangements: the first was a loan to the *Express* of £25,000; the second was a promise to Blumenfeld personally that he would be 'looked after' if his editorial advocacy of a policy that might be unpopular with the then proprietor of the *Express* should cost him his job. So that he might be in a position to fulfil this promise if necessary, Aitken bought a London evening newspaper, the pink-coloured *Globe*; its editorial chair could be made available for Blumenfeld at short notice. He did not have to pay much for the *Globe*: it was losing money when he bought it. By the time he had spent some £50,000 on keeping it alive, he was really anxious to get rid of it; moreover, he now knew that he could acquire the *Express*, so he no longer needed the *Globe*. Unfortunately for him, nobody wanted to buy it. In the end, he actually had to pay Mr Dudley Docker, the Birmingham industrialist, £5,000 to take the *Globe* off his hands. When doing so, he bet one of Docker's associates £500 that the paper would still not pay: he won this bet, thus reducing by £500 his net loss.

---

[1] This was when Jack Sandars had written to Balfour about 'the little Canadian adventurer' and had said, with some exaggeration, that he 'practically own[ed]' the *Express*. Blumenfeld had first become aware of Beaverbrook a little earlier, at a dinner of the Canada Club, when Sir Thomas (later Lord) Shaughnessy, President of the Canadian Pacific Railway, had pointed him out to Blumenfeld as 'a remarkable man—the only man I know who has ever beaten the Canadian Pacific Railway in a commercial deal'. Blumenfeld sent a reporter to interview him next day.

For most of the last two years of the war, whether in office or not, he was too closely immersed in politics to take an active part in the running of the paper. 'I may claim to have become a full-blooded journalist,' he wrote later, 'just before the General Election of 1918.' This is one of the rare examples of the use by Beaverbrook of the English trick of meiosis; for few ordinary journalists, 'full-blooded' or not, are occupied in such high-level intrigues as those already mentioned— arranging private dinner-parties at 10 Downing Street and at Winston Churchill's house in order to procure the electoral support of other press-lords. It was not until the foundation of the *Sunday Express* that he started to go to work regularly each day in the *Express* office.

He did not plunge into his greatest journalistic venture without forethought. It had long been in his mind that he would need a Sunday as well as a daily newspaper. A few months before the end of the war he had nearly bought the *Sunday Times*: the Berry brothers were willing to sell it to him for £200,000. Lloyd George intervened personally to prevent the deal: Beaverbrook was still in the Government, and there had been enough trouble already about ministers who owned newspapers. When Beaverbrook was free once more to buy, the *Sunday Times* was no longer for sale. On December 29th, 1918, therefore, he founded the *Sunday Express*. Its birth was not painless: on the very eve of publication of the first issue, Lord Riddell, proprietor of the *News of the World* (with which the *Express* had a 'stand-by' printing agreement) notified Beaverbrook that the presses on which the paper was to be printed would be required by the *News of the World*. This attempt at abortion was unsuccessful: Lord Riddell received an emphatic reply, and the *Sunday Express* appeared. On that Saturday night Beaverbrook dined at the Savoy with Lady Diana Manners (later Cooper), and Mrs Edwin Montagu; after dinner they went to the *Express* office, and Lady Diana set in motion the press that printed the first copy. The first issue contained the first of a series of articles by Lady Diana, and recorded the overwhelming election victory of the Lloyd George Coalition. The first editor was Mr Vivian Carter.

The optimistic Blumenfeld thought that it might cost Beaverbrook £20,000 to get the *Sunday Express* going. It cost £150,000 in its first year, £300,000 in its second year; the circulation, which had started at 300,000, sank to 155,000.

At this point Beaverbrook felt that he had better run the *Sunday Express* as well as the *Daily Express* personally. He stepped in. There were several changes of editorship, in quick succession. He decided to acquire the then editor of the *Star*, Mr James Douglas; though the salary he paid him was modest by present Fleet Street standards (£3,000 a year), it was twice what the *Star* had been paying. 'Douglas,' Beaverbrook has said, 'brought the human sympathy that was needed. I was lacking in that human sympathy.' On one notorious occasion, this human sympathy took the form of a puritanical demand for the withdrawal or suppression of an allegedly pornographic work of art, Miss Radclyffe Hall's earnest novel, *The Well of Loneliness*.

Douglas, however, was a writer rather than an editor. It was in 1921—a year before the *Sunday Express* at last began to make good its losses—that Beaverbrook gave their first major opportunities to two gifted Canadians, Mr Arthur B. Baxter (now Sir Beverley Baxter, MP) and Mr E. J. Robertson.

Baxter, a former piano-salesman and amateur opera-singer, had first asked Beaverbrook for a job towards the end of the war, when he was helping Brigadier-General A. C. Critchley to train Canadian cadets in England. Beaverbrook was 'not interested'. After the war, in June 1919, Beaverbrook was going to Canada and Baxter happened to be going home in the same ship. Both Beaverbrook and Baxter have often told the story of their mid-Atlantic encounter, and it has no doubt gained something in the telling. According to them, Baxter sang an air from HMS *Pinafore* at a ship's concert—and Beaverbrook sent him a note saying, 'On hearing you sing, I am convinced that you should be a journalist'. So Baxter was hired. He knew nothing about journalism, but (as his dramatic and film criticism in recent years has shown) he had a sense of drama and a facile and vivid pen. After a novitiate in the features department, he became managing editor of the *Sunday Express*. On his first Sunday in charge, the front page did not look promising: in the first edition it had been filled up so generously with overmatter that there were no fewer than seven news-headlines referring to coal. Beaverbrook decided to go to the office himself every Saturday evening from then on, and held conferences in his Hyde Park Hotel suite every Friday night and every Monday night—the latter being an inquest.

A succession of scoops attracted much attention. One of the most sensational appeared on February 12th, 1922, under the heading 'The Greatest Scandal of Modern Finance'. It reported the disappearance of Mr Gerard Lee Bevan, Chairman of the City Equitable Fire Insurance Company; the liabilities of the various enterprises with which he was concerned were said to total £4,250,000. Other circulation-building scoops of the 1920s included a series of five articles by H. G. Wells describing a visit to the Soviet Union (which put up the *Sunday Express* sales by 80,000) and Mrs Thompson's letters to her lover, the murderer Bywaters.

In 1924 Baxter was transferred to the managing editorship of the *Daily Express*, under Blumenfeld, who was designated editor-in-chief (i.e., revered figurehead). In 1929 Blumenfeld retired, and Baxter assumed sole charge. By 1934, says Beaverbrook, 'Baxter was beginning to take a larger view of life, so I sent for Christiansen' (Mr Arthur Christiansen, a young journalist then in charge of the Manchester edition of the *Daily Express*). Beaverbrook's account of the dialogue between himself and Baxter, occasioned by the introduction of Christiansen as a joint executive editor, is as follows:

Baxter: 'In that case I resign.'

Beaverbrook: 'In that case I accept your resignation.'

Baxter: 'In that case I withdraw it.'

Beaverbrook: 'In that case I ask you to vacate your office in six months.'

They were an uncomfortable six months in the *Express* office. Neither editor knew which of them had, even nominally, the final power to take decisions. This is the sort of situation in which Beaverbrook is always at his most unpredictably impish: to Baxter he would say, 'You'll have to be careful not to let this fellow Christiansen have his head too much at first'; to Christiansen he would say, 'You'll have to watch that fellow Baxter—don't let him sit on you'; or, in each case, words to that effect. It was a new adaptation of Burke's theory of the go-between.

Next year Baxter became an MP (with the help of Beaverbrook's Empire Crusaders, defeating Mr Duncan Sandys for the Conservative nomination in the safe Conservative constituency of Wood Green). After various vicissitudes he returned to Beaverbrook's employment. On one occasion during the Second World War he attacked him in the House of Commons as possibly responsible for the loss of Crete; on other occasions he has championed him; Beaverbrook finds his company agreeable, and he seems likely to be bound to him for life in a love-hate nexus characteristic of Beaverbrook's relations with those around him.

Modern mass-circulation newspaper-publishing is big business. Therefore, on such a newspaper, the editor does not hold the supreme position that he held in an old-fashioned 'organ of opinion': the man in charge of the complex techniques of management and production is even more highly regarded, and rewarded, than the editor. To do, ultimately,

L

this responsible work Beaverbrook found the ideal man in
E. J. Robertson—a man shy yet tough, cautious yet bold,
with an extraordinarily correct financial intuition.

Beaverbrook remembered Robertson before the 1914 war
—an alert bell-boy at the Queen's Hotel, Toronto, who had
carried his bags upstairs and wanted a job as soon as he had
finished working his way through college. 'I was his idea
of success,' says Beaverbrook. During the war Robertson
crossed the Atlantic as a soldier. He fell ill with spinal menin-
gitis; one of those who visited him in hospital was Beaverbrook's wife. In January, 1919, when he was waiting to
return to Canada for demobilization and to continue his
law studies, Beaverbrook (whom he had worked with during
the war at the Canadian War Records Office) offered him
a job on the *Express*. He joined it as assistant to the general
manager.

The lasting success even of a 'popular' newspaper does not
depend simply on a mechanical increase in circulation. That
can often be inflated artificially, for a time, by stunts of one
kind or another, by 'competitions' which are thinly disguised
raffles, by 'free gift' schemes. In its time the *Express* has
indulged in many such stunts. As early as 1920, however,
Beaverbrook began to learn that stunts alone were not
enough. In June of that year the circulation of the *Daily
Express* shot up rapidly because of an extraordinary run of
luck in the racing tips. On June 2nd (when the tipster gave
two winners) the circulation was about 530,000. By the end
of the month thirty-three winners had been tipped, the punters
were grabbing the paper as early as they could get it, the
circulation had gone up to more than 700,000—and thousands
of regular readers had changed to other papers, having lost
patience with a paper that was so often unobtainable at their
bookstalls. Then the run of luck stopped; the circulation sank
to 550,000; and the hard core of regular readers began to be
consolidated again.

It may be noted in passing that an average score of a winner a day in the month of June would not now seem miraculous in a big popular newspaper. Each paper employs as many as four or five tipsters: since these are shrewd and well-informed full-time racing men, it would be surprising if they did *not*, between them, pick some short-priced winners fairly often and bring off an occasional long shot.

In 1921 the circulation of the *Daily Express* rose by 100,000. In 1922 demand began to exceed supply: 'the existing machinery was incapable of turning out the requisite number of copies'. By August, 1922, when the sale had reached 942,591, it actually became necessary to cut circulation: the extra arrangements for printing and distribution were costing too much. More advertisements, too, meant more pages—sixteen instead of twelve; and this in turn slowed down production. One evening a decision had to be taken which reduced by 300,000 the number of copies to be sold next morning.

One morning in the early 1920s Beaverbrook went into his wife's room. She was studying the *Daily Mail*. He asked her what she found so interesting in it. 'I'm reading the drapers' advertisements,' she said. He took the hint: soon the big drapery stores, whose customers are mostly women, began to advertise extensively in the *Daily Express* also. One of them was Selfridge's, whose American founder, Mr Gordon Selfridge, was an old friend both of Beaverbrook and of Blumenfeld; his order was booked by Beaverbrook himself—the only occasion in his publishing career on which he personally sold space.

When the proposal to set up a Royal Commission on the Press was being debated in 1946, in and out of Parliament, a good deal of time was spent on the question of the influence of advertisers on newspapers. Supporters of the mass-circulation press—especially those of them who had no personal experience of work in a newspaper-office—were hotly indignant at the 'monstrous aspersion' that the editorial policy or the methods of news-presentation of any newspaper could ever be influenced by pressure from advertisers. Of all the charges made against newspapers—charges of distortion and suppression of news, of 'monopolistic tendencies', of vulgarity, of 'intrusion into private grief'—this was the one to which the newspapers themselves seemed most sensitive, no doubt because, if proved, it would tend to weaken the valuable myth of press freedom.

In the House of Commons debate on October 29th, 1946, Baxter, then MP for Wood Green, was indiscreet enough to be the first to explore this aspect of the topic. After 'many years of editorship in Fleet Street', he assured the House that it was 'not true' that the advertiser had influence. [Honourable Members: 'Oh!'] Beaverbrook's son, Max Aitken, then MP for Holborn, declared—in what was described as an 'extremely well-written speech'—that advertisers had 'not the slightest influence on the editorial columns of the papers'. Other MPs with inside knowledge of newspaper offices, though not in executive positions, took a different view. Mr J. P. W. Mallalieu thought Baxter and Aitken 'too innocent to live', and testified: 'I have had a long experience in a part of newspaper work where one is especially subject to pressure by advertising interests—on the financial side . . . There was never one week . . . when, in one way or another, the pressure of advertisers was not exercised upon me.'

At the time of the Munich Agreement Mr Arthur Mann had been editor of the Conservative (but anti-Munich) *Yorkshire Post*. He told the Royal Commission: '. . . many members of the Conservative Party interested in big business thought there would be a better chance of business prospering if good relations with Hitler were maintained . . . Apart from efforts made by the [Conservative] Central Office to get papers of a Conservative leaning to support the policy of appeasement, that did happen, I think . . . There is nothing unusual in that. Influence was brought to bear on newspapers but not by advertisers as such.' But—whatever 'as such' may mean—it had never been suggested that the influence was always, or usually, direct; and it does not seem unduly suspicious to suppose that those Conservatives 'interested in big business' who chose, or were chosen, to approach Conservative newspapers may have included some connected with firms apt to spend a good deal of money in newspaper advertising.

In its conclusions on the subject, the Royal Commission,[1] while 'glad to record' that attempts at influence by individual advertisers 'appear to be infrequent and unsuccessful', did at least dare to say: 'So long as newspapers do not pay without advertising revenue, a newspaper may well think twice before it adopts any policy which is likely to reduce advertisers' demands for its space'—precisely the substance of the original criticisms, which had caused such shocked and sanctimonious protests.

The Royal Commission might have been less cautious if it had been aware of a lecture given by Beaverbrook in his early days as a newspaper proprietor, when he had not yet learned that candour on such matters should be exercised with due economy.

This lecture was delivered at the Victoria Hall, Sheffield, on Sunday, May 14th, 1922. Its subject was boldly announced as 'The Sensational Press'. On the ethics of policy-making, Beaverbrook stated: 'It is the duty of newspapers to advocate a policy of optimism in the broadest sense'. According to the *Sheffield Daily Telegraph* report he said: 'If he [the advertiser] insisted on asserting his authority he could do so in many cases. He did not do so.' He added, however, that the advertiser 'had got the right to expect that the newspapers would reasonably conform to a certain policy, and [sic] otherwise the newspapers did not offer a satisfactory medium to him'. This passage—with its implication that the advertiser did

---

[1] Cmd. 7700, para. 527.

149

not assert 'his authority' only because newspapers were so well-trained, anyway, that there was no need for him to do so—was omitted from the *Daily Express* report of the lecture.

Distress may have been caused to Beaverbrook as a Calvinist by some local reactions to this event. Sabbatarian correspondents pointed out in the Sheffield papers that the Victoria Hall was supposed to be a mission-hall, that 'The Sensational Press' was 'not a sacred subject', and that to lecture on it was not 'a work of necessity'. One even wrote: 'The Victoria Hall authorities did more in that one solitary Sunday afternoon to bring about the downfall of the Christian Sabbath than all its avowed enemies could have accomplished in five years'.

Such comments as these stung him into remarking, in an article in the July issue of *The Brotherhood Outlook, a Journal of Goodwill towards Men*: 'Hypocrisy is a menace to which the Brotherhood is particularly exposed'. The same article (on 'My Religion') contains some valuable clues to the stage of spiritual development which he had by this time reached: 'I might describe myself as a type of the Nonconformist mind which has passed out of its Nonconformist environment . . . I have chosen to preach my own idealism of conduct—one which, though differing from some other forms of idealism, is just as difficult to attain . . . Honesty is the especial virtue of the business world.'

At this time he was lecturing and writing quite frequently; he was indeed beginning to practise once more for himself the art of manipulating words as he had previously learned to manipulate, in turn, bonds and politicians. Some of his early essays were a trifle clumsy: his financial friends thought the metaphor unfortunately ambiguous when he wrote of the City of London as 'the unrivalled mistress of the world of commerce'. But his style was as special to himself as the idealism which he had claimed to preach, and as vigorous as his conversation; and it was clear that he was acquiring a kind of finesse in this art also when he could write (in the *Sunday Express* of July 2nd, 1922): 'I am not, strictly speaking, the proprietor of a newspaper; but I am the principal shareholder in two, and share with the directors many of their troubles, chiefly because the other shareholders are too wise to allow this weight of worry to be imposed on them'.

A quarter of a century later, giving evidence before the Royal Commission, he was to express a similar idea in blunter words. He had been testifying to the 'latitude' he had given his editors on matters of policy, saying that they were by no means always in agreement with each other or with him. Asked what had happened on occasions on which they had taken a view different from his on Empire matters, he replied: 'I talked them out of it'. Asked, further, if it had been by his decision that his papers had unanimously opposed Marshall Aid, he replied: 'No, that is my teaching. That comes from my co-operation with my colleagues, we are all thinking together and thinking alike.' By the time of the Royal Commission E. J. Robertson was Chairman of London Express Newspaper Ltd.[1] He was undoubtedly being strictly accurate, as well as loyal, when he told the Commission that Beaverbrook 'never made the slightest attempt to override the decisions' of members of the staff responsible for policy: for, as the Royal Commission remarked, 'These men were originally selected for their posts ... because they shared Lord Beaverbrook's views.' This felicitous situation 'demonstrates', said the Royal Commission, dead-pan, 'how a tradition is created'.

*　　*　　*

The lecture which had so sorely disturbed the Sabbatarians of Sheffield contained a political allegory more appropriately biblical than its main theme. This was based, of course, on the

[1] Now Beaverbrook Newspapers Ltd.

Old not the New Testament—on the grim, dramatic story of
Haman and Mordecai in the Book of Esther:

After these things did king Ahasuerus promote Haman . . . and
set his seat above all the princes that were with him. And all the
king's servants, that were in the king's gate, bowed, and rever-
enced Haman . . . But Mordecai bowed not, nor did him reverence . . . And when Haman saw that Mordecai bowed not, nor
did him reverence, then was Haman full of wrath . . . Haman
said moreover, 'Yea, Esther the queen did let no man come in
with the king unto the banquet . . . but myself; and tomorrow am
I invited unto her also with the king. Yet all this availeth me
nothing, so long as I see Mordecai the Jew sitting at the king's
gate.'

Then said Zeresh his wife . . . 'Let a gallows be made of
fifty cubits high, and to-morrow speak thou unto the king that
Mordecai may be hanged thereon: then go thou in merrily . . .
unto the banquet.' And the thing pleased Haman; and he
caused the gallows to be made . . .

So Haman came in. And the king said unto him, 'What shall
be done unto the man whom the king delighteth to honour?'
Now Haman thought in his heart, 'To whom would the king
delight to do honour more than to myself?' And Haman
answered the king, 'For the man whom the king delighteth
to honour let the royal apparel be brought . . . and the horse that
the king rideth upon, and the crown royal which is set upon his
head . . .' Then the king said to Haman, 'Make haste, and take
the apparel and the horse . . . and do even so to Mordecai the
Jew, that sitteth at the king's gate' . . .

And the king said again to Esther . . . at the banquet of wine,
'What is thy petition, queen Esther?'. . . Then Esther the queen
answered and said, . . . 'Let my life be given me at my petition,
and my people at my request. For we are sold, I and my people,
to be destroyed, to be slain, and to perish' . . .

Then the king Ahasuerus answered and said unto Esther the
queen, 'Who is he, and where is he, that durst presume in his
heart to do so?' And Esther said, 'The adversary and enemy is
this wicked Haman'. Then Haman was afraid . . .

And the king arising from the banquet of wine in his wrath went into the palace garden: and Haman stood up to make request for his life to Esther the queen; for he saw that there was evil determined against him by the king.

Then the king returned out of the palace garden . . . and Haman was fallen upon the bed whereon Esther was. Then said the king, 'Will he force the queen also before me in the house?' As the word went out of the king's mouth, they covered Haman's face.

And . . . one of the chamberlains said . . . 'Behold also, the gallows fifty cubits high, which Haman had made for Mordecai . . . standeth in the house of Haman.' Then the king said, 'Hang him thereon'. So they hanged Haman on the gallows that he had prepared for Mordecai. Then was the king's wrath pacified . . . And the king took off his ring, which he had taken from Haman, and gave unto Mordecai . . . And Mordecai . . . was great in the king's house, and his fame went out throughout all the provinces: for this man Mordecai waxed greater and greater . . .

This account of the ruthless seesaw of high politics must always have appealed powerfully to Beaverbrook. 'The man whom the king delighteth to honour' is a stock figure in the more dignified leading articles at the time of the New Year or Birthday honours list: the ironic original context of the phrase, and the sudden catastrophe that it foreshadowed, are not always remembered. Beaverbrook knew from bitter personal experience how empty, and how disastrous, words that seemed to imply promotion could be: the story of Haman's downfall must have stirred him like a twinge in a favourite wound.

It is possible only to guess at the precise modern application that he gave to his parable. According to the brief summary of this part of his lecture in the *Sheffield Independent*, he was talking of the Prime Minister of the day, Lloyd George, and of the respect in which he was widely held; but '*he thought there was also a Mordecai sitting in the gates who would not take off his hat'*. If this dark saying was reported to the intuitive Celt whose seat in Downing Street seemed unassailably 'above all the princes that were with him', he may well have shivered slightly, as it is said that a man does when a ghost walks over his grave. Beaverbrook himself later told an inquisitive friend that he had been thinking of Northcliffe when he spoke of Mordecai; but, in the context of the allegory, the parallel with Law seems more exact. For in a short time Bonar Law—no longer in office but still a Privy Councillor, 'sitting at the king's gate'—was to behave as disrespectfully as Mordecai towards the Liberal Haman; and it seems hardly too far-fetched to identify Beaverbrook himself with Esther, linked in racial kinship with Mordecai, Esther the organizer of political dinner-parties, the destroyer of prime ministers . . .

No one knew better than Lloyd George, after all, how much mischief to a man in office there could be in the conjunction of Beaverbrook with Law; and his relations with Beaverbrook had been precarious in recent years. There had been the coolness towards the end of the war, and the reconciliation when the 'coupon election' was pending: Beaverbrook had supported him in this, and had been almost alone in forecasting the overwhelming victory that had been won. But since then the *Express*, under Beaverbrook's direction, had conducted several campaigns against the Government—the more embarrassing to Lloyd George, perhaps, because some of them were 'radical' in character. One campaign was for the taxation of war fortunes, by means of a special 'once-only' levy. Another was against Churchill's intervention in Soviet Russia. A third was against the embargo on Canadian cattle.

In 1920—again on account of an *Express* article to which Lloyd George took exception—there was 'a complete break' between them. In 1921 an attack began on Lloyd George's policy of encouraging the Greeks in 'their wild dream of an

adventure towards Constantinople'. The dispute thus opened
—not only by Beaverbrook—was to be the main cause of
the fall of Lloyd George's Government in the autumn of
1922. In 1921, too, Bonar Law resigned office. 'I had to
get Law out of George's Government,' Beaverbrook has
since said (but it was on medical advice also). The Coalition
was beginning to come apart at the seams.

In the winter of 1921–2, however, there was another brief
rapprochement. At that time the winter rather than the summer was the fashionable season on the Riviera: both Lloyd
George and Beaverbrook were there, and they saw a certain
amount of each other. A gossip in the *Tatler* babbled:

> Mr Lloyd George is, of course, *the* great attraction . . . crowds
> of people flock after him all day long . . . The Premier played a
> foursome with Mrs Stern against Major Stern and his secretary,
> Miss Stevenson, and afterwards they all lunched in the club-
> house with Mr Winston Churchill . . . It seemed so strange at
> lunch without the Grand Duke Michael and I hear now that
> they (the Grand Duke and Countess Torby) will not be out at
> *all* this season, which sounds dreadfully sad . . . The Grand
> Duke Cyril was playing golf too, also Sir Alan and Lady Johnson,
> Mr Napier (the motor man), Colonel Brinsley Fitzgerald,
> Captain 'Freddie' Guest, and ever so many more . . . Mr Lloyd
> George went . . . to dine with Lord Beaverbrook, his son-in-law,
> and Sir Frederick Bowater at the Hotel Beausite; he certainly
> is tremendously energetic, and always laughing . . .

During his Riviera holiday, Beaverbrook had the mixed
pleasure of reading the reviews of his book, *Success*; some of
these were enthusiastic, some acidly severe. After the *Express*
campaign for the taxation of war fortunes, it was a little hard
that the *Cape Times* should have described this almost school-
boyishly open and unpretentious little book as 'a first-class
handbook for those who want to be war profiteers in the next
war'. The *Educational Times* quoted with derision the ham-
handed but indubitably truthful judgement: 'Shelley had

155

genius, but he would never have been a success in Wall Street'. (This sentence was removed from later editions of the book.)

In April, 1922, the sun still shone, somewhat bleakly, on Beaverbrook's friendship with Lloyd George. The *Sunday Express* deprecated 'all attacks on the personal honesty and integrity of the Premier by expensive newspapers with small circulations'—the kind of admonition which may make its beneficiary slightly uneasy, as Brutus might have felt if he had overheard any of Mark Antony's oratorical tributes to his honour. The knife which had disposed of Balfour and of Asquith was now being reground for early use. The Sheffield lecture contained the first hint of the impending slaughter; Lloyd George may have felt like the priest of Nemi as Sir James Frazer described him in a famous passage in *The Golden Bough*.[1]

Beaverbrook's best friend would hardly picture him as a disinterested Olympian, immune from the frailties and passions of man: on the contrary, like the gods of Greek folklore rather than those of the Epicurean philosophy, he is apt to pursue his purposes with earthy zest and in a Protean succession of manifestations that may sometimes be confusing even to himself. Thus, when it began to seem necessary to him that Lloyd George should be 'destroyed', as Asquith had once been destroyed in favour of Lloyd George, he convinced himself that the origin of the quarrel was Lloyd George's failure to be the 'Empire man' that Beaverbrook had once hoped that he might be. This was, truly, one of his motives. Another, conscious or unconscious, may have been a personal desire to replace the fickle Lloyd George by Bonar Law, on the steadiness of whose friendship he could count. Moreover, Law at Downing Street would be a living proof that the son of a New Brunswick manse could rise to the highest office in the Empire; and he was twenty-one years younger than Law;

[1] Quoted on p. 137.

and Lloyd George, anyway, by promoting that accursed peerage, had been, even if inadvertently, the main frustrator of his life's ambition.

Lloyd George was already unpopular with other Conservatives on account of the Irish settlement (on which Beaverbrook had supported him). In the summer of 1922, despite the Government's apparently impregnable majority, an issue of foreign policy which was to prove disastrous to Lloyd George became urgent. Britain was still technically at war with Turkey. Lloyd George and other Liberals had encouraged the Greeks, who now advanced into Asia Minor.

In August, at Deauville, Beaverbrook discussed this situation with the Aga Khan, and through his introduction arranged to meet the new Turkish leader, Mustapha Kemal, in Angora (now Ankara). Before starting for Turkey, he invited Lloyd George, Churchill, and Birkenhead to Cherkley. His mission to Turkey was to be, ostensibly, journalistic: he announced that he was going there 'at the request of the editor of the *Sunday Express*'—a statement more convincing, perhaps, to the unsophisticated newspaper-readers of the early 1920s than it would be today. The atmosphere of the week-end gathering at Cherkley was uncomfortable. Beaverbrook tried to persuade Lloyd George to give him some representative status—'some kind of power to negotiate', as he put it. The suggestion, made long before the roving American ambassador-at-large had become a familiar figure on the international scene, was embarrassing and indeed amateurish: Lloyd George was 'indefinite and evasive'; and, as he apprehended, the highly professional Foreign Secretary, Curzon, was 'greatly exercised' by such meddling. The *Morning Post* published 'detailed and alarming accounts' of Beaverbrook's movements. He had to be content with a general assurance from Lloyd George that he would listen to what he had to say on his return.

When he got to Turkey, the situation had changed dramatically: the Greek forces were routed, the Turks dominant. Beaverbrook hurried back to England, told Bonar Law, 'These men [Lloyd George and his supporters] mean war', and published a short letter saying that his projected *Express* articles could not now appear, as he disagreed with the Government's policy but did not want to embarrass the Cabinet during delicate negotiations. This explanation seems out of character. Possibly Bonar Law was counselling reticence; possibly this unwonted reticence was conditional on a corresponding outspokenness on the part of Law—for Law did indeed now issue a letter, since widely regarded as the decisive prelude to Lloyd George's downfall, declaring that Britain could not act as 'the policeman of the world alone'.

There was a Conservative Party meeting at the Carlton Club. Bonar Law had been inactive since his retirement from the Government in the previous year. There was strong pressure, mainly from the Right, for Conservative withdrawal from the Coalition. Had Bonar Law not gone to the Carlton Club meeting, the Conservative ministers—led by Austen Chamberlain, who had succeeded Law as leader of the Party —might have persuaded the Party not to withdraw; or—in Beaverbrook's view—the Party would have been split. Law, whose poor health had not been merely an invented pretext for his retirement from office, was more than ever anxious for a quiet life: on balance, the want of quiet to be anticipated from attendance at the meeting was slightly less than the want of quiet actually suffered under the domestic nagging of Beaverbrook. So at least it may be supposed. It has been shown already that there were varying estimates of the strength of Law's ambition. His opponents saw him at this time almost as Beaverbrook's creature. A Socialist weekly, the *New Leader*, wrote: 'This last week, when Bonar Law was timidly preparing to resign rather than make his speech against Mr Chamberlain, ... Lord Beaverbrook took the

decision for him.' At any rate, Law went to the meeting[1];
his speech reinforced a powerful and ingenious argument by
Baldwin for secession from the Coalition; the Party decided
to secede; and a General Election followed.

In a *Sunday Express* article entitled simply 'The Crisis'
(October 22nd, 1922), Beaverbrook said that Law was standing for the Conservative rank-and-file in 'striking down Lloyd
George and the third Coalition as he had stood for them in
overthrowing Mr Asquith and the first'. Others, including
some Conservatives, were dismayed by Law's re-emergence
from the limbo which seemed to be his natural environment.
Some even refused to accept the conventional view that,
whatever might be thought of Beaverbrook, one so dull and so
dim as Law could hardly be other than respectable. The *New
Witness*, the organ of Belloc and Chesterton, was most scathing of all. It said outright that Law stood for corruption
and plutocracy: 'he represents that colonial commercialism
of the Beaverbrook school which does not differ in the least
... from the cosmopolitan commercialism of the Mond and
Montagu school.'

Beaverbrook was used by now to the rough-and-tumble of
everyday press controversy and attack; but such phrases as
these were extraordinarily offensive. Journalists employed on
the *Express* were not surprised, in the years that followed, to
find the names of Belloc and Chesterton among those included in each revision of the office 'white list' (a euphemistic
nickname for the black list of persons not to be mentioned,
for various reasons, in the newspaper). The ban was enforced
so strictly that Chesterton's death in 1936 provided the first
occasion on which a columnist who had often wished to write
about him was allowed to do so; while another contributor,

---

[1] Some believed that it was Law's sister Mary who had persuaded him to
go. This is not inconsistent with the view that Beaverbrook's influence was
effective: it has already been shown (p. 66) that Mary Law had got over her
original dislike of him, and on many occasions he got his way with Law not by
bluntly urging a certain course on him but by more subtle and indirect means.

an ardent admirer of the verse of Belloc, was allowed to quote a few lines of it now and then on condition that Belloc's name was not printed and that the lines were attributed merely to 'the greatest living poet'.[1]

Polling-day was November 15th, 1922. It was preceded by a campaign of great bitterness. Beaverbrook made his contribution to the raising of the temperature—in particular, by backing independent Conservative candidates in constituencies in which local pacts had been made between Coalition-minded Liberals and Conservatives. One such 'sponsored' candidature was that of Mr Ralph Hall Caine, son of the famous novelist, who fought and beat Captain Freddie Guest, once Lloyd George's Chief Whip and an old personal friend of Beaverbrook's. (They had actually dined together, with Birkenhead, on the night of the Carlton Club meeting; the dinner was marred by sharp disagreement.)

As it turned out, neither the pacts nor Beaverbrook's interventions to break them affected the result of the Election decisively; Law and the Conservatives were returned with a majority of seventy-one seats. Law proceeded to form a government replete with that mediocrity which hostile critics considered his most striking quality: 'another *Who's Who* government', they called it, after an anecdote of Disraeli, deaf and aging, who had exclaimed 'Who? ... Who? ... Who!' as each dim name in some new administration was recited to him. At any rate, Mordecai, if Law may be so identified, had succeeded to the honours and dignities of

[1] In evidence before the Royal Commission on the Press, spokesmen for the *Express* management sought to rebut the evidence of this use of the 'white list' provided by a number of responsible journalists with personal experience in the *Express* office over a number of years. They put in notes to show, e.g., that Belloc's name had been printed nine times in the fifteen years or so during which it had been said to have been on the 'white list', and Chesterton's sixty-nine times during the same period (which lasted for seven years after Chesterton's death). The Royal Commission admitted that 'if a newspaper in fact kept a list of persons who, either on the whim of a proprietor or for political reasons, were not to be mentioned in its columns that might seriously prejudice the free expression of opinion . . .'

Haman. Mordecai's friend could surely look forward at last to the fulfilment of his hopes; as he had once lurked in another room at Pembroke Lodge, so he would now be closer than anybody else to the 'unknown premier' in Downing Street.

Dis aliter visum. Beaverbrook was still to be close to Law indeed, but in a more melancholy office; for by the spring of 1923 it became clear that Bonar Law was a dying man. For a month and more Beaverbrook fought against the inevitable diagnosis, and strove almost to will his friend back to health: for once, his will encountered a force in Law stronger than itself. His desolation was desperate: he was losing at once his most intimate friend and his greatest political opportunity. It is hardly surprising that when others, perturbed by Law's growing disability, discussed seriously how soon he ought to be replaced, and by whom, the *Sunday Express* denounced them in savage terms, in an article attributed to its political correspondent:

> Lord Birkenhead wants to return to high office, Mr Winston Churchill is tired of sketching and polo as life's great aim. . . .
>
> The Savoy Hotel welcomed in a private room last Thursday at luncheon time some of the principal modern gunpowder plotters. The party consisted of no less personages than Mr Lloyd George, Mr Winston Churchill, and Lord Birkenhead, who whispered 'soft somethings' to each other. . . .
>
> An attempt was made to mobilize the Press to make a direct attack on the stability of the Government, because it is alleged that the Prime Minister is in an enfeebled condition. Actually the only ground for this contention is the fact that Mr Bonar Law is suffering from a bad throat. . . . On Sunday last the Press bombardment began. . . . The success of this manœuvre has not been marked. . . .
>
> The aim of the plotters was and is perfectly well defined. Mr Bonar Law, having twice beaten them as a live man, must be politically slain. . . .

On the same day another article in the same paper, signed by Beaverbrook himself, proclaimed defiantly that Law's

M

Government was 'the best Government which the present generation has seen'. Complaints of inaction were nonsense: this was 'tranquillity', an admirable example of non-interference by the Government in matters that should be left to private initiative.

In a life whose dominant pattern has been one of vigorous achievement followed instantly by profound frustration, there can have been few moments at which the circumstances were so acutely ironical as they were now. The *tableau vivant* was familiar: the lethargic leader, the brisk outsiders plotting to oust him, even once again—most despicable of all!—the 'attempt . . . to mobilize the Press'. Only some members of the cast were different; and, in particular, he who had been on previous occasions the chief go-between and most adventurous of plotters, now learned what it felt like to be inside the crumbling stronghold, impotent, while others, assisted by a grim fate, worked for its destruction.

Yet in his utter dedication to Bonar Law, in his refusal to desert him when the hope of recovery had passed and his own interest might have led him to seek a sensible accommodation with Birkenhead and the rest, there is a certain decency, if not nobility. If he were a less fervent patriot, it might be said that he was here illustrating that principle of friendship which Mr E. M. Forster later summed up in the dictum: 'If I had to choose between betraying my country and betraying my friend, I hope I should have the guts to betray my country'.[1]

The *Sunday Express* attack on the plotters was published on April 22nd, 1923. During that week-end even the uncongenial Curzon was called in to sustain the legend that Bonar Law could continue in office. Law, he said publicly, had told him 'that the loss of his voice was rapidly disappearing'; his 'general health' was 'stronger than when he took office'. Curzon can hardly have believed this himself: if he said it at Beaverbrook's instigation, he may well have forfeited some

[1] *Two Cheers for Democracy*, p. 78.

of such credit as he had with the Birkenhead faction, and he was to be one of the two candidates for the succession to Law. But then, Curzon was notoriously inept in his timing, no doubt because he had an intellectual distaste for politics as such. 'Politics are a dirty game,' he once wrote, 'and the mud which others stir seems to settle with an almost malignant monotony on me.'

Only one week later, again in the *Sunday Express*, Beaverbrook was obliged to announce that Law was 'going to take a holiday till after Whitsuntide'. The 'relaxed condition of his throat' made 'complete rest' essential. Rumours of permanent resignation were denied. Curzon was to act as Deputy Prime Minister.

Law went to Aix-les-Bains. On May 17th Beaverbrook left London hurriedly to join him there. The *Daily Chronicle* reported 'grave concern' and 'rumours of resignation'. On May 20th Beaverbrook was writing sombrely in the *Sunday Express* that whether Law's tenure of office were to be long or short, it was 'already . . . illustrious'. The nation, he said, 'waits anxiously for news'.

The news came next day. Sir Thomas Horder insistently advised immediate resignation; a 'slight operation' had to be performed on Law's throat. As so often, an Old Testament echo crept into Beaverbrook's comment. 'A certain glory has departed,' he wrote, 'and cannot be replaced.' The exaggeration may have been comforting to himself or to the dying man.

The summer wore on sadly for them. Beaverbrook refused social and political engagements to be near Law by day and by night. In the afternoons they played bridge; each evening Beaverbrook stayed to dinner. This must have been a distressing obligation. There was no secret about it now: the complaint in Law's throat was cancer.

Law died at 3 a.m. on October 30th. A few hours earlier, his last, murmured words to his friend had been: 'You are a curious fellow'. Beaverbrook arrived at his house 'shortly after 3.5 a.m.'. The pall-bearers at the Abbey funeral were the Prince of Wales, the Speaker of the House of Commons, the new Prime Minister (Baldwin), Balfour, Asquith, Carson, Beaverbrook, Austen Chamberlain, Ramsay MacDonald, and Lord FitzAlan. Four years later, when a photograph taken outside the Abbey on this occasion was published in Asquith's *Memories and Reflections*, Beaverbrook may well have noticed that the photograph had been trimmed so that he, alone of the pall-bearers, was omitted from it. If this was intentional, he may have felt that it was an unkind return for the subscription of £1,000 a year which he had contributed towards Asquith's private pension.

Though it had been anticipated for so many months, Beaverbrook felt the shock of Bonar Law's death deeply. It made a void in his life. He fumbled for comfort, and was at a loss where to turn for it. He issued a pathetically ridiculous instruction to his newspapers: Bonar Law was always so to be referred to, *tout court*—never as 'the late' or 'the Rt Hon' or as 'Mr Law'. He inherited Law's private papers and was able, in due time, to hand them over to the University of the province that both of them had come from, and to watch the resources of scholarship applied to their analysis. This was poor consolation as yet; in low spirits, he set off for a visit to the United States and Canada.

There is an interesting passage in Mr G. M. Young's *Stanley Baldwin*,[1] in which the author describes a conversation between himself and Baldwin. The post-war Lloyd George Coalition, Baldwin had remarked, was 'charged with mischief':

> The Inner Ring, Lloyd George, Churchill, Birkenhead, and Beaverbrook, were at odds with the official prescribed policy, and were irrepressibly vocal at awkward moments. 'But', I once said, 'in the end you won them round . . . All but Beaverbrook. What was between you?' 'Bonar Law', he answered.

[1] p. 30.

'We fought for the soul of Bonar Law. Beaverbrook wanted to make him a great man after his own fashion. I showed him there were better things to be.'

Beaverbrook was once asked if this was indeed why he and Baldwin had never been reconciled to each other. 'I never wanted to be reconciled to him,' he replied. 'Baldwin could do many diabolical things and get away with them. He used to make me so frantic. . . .'

One incidental irony contributing to this wild or sullen fury was the fact that Beaverbrook himself had actually helped to start Baldwin on his career. In 1916, when Bonar Law became Chancellor of the Exchequer, he asked Beaverbrook to recommend a back-bench MP to serve as his Parliamentary Private Secretary. Beaverbrook suggested three names; they decided on Baldwin because he was 'rich, reticent, and neutral in character'. They were right about the first two qualifications.

The man who has succeeded in making his adversary 'frantic' is already half-victorious. If Beaverbrook had won the battle for Law's soul, Baldwin's revenge in other fields was to be decisive and lasting.

CHAPTER EIGHT

MR BALDWIN YAWNED

The strongest poison ever known
Came from Caesar's laurel crown.
WILLIAM BLAKE

BEAVERBROOK was now in what should have been, in every sense, the prime of his life—forty-four years old, a multi-millionaire, securely established in Fleet Street; in politics, a figure whom few could afford to disregard. Though he never bothered to acquire mere polish, social life in London had planed down some of his rough edges: when a charming pair of American actresses, the Dolly Sisters, came to London to appear at the Hippodrome, they found him an invaluable *arbiter elegantiarum.*[1] Except when he was mourning the loss of Bonar Law, he was, outwardly, the very pattern of a successful man, radiating confidence.

This was a superficial impression. He had not achieved the inner certainty—the integrity, in the strict sense of the word—which springs from singleness of purpose; he was confused about ends, and he was confused about the means to secure such ends as did seem clearly desirable. If the New Testament had been drummed into him as diligently as the Old had been, he might have applied to his own life the lesson of Luke xi, 34: *When thine eye is single, thy whole body also is full of light.*

One of the leading humanists of that time, H. G. Wells, saw shrewdly through the mask of success. Beaverbrook's 'doubts will grow', wrote Wells[2]—and added: 'He has attained nothing so far but wealth and considerable power,

---

[1] 'He told us to make ourselves agreeable to personages of our own sex in high society, and to accept invitations only from them. To be taken to exclusive homes by anyone of male persuasion, no matter what his standing, might prove fatal to a successful social career . . . In London it was always best to make haste slowly.' (Miss Rose Dolly, in the *World Magazine.*)

[2] In *T.P.'s and Cassell's Weekly*, November 24th, 1923.

nothing in fact except to secure opportunity . . . only by the use of his present opportunities can he or anyone judge the ultimate quality of his life.'

Beaverbrook himself occasionally showed that he was conscious of an unresolved conflict within him. 'Journalism,' he wrote, 'is the most fascinating of all professions, and if I had my time over again I would give my whole life to it.' He had not yet worked out a reasonable distribution of his energies between politics as such and newspaper production; he was finding out by trial and error, as he went along, the extent to which the two activities overlapped, and which of them to concentrate on in each situation that arose. Twenty-five years later he would have handled quite differently, for instance, his campaign against Lloyd George's pro-Greek policy: if he had seen fit to go personally to Turkey as a self-appointed, unofficial diplomat, he would not have been so naïve as to undertake a journalistic commitment as part of the mission; more probably, he would not have gone to Turkey at all but would have stayed in London, busying himself behind the diplomatic and political scenes, while one of the highly trained *Express* correspondents sent dispatches for whose publication Beaverbrook could, if necessary, disclaim responsibility.

Another Middle-Eastern excursion, though it led to one of those public controversies which Beaverbrook has always found diverting, might also not have been embarked on at a more mature period of his life. He had from time to time felt a desultory antagonism to the Zionist cause; and in the spring of 1923, taking with him James Douglas of the *Sunday Express*, he set out for Palestine. He said afterwards: 'I went to Palestine to form my own conclusions on the spot'. As he had been attacking Zionism vigorously for more than a year before going, the conclusions were probably not difficult to form. Chesterton observed in the *New Witness* that this was 'one of the strangest pilgrimages ever undertaken to the Holy Land'.

His first cable from Palestine appeared in the *Daily Express* on March 14th. He quoted official figures to show how greatly the Jews then in Palestine were outnumbered by the Arabs. His message ended with the words: 'I trust that you will give publicity to this declaration'. His trust was not misplaced. Douglas (who would not have withheld his own dispatches from his travelling-companion) committed himself, in the *Sunday Express*, to a judgement that may be said to have been premature: 'The Arab nation are ironically watching the last agonies of the great Zionist delusion'.

The spectacular establishment of the State of Israel makes retrospective argument about Zionism academic. In 1923—ten years before Hitler's accession to power—it was possible to argue respectably against Zionism and to discuss 'the Jewish problem' without being suspected of anti-Jewish prejudice; many Jews were themselves non-Zionist or anti-Zionist.

Beaverbrook, however, did not escape the imputation, even though he insisted that he knew and admired many Jews in business and politics, and even though an anti-Semitic extremist, Joseph Bannister, attacked the *Express* as 'one of the most Kosher organs in London' and Beaverbrook because he had supported 'the stockjobber Isaacs' for Viceroy. Jews took Beaverbrook's disclaimer as a variant of the familiar anti-Semitic tag: 'Some of my best friends are Jews, but . . .' The *Jewish Chronicle* accused him outright of 'anti-Semitic bias', saying: 'This anti-Jewish sentiment as an element in the campaign Lord Beaverbrook . . . has denied with such vehemence as could only arise in one who was conscious that the offence charged against him was well-founded.'

A protestation of innocence is not necessarily evidence of guilt; but, if there was no taint of racial prejudice in this campaign, Beaverbrook cannot be acquitted of some ingenuousness in his method of promoting it. It began with a *Sunday Express* article, headed simply, in large capitals, THE JEWS; and this article began with a notable instance of *petitio principii*—'Why is there such a marked recrudescence of feeling against the Jews?' Like most questions which are begged, this one was answered in the way that happened to suit the questioner: public 'feeling against the Jews', real or imagined, had one cause only—Zionism. This article was soon followed by a favourable review in the *Evening Standard* of the 'serious and logical argument' in Belloc's book, *The Jews*; and space was found in the *Sunday Express* for an effusion by the pathologically prejudiced T. W. H. Crosland —who could actually write 'Judas was a Jew' without bothering to mention the racial origin of the One whom Judas betrayed. This contribution was entitled 'The Fine Old Hebrew Gentleman'.

It is fair to add that the advocates of Zionism reacted to the campaign with more zeal than skill. A neutral referee would be obliged to award some points at least to Beaverbrook.

To start with, the *Jewish World* suggested that the High Commissioner (Sir Herbert Samuel) would be 'fully justified' in barring Beaverbrook and Douglas from Palestine as undesirable aliens and mischief-makers—a suggestion naturally seized on with avidity as evidence that Zionists were intolerant and had something to hide.

Then, in their eagerness to rebut such a case as Beaverbrook might have, Zionist publicists allowed themselves to be trapped into challenging his veracity on a point of fact which he would hardly have made if there had been no basis at all for it. He was reported to have told an Arab delegation in Palestine that he had first been 'converted to anti-Zionism by a deputation of British Jews'. He did not say who they were, or where or when he had met them; the bare statement was enough to excite strong protests and denials. Challenged to name the Jews in question, he refused to do so on the ground that they would be victimized by the powerful Zionists; but he said that their names were known 'to the

169

boardroom of the *Jewish Guardian*', to Sir Alfred Mond,[1] to 'an employee of the Zionist Government in Palestine', and to Balfour.

This was getting nearer home. Not surprisingly, the clamour of indignation was redoubled. Sir Alfred Mond repudiated Beaverbrook. Thirty-five 'Arab notables' repudiated Beaverbrook. The Zionists must have thought that he would soon be on the run—or they would surely have made a few private enquiries before pressing their challenge further.

It was two months before he replied to it again. (This episode coincided with the illness and resignation of Bonar Law, by which Beaverbrook was more intensely preoccupied.) His delayed reply was devastating. He now gave names, with details so circumstantial that it was clear that his original statement had been true. The 'deputation of British Jews' who had converted him to anti-Zionism had come to him when he was Minister of Information: they had been concerned by the exclusively Zionist character of the Jewish propaganda section of the Ministry, and had persuaded him to add a non-Zionist Jew to the staff. The deputation had consisted of two men of outstanding eminence in Jewry—Mr Lionel de Rothschild and Sir Charles Henry, MP. Moreover, Sir Charles had been fortified in his approach to Beaverbrook by the approval of the Prime Minister himself: before coming to the Ministry of Information, he had taken the precaution of seeing Lloyd George and obtaining his informal assent to a reorientation of official propaganda on Palestine. As it turned out, nothing came of this *démarche* while Beaverbrook was still in office, for he was called to order by a letter from the Foreign Secretary, who had soon heard of this meddling:

Dear Beaverbrook,

The policy of His Majesty's Government in Palestine is that laid down by the Foreign Secretary in his last speech. Until it

[1] Later Lord Melchett.

is altered officially, it is in no way affected by conversations
between Sir Charles Henry and the Prime Minister.

Yours sincerely,

Balfour.

The *Jewish Chronicle*, which had been exultantly scornful,
was now nonplussed. It deplored such conduct by distinguished Jews—conduct which, it said, 'goes to the very roots
of our communal organization and of the amenities that must
subsist between Jew and Jew, if the community is to endure'.
The Editor of the *Jewish Chronicle* met Beaverbrook personally, and took him to lunch with Dr Weizmann, whom he
found 'a splendid man'. The attack on Beaverbrook was not
pursued by the Jewish press or, so far as public records show,
by Sir Alfred Mond: at the time of his repudiation of Beaverbrook, he had, no doubt, genuinely forgotten ever having
been cognizant of the incident at the Ministry; but Beaverbrook was able to pin him down with dates and quotations
from letters.

This is one of numberless incidents in Beaverbrook's life
which illustrate the usefulness of his invariable habit of keeping and filing all letters received and copies of all letters
dispatched. He keeps almost as much paper as he destroys:
as any of his housemaids would testify, that is a good deal.
Any of his secretaries, likewise, would testify that considerable filing-space is needed for half-a-century's business,
political, general, social, and private correspondence. He also
has a passion for acquiring and preserving the letters and
diaries of his great contemporaries—Lloyd George, Bonar
Law, R. B. Bennett, and many others. He has lately bought
the papers of Lord Wargrave—now almost forgotten, but a
key figure in the Conservative Party a generation ago. He
owns, too, a number of Asquith's private letters—some of
those, perhaps, which Lloyd George used furiously to allege
that Asquith would write hour after hour, in his dignified
Victorian long-hand, while presiding at Cabinet meetings.

171

Beaverbrook does not collect these papers merely to indulge his own curiosity, powerful though this trait is in him (as in all successful newspapermen). Except when they are too intimate in character and persons referred to in them are still alive, he makes them available for research, and even commissions books based on them. They are indeed the raw material of history. So, without doubt, would be much of the contents of Beaverbrook's own files. Yet it is his present intention that most of these shall be destroyed after his death. Historians will hope that he may reconsider this decision and leave his papers—if necessary with a fifty-year embargo on the publication of private material in them—either to the University of New Brunswick or to some other institution more accessible to the generality of scholars.

*   *   *

In August, 1923, he first coined a phrase which was to be reiterated often for the education of *Express* readers: Splendid Isolation. The *Chicago Tribune* and other newspapers in the Middle West of the United States exploited the strong anti-European sentiment latent in the New World, even among citizens of European origin and ancestry, many of whom had escaped from hardship and poverty in their native lands: so, too, Beaverbrook was disposed even more powerfully by somewhat different impulses—his own sunless Scottish-Canadian background, his want of understanding of the Mediterranean sources of Christian and European culture—to cry aloud to the British people and Government: 'Leave Europe to the Europeans'. Above all, the suggestion that the Straits of Dover were wider than the Atlantic Ocean fitted in well with the protectionism whose necessity he had dimly apprehended, as a boy, when his elders had told him of the burning of the effigies of those uncousinly Britons who had sought to buy timber from the Baltic. There is the essence of Protestant utilitarianism in his advice *To the Young Men of England*: 'If you serve yourself well, you will serve the State

172

well too'. Dr Rosenberg himself never proclaimed the doctrine of a *Herrenvolk* with more conviction than Beaverbrook in his more lyrical passages on 'the teeming energies of the Imperial race'.

For years he pestered the Conservative leaders, one after another, to proclaim the full doctrine of Imperial Preference, including taxation on foods imported from non-Empire countries. One after another they shied at the electoral risks implicit in the doctrine, and sent emissaries begging him not to embarrass the Party to which he was, after all, nominally attached. 'For my own part,' he growled, 'if my action is to be so limited and circumscribed by party exigencies that I am debarred from expressing my real views on the needs and future of the race and the Empire, I would at once quit public life altogether and return to the Canadian village from whence I came.' This threat seems not to have been taken seriously; if it was, it merely caused the Conservatives to redouble their resistance to his efforts.

Meanwhile, he continued to bounce resiliently between public newspaper controversy and private political negotiations, perhaps unconsciously seeking an equilibrium. Within a year of the Election of 1922, Baldwin had decided that another Election must be fought. Beaverbrook (and others) were strongly opposed to this 'rushing' of the Election. They warned Baldwin that 'Bonar Law's carefully constructed majority would be wantonly squandered'. Despite another stern Old Testament analogy by Beaverbrook (comparing himself with the prophet Micaiah and Baldwin with Ahab before the battle of Ramoth-Gilead), Baldwin preferred to listen to those Central Office experts who prophesied 'smooth things'.

There was much excitement and indignation in official Conservative circles when it was disclosed that, just before the Election, Austen Chamberlain, Birkenhead and Churchill had been spending the week-end with Beaverbrook at Cherkley.

Official Liberal circles were equally perturbed when it was learned that Lloyd George—who had been reconciled with Asquith and his followers only a few days before—had also been present at this gathering. The week-end party was represented—'absurdly enough', said Beaverbrook—as a 'sinister intrigue'.

Whether it was so or not, relations between Baldwin and at least one of the Cherkley guests were so poor that when Baldwin—still Prime Minister—wrote to ask Birkenhead to come to see him for half-an-hour, Birkenhead replied that he was 'too busy'. This and other manifestations of independence caused such acute concern to the Party managers that Beaverbrook felt obliged to write a letter to the *Morning Post* emphatically disclaiming hostility to Baldwin. Baldwin, he said, had merely 'made a profound error', in rushing the Election and in shirking Imperial Preference; but he would do his best, none the less, to help Baldwin win the Election. In next day's *Sunday Express* he clarified his attitude further, under the headline—scarcely calculated to inspire and attract the floating voter—'Making the Best of a Bad Election'. The discovery of his private political house-party at Cherkley had evidently piqued him. 'I have had journalistic spies placed on my doorstep,' he protested, 'in order to record in the Press the names of all who visit me.' Many who have since then suffered similar intrusions must wish that they also could have expressed their resentment so publicly.

Ten days later his rôle was still that of the injured party. He complained of a 'shower of vituperation and insinuation' unparalleled since 1909: those who accused him and his friends of being animated by low personal motives were all 'extremists' of the Right or of the Left, or 'turncoats'. He advised voters to vote simply on the Imperial issue, irrespective of party altogether: they should vote against Labour 'every time', but should prefer an Imperialist, however labelled, to a 'narrow-minded' Baldwinite Tory.

With all this going on, it is hardly surprising that the Conservative majority was lost, as Micaiah had foreseen that it would be; the Labour Party came to office (though not with a clear majority of seats) for the first time. As happens when an election is lost, each faction on the losing side was able to blame the other. The Right-wing *National Review* sourly said that the Coalition had been 'sufficiently crooked' and that it was preferable to lose elections honourably under Baldwin than to win them *talis auxiliis*—a view rather loftier than that of the Party managers, who simply preferred winning elections. In the course of a prolonged post-mortem, Beaverbrook declared in print that Baldwin, having rushed his party to disaster, ought to resign. But he still insisted that he had no vendetta against Baldwin. As he put it (and such egotistical, tongue-in-cheek brazenness must have been infuriating to those who took their public life seriously): 'I have always been ready to agree with Mr Baldwin when he is right'— i.e., when his policies happened to suit Beaverbrook.

In the first few months of 1924, the main emphasis of Beaverbrook's propaganda shifted slightly. He seems to have begun to despair of ever converting the official Conservative leadership to his Imperial policy. Instead, he began to play with an idea that has often been canvassed in modern English politics, but never successfully realized: the idea of a centre party, a coalition of moderate men agreed on some major item of policy—in this case, of course, Imperial Preference. In pursuit of this idea, Beaverbrook wrote glowingly of the necessity of Liberalism and even of the Liberal Party (which a few years earlier had seemed to him to be a 'party of spoilers . . . tottering to its fall'). It was 'quite unthinkable', he now wrote, that the Liberal Party 'should be wiped out of existence in twenty or thirty years'. (Less than thirty years after the publication of these words, the representation of the Liberal Party in the House of Commons, then 159, had been reduced to 6.) Closely associated with Beaverbrook in this agitation for Liberal-Tory fusion (minus the non-imperialist elements in each party) was Birkenhead.

The climax of their efforts was reached in the by-election in the Abbey Division of Westminster. Winston Churchill was induced to stand as an Independent against the official Conservative and Liberal candidates. His programme included Imperial Preference and 'Conservative Social Reform'; he had the backing not only of Beaverbrook and Rothermere, but of Lord Wargrave and other influential Tories. Birkenhead wrote in his support in the *Sunday Times*, Lord Burnham in the *Daily Telegraph*. Sir Charles Oman, the eminent Oxford Tory historian, said, more equivocally: 'Winston will, of course, be a great force in the House, and a most useful battering-ram against Socialism. But I am afraid he will push himself on to the front bench too soon.' It was felt by many that the Centre Party was now in being, round Churchill's candidature. Both the campaign and its result were profoundly disturbing to the head offices of the parties: Churchill did not, indeed, win, in so safe a Tory stronghold, but he polled only 43 votes fewer than the official Tory candidate's 8,187.

Though this result was correspondingly gratifying to the rebels, it was galling to Beaverbrook to reflect that victory—those few more votes—might have been achieved if he had been able to throw all his propaganda resources into the campaign. He was prevented from doing so by an unusual—an unheard-of—domestic incident: the Editor of the *Evening Standard*, E. R. Thompson,[1] did not hold with Churchill's candidature and actually dared to refuse to support it editorially in the newspaper. Moreover, he warned Beaverbrook that if he were forced to print editorials that he disagreed with, or if he were sacked or suspended, he would write a letter to

---

[1] Better known by his pseudonym, 'E. T. Raymond'; father of the late C. V. R. Thompson, for many years chief *Daily Express* correspondent in New York.

The Times complaining of Beaverbrook's dictatorship. It was an ugly, and a delicate, situation; in view of the possible electoral repercussions of such an exposure, Beaverbrook decided to do nothing about it until after polling-day. Then, of course, Thompson was sent for: such mutiny could not be tolerated. Fortunately the interview, though stormy, was brief: in the course of being sacked, Thompson had a heart attack and died.

At this time several brilliant Radical cartoonists were drawing in the British newspapers. Will Hope in the *Daily Herald* and David Low in the *Star* both satirized what they called the 'Plot Press'. It was shortly before the Abbey by-election that Low invented two figures who were to become as familiar in his drawings as Colonel Blimp at a later date: the figures of Beaverbrook and Rothermere as the Wicked Uncles of the fairy-story, with Baldwin as a Babe in the Wood (and Mr Garvin, of the *Observer*, as a bird bringing leaves to cover him with).

The fact that Low could plausibly portray Baldwin and Beaverbrook in these respective characters is itself a simple illustration of Baldwin's overwhelming superiority to Beaverbrook in the art of politics. Beaverbrook was a Wicked Uncle, a plotter, a manipulator—and everybody knew it and could see it. Baldwin, though more indolent by temperament, was at least Beaverbrook's equal in manœuvre—and his mastery lay in the invisibility of his movements. The public, like the cartoonists, really believed that he was a plain, solid, rather stupid, but honest, average Englishman, a Babe in the Wood of politics, beset by Wicked Uncles.

Baldwin was no Babe in the Wood. He was a Fabian, rather, slow to move, unobtrusive when moving; but his might have been the motto of the Fabian Society—'When I strike, I strike hard'. It was now his turn to sharpen a long knife. Whatever the truth about his tussle with Beaverbrook for Bonar Law's soul, whether or not it be the case, as

Beaverbrook has always claimed, that the first disagreement between them was on public policy—on the American debt settlement of 1923—Baldwin must have felt that Beaverbrook's sponsorship of unofficial candidates for Parliament was the one crucial action that made reconciliation impossible.

At any rate, he now struck hard—and chose in doing so, no doubt with conscious irony, to invade Beaverbrook's own territory and to make his attack not in Parliament but through a popular newspaper.

On May 18th, 1924, the *People* published a long exclusive interview with Baldwin which it was able in its next issue to refer to—without, for once, exaggeration—as a 'bombshell' and as 'the greatest political sensation of modern years'. The interview was headlined, in the ample manner of sub-editors before the age of newsprint-rationing and with a plenitude of full points and five-em rules:

Baldwin Turns and Rends
His Critics.

Sensational Disclosure
to *The People*.

Why the Trust Press Attacks
Him.
Party's Great Social
Programme Revealed.

By Our Political Correspondent.

The first part of the interview was unexciting. It consisted largely of the sort of platitudes uttered on such occasions by leaders of all parties. A 'great social programme' was, if not 'revealed', at least alluded to in hopeful generalizations. The first point which the ordinary Conservative reader might have found unconventional was one of Baldwin's replies to

178

questions on this aspect of the interview: 'Every future Government must be Socialistic, in the sense in which our grandfathers used the word. Personally, I don't know what Socialism means, but'—and he relapsed into *clichés* about the removal of abuses and the tackling of social and economic evils.

Then he said, or so the Political Correspondent reported: 'The lot of a leader in opposition is a difficult one'. From this point onwards the interview was, indeed, sensational. Baldwin was quoted directly as saying:

. . . When I spoke at the Carlton Club meeting [on the decision to withdraw from the Coalition], I never expected that we [i.e. those who favoured withdrawal] should win. I took my political life in my hands and I was prepared to retire from politics. I did not know that Bonar Law would lead us. In fact the night before I spent two hours with him, and he had sealed a letter to the Chairman of his Glasgow Association telling him that he would not stand for Parliament again. In that mood I left him.

And then we won. I spoke because I was determined that never again should the sinister and cynical combination of the chief three of the Coalition—Mr Lloyd George, Mr Churchill, and Lord Birkenhead—come together again. But today you can see the signs of the times.

But I didn't expect the exiled Conservative ex-Ministers would take things as badly as they did. Before the election last year, I welcomed Mr Austen Chamberlain back, and I accepted his friends, though I could easily have stopped their return to our councils.

With Austen came Lord Birkenhead, who had attached himself to the strings of Austen's apron the year before very cleverly. And Austen is one of those loyal men who could not see disloyalty or intrigue even if it was at his elbow. But I am under no illusions as to Lord Birkenhead. If his health does not give way he will be a liability to the Party. But can a leader in opposition shut the door to an ex-Minister?

And at the same time I am attacked by the Trust Press, by Lord Beaverbrook and Lord Rothermere. For myself I do not mind. I care not what they say or think. They are both men that I would not have in my house. I do not respect them. Who are they? . . .

This Trust Press is breaking up. The *Daily Mail* is dead; it has no soul. Northcliffe, with all his faults, was a great journalist, with a spark of genius. But this man! . . .

The last time I spoke to Lord Beaverbrook was at Bonar's funeral. He had contracted a curious friendship with Bonar and had got his finger into the pie, where it had no business to be. He got hold of much information which he used in ways it was not intended. [*Sic*]

When I came in, that stopped. I know I could get his support if I were to send for him and talk things over with him. But I prefer not. That sort of thing does not appeal to me.

As I said, I do not mind attacks on myself. I often wonder if my silent contempt irritates them more than if I were to speak out. I suppose it is my lot to suffer disloyalty. But there are limits.

Take the article in the recent number of *English Life*.[1] That's a pretty dirty bit of work. It is written by 'A Conservative ex-Minister' and I am pretty certain that if it is not written by the man I suspect, it was certainly inspired by him. It was a stab in the back . . .

Besides, all this intrigue—this Churchill plotting—is bad for the party, for all the young men who are looking to Toryism for the salvation of the country. What do these intriguers want? Simply to go back to the old dirty kind of politics! Not while I'm leader of the Party.

So spoke Baldwin, according to the Political Correspondent of the *People*, who added only one descriptive sentence to round off his scoop:

And Mr Baldwin yawned with disgust and weariness at discussing for so long so unpleasant a subject.

[1] This article, entitled *The Jelly Bulwarks of the Conservative Party*, had referred to 'Diehards . . . gibbering anguish when they encounter Lord Beaverbrook's very sulphurous criticism', to Baldwin's leadership as 'impotent', and to a private decision of the Shadow Cabinet. It had alleged that Baldwin had 'hastened to Lord Balfour's house at midnight' to suppress a letter by Balfour backing Churchill in the Abbey by-election. The article was anonymous; its author was, in fact, Birkenhead.

If Baldwin was yawning, others were sitting up with a start that Sunday morning and rubbing their eyes. Those who approved of what Baldwin was reported to have said, and those who were against him, were agreed that no more savage attack by a political leader on colleagues belonging to his own party had ever appeared in print. The allusion to Birkenhead's 'health' was especially feline, in view of his notorious addiction to the bottle. It may be surmised that the telephones were exceptionally busy that day in Downing Street and the Fleet Street editors' offices and at Cherkley and half-a-dozen other political country houses. The Party managers were in despair: much as they deplored the activities of Beaverbrook and his friends, they just could not afford to have all this dirty linen washed so publicly. Baldwin would have to put the matter right.

He put it right—in so far as the memory of such words could ever be obliterated—in a conventional and not particularly courageous way, by the use of a technique, common among politicians, known to newspapermen as 'blaming the reporter'. He issued a disclaimer through the Press Association and —on the advice of an eminent Tory lawyer, Sir Douglas Hogg[1]—wrote a personal letter to each of the colleagues who might have felt that they had been libelled in the interview. These personal letters were unqualified and uncompromising in their repudiation of the *People* interview: '. . . I hope you know me well enough to be certain that I never gave expression to the personal reflections on yourself which are there reported. I am deeply distressed that I should have been so grossly misrepresented.' Each of the men to whom such a letter was sent replied to it more or less cordially, accepting Baldwin's disclaimer, save one of them only—Beaverbrook. He sent no reply.

Possibly he had already learned enough about the newspaper trade and art to know that no correspondent would

[1] Later Viscount Hailsham.

have dared to invent so extraordinary a pronouncement by a party leader, and that no editor would have dared to publish it, quoted at length in direct speech, if he had not been convinced of its genuineness. On internal evidence alone, indeed, the interview carries conviction to any journalist reading it many years later; it simply could not have been faked. A commentator in the *Daily Herald* at the time remarked: 'Those who know the Conservative leader well say he talks just in that blunt, crisp way'.

In any case, even the most prompt and sweeping disclaimer cannot undo all the effect of such an interview, circulated without denial among millions of people for a whole day. Nor did the *Morning Post* make things easier by gloating at length the next day on the caustic quality of Baldwin's alleged rebuke to his critics, and heartily endorsing it. There were in the interview, said its editorial, 'some things which we should not wish unsaid, whether they were said by Mr Baldwin or came from the fertile brain of the journalist'. The interview 'takes on, by its imaginative force, the higher similitude of fiction'; and (as in Defoe's account of the Plague) there was 'so much truth in what [Mr Baldwin] is alleged to have said, that it is almost as good as if he had said it'.

If it be accepted that Baldwin was not, in fact, 'grossly misrepresented' by his interviewer, the only point that remains at issue is whether he knew that he was talking for publication or whether he was merely 'thinking aloud' in a confidential way—'off the record', as it is now called. (This, be it noted, is not what Baldwin claimed. If he uttered at all, even off the record, the words attributed to him, he might have said that their publication was unauthorized, but he could hardly have claimed, as he did, that he had never said anything of the kind.) According to the *Morning Post*, 'the interview, as for publication, ended' at the point at which it began to be really interesting; 'and what followed was compiled from statements of the interviewer himself, supplemented by conversational comments by Mr Baldwin, who, at this period of the conversation, became a listener rather than an interlocutor'. This may be true of some passages; but it is hard to believe that the interviewer would have originated such references as those to Beaverbrook's friendship with Law and the *English Life* article.

The *People* had been founded as an independent Conservative paper by the Duke of Northumberland and others on the Right wing of the Party, and was at this time controlled by a Canadian financier, Colonel Grant Morden. He was a man not indifferent to the prospect of honour and advancement, and the elevation of newspaper proprietors to the peerage was in those days almost an accepted convention. Grant Morden was, therefore, subjected to the heaviest possible pressure—political, financial, legal, and social—from people with whom he wished to stand well. It was essential, they told him, that the Baldwin interview should be repudiated editorially, with a grovelling apology. Moreover, it was even suggested that the Editor and the Political Correspondent responsible for this outrage should be sacked. They were, respectively, Mr Hannen Swaffer and Mr Freddy Wilson.

Since the *People* is a Sunday newspaper, the pressure on Grant Morden was kept up for the better part of a week. By Friday night or Saturday morning, at the latest, a decision had to be taken. On the Friday, Grant Morden said to Swaffer: 'I'm finished'. Swaffer, chivalrously—for he might have been committing professional suicide—replied: 'Disown me'. His generosity touched Grant Morden, who rallied, saying: 'By God, I'll fight 'em'. And so he did. The next Sunday's *People* published a long statement giving circumstantial corroboration of the authenticity of the interview: it was shown that this had actually been arranged by officials of the Conservative Central Office so that Baldwin might have an opportunity of advertising the Party's social programme and also (according to the *People*) of replying to his critics. The Political Correspondent wrote that Baldwin had seemed to him 'a slow-thinking, very honest, earnest, likeable man . . . trying to tackle a very difficult subject with rather uncorrelated knowledge'. A long editorial justifying publication ended with a perfunctory expression of 'regret for any personal pain' that had been caused.

This bold resistance is in welcome contrast to the readiness with which some newspapers have capitulated to pressure in similar circumstances. Grant Morden and Swaffer were not, indeed, absolutely alone in their fight. They had powerful, if private, allies: Beaverbrook and Birkenhead both accepted Swaffer's word that the interview was authentic; so did the newspaper's legal adviser, Sir William Bull. None the less, Grant Morden is entitled to some credit for his gesture in defence of press freedom—and the credit is not appreciably diminished by the fact that, according to Swaffer's recollection, the newspaper's funds were low at that time and it would have been difficult, if he and Wilson had been sacked, to find the substantial compensation to which their contracts would have entitled them. It is probably a coincidence that Grant Morden died a commoner.

Thirty years have passed, and most of the participants in this fracas are dead. In objective retrospect, it seems not only almost certain that Baldwin said the words attributed to him but also likely that he knew that they were to be published. He could hardly have failed to notice that the interviewer was taking notes during the latter as well as the former part of their conversation; if he did notice this, it was open to him—and it would have been usual—to say, at some point, 'You realize that this is not for publication'. It has never been suggested that he said this.

It follows, then, that the whole episode was an exercise in political warfare of the utmost ingenuity and daring. Baldwin indulged in a calculated indiscretion: when this had created the desired effect, he simply evaded the consequences by sacrificing the journalist who had been the recording instrument. He had indeed hit on a technique of character-assassination that had no come-back and was, accordingly, at once more simple and more cunning than anything devised since by Goebbels or by Senator McCarthy. Only a politician with the status of a party leader and a carefully built-up reputation for homespun honesty could have brought it off; and this, no doubt, is what Beaverbrook meant when he said that Baldwin 'could do many diabolical things and get away with them'. Whether an action seems 'diabolical' or not depends on the point of view.

At least the assassin, however noble, should not be seen as a Babe in the Wood. That is to misread history. Baldwin yawning in disgust at the end of a single interview had more power in him, and more guile, than Beaverbrook could command in a thousand frantic editorials.

CHAPTER NINE

HUNTING THE TIGER

Two pairs of eyes meet one another glowing—
They hunt, the velvet tigers in the jungle.

W. J. TURNER

ONLY A YEAR or two before the *People* interview, Baldwin would not have been recognized by nine out of ten passers-by in Whitehall. When he succeeded Bonar Law as Prime Minister in 1923, the term 'The Unknown Premier', said to have been applied to Law by Asquith as the *cortège* passed the tomb of the Unknown Soldier during the Abbey funeral, would have applied equally well to Baldwin.

Beaverbrook underestimated him, but he was not alone in doing so. The recent fashion in politicians had been for men of obvious brilliance, noisy men, men of stinging wit or ardent rhetoric. The sudden—and, to outsiders, puzzling—emergence of a leader cut to an altogether different and homelier pattern misled almost everybody. Curzon, from whom Baldwin's call to Buckingham Palace had snatched the premiership he expected, bitterly said, again and again, that he had been passed over for 'a man of the utmost insignificance'. Lloyd George reckoned him, says Dr Thomas Jones, 'as of little or no account', and referred to him, disparagingly, as 'honest to the verge of simplicity'. (He probably did not know that Baldwin habitually referred to him, in conversation, as 'The Goat'.) Perhaps a writer in the *Daily Herald* showed more understanding that the visible *persona* was not the whole man when he wrote: 'If Mr Bernard Shaw is right in saying that every man must have a pose of some kind, Mr Baldwin may be congratulated on having chosen one which is attractive to spectators and relaxing to opponents'.

As Beaverbrook was to learn, it was unwise for Baldwin's opponents to relax for a moment. They should have studied

186

him more closely, on and off duty. Had they done so, they would soon have sensed that this was no humdrum, bucolic John Bull: though he has been depicted as given to idleness and procrastination, his resolution, or obstinacy, could be as tough as the iron from which his fortune came; he could spin a length of purple prose with Borrow or Stevenson (and discover, in Mary Webb, a novelist ideally suited to the taste of the middle-class female elector); he 'did good by stealth' (as in his semi-anonymous gift to the Treasury of one-fifth of his estate, £120,000) and may have blushed to find it, invariably, fame; he even, in unguarded moments, let slip epigrams that seem to have been original and were dangerously nearer to wit than to humour (such as his remark that the word *intelligentsia* bore 'the same relation to intelligence that the word gents does to gentlemen'). When he was in fighting mood, his wife used to murmur admiringly 'Tiger Baldwin . . . Tiger Baldwin'.

The years of Baldwin's leadership happened to coincide with a period in Beaverbrook's life in which he was bored and lonely. The void caused by Bonar Law's death has already been stressed; and in 1927 he suffered two bereavements that touched him even more closely.

In August his mother, travelling to Scotland by train, opened the blind of her sleeper to get a glimpse of Newcastle, after which her home-town in New Brunswick had been named. The blind was stiff: the exertion brought on a heart-attack, from which she died.

Then, in the winter, Lady Beaverbrook, too, died, 'from heart failure following an illness which first developed during a holiday at Le Touquet in the summer'. All who knew her still speak of her as the most gentle and beautiful of women. Birkenhead, in an obituary tribute, wrote of her 'simple and exquisite charm':

> She had a breeding, a beauty, a poise, and a judgement which would have recommended her to any society in Europe at the

most critical moment of that society . . . She was essentially womanly, and being womanly she was incredibly understanding. She made allowances easily and generously . . .

This loss was not only a shock to him; it was a challenge. He was used to challenges in business and in politics: he was surprised and baffled to find himself unable to meet and deal with this challenge in his personal life. He went on with necessary business more or less mechanically, and made more spare time than ever before for the unfamiliar task of holding his home together. Soon after this, his daughter Janet married; but his two sons, Max and Peter, were still at school, and he tried to look after them himself. In later years, he did not feel that he had gone about this in the right way, or made much of a success of it: when a holiday abroad was indicated, he chose such unsuitable places as Deauville; when he took them travelling in Canada and the United States, he was always wanting to talk shop with old cronies and never quite knew what to do about the boys. Neither of them, however, seems to have come to much harm from these unusual vacations; and they probably acquired, in the course of them, a good deal more worldly knowledge than was available to the other boys, or indeed to the masters, at Westminster School.

By now he knew without doubt that his newspapers were going to be immensely successful. Their sales were told in swelling millions. A Manchester edition of the *Daily Express* was started in March, 1927, with a manifesto containing Beaverbrook's favourite quotation from the Presbyterian Shorter Catechism ('*The Eighth Commandment forbiddeth whatsoever doth or may unjustly hinder our own or our neighbour's wealth or outward estate*') and a thought-provoking comment on it ('*This means that all our activities to our own advantage are good unless they directly damage other people*'). A Scottish edition was announced in November, 1928, when Beaverbrook wrote:

. . . I have put eight years of my life into making the *Daily Express* whatever it is. I am the creator of the structure . . .

But my share in the work is done. I am like a ship-builder who has built a ship but will not be her captain. As the vessel glides down the slip-way he says 'Farewell' . . .

I planned the *Daily Express* . . . but the staff are more competent than I am to manage it.

I can conceive and create but I cannot conduct. This has always been my case. I conceived and created the Canada Cement Company. I never should have been competent to manage it, and I never tried. I simply handed over my little orphan to Mr Frank Jones, the best business manager on the other side of the Atlantic . . . So on the very last day of the month of November, 1927, I said 'Good-bye' to the *Daily Express* office for ever . . .

This is one of the first and more elaborate examples of an extraordinary phenomenon—Beaverbrook's constantly reiterated pretence that he has no control over the management or policy of his newspapers. In 1928 he also wrote (in a letter to the *Morning Post*): '. . . I have long ceased to interest myself actively in any kind of management or business, except in the case of one or two private companies. It is true that I own the share control of the London Express Newspapers. . . . But this does not imply that I am responsible for the policy of the *Daily Express*.' A few weeks before his valedictory introduction of the *Scottish Daily Express*, he had written an interesting letter to *Time and Tide* in reply to an article about him which had said, *inter alia*: 'He gives lavish parties to escape boredom, and is bored at them'. Correcting certain misstatements about his financial associations with Lord Rothermere, he wrote:

When I was young I never contradicted anything. Now in the waning sunset of my old age[1] I intend to contradict, if I have time, ever so many statements about me which are not accurate . . .

[1] He was forty-nine.

I believe the *Daily Express* should not pay its maximum possible dividend until it is a perfect newspaper. Anyone who does not agree with the conception should not invest in the *Daily Express* . . .

I think it only right to say . . . that I am neither a Director nor employee of the *Daily Express* Company, and take no part in its management or direction.

The writer of the *Time and Tide* article, replying to this letter and commenting on its last claim, cited a novel by Arnold Bennett, *The Strange Vanguard*, and a character in it, 'Lord Furber', who was supposed to bear some resemblance to Beaverbrook, and quoted the sentence: 'After this enormous whopper he paused to recover, afraid lest he might be going too far'.

On June 19th, 1929, an announcement appeared: 'Lord Beaverbrook has made a gift of his controlling share interest in the London Express Newspaper Company to and for the benefit of his elder son, William Maxwell Aitken'; and a photograph of 'young Max' in the *Daily Express* was captioned, perhaps ingenuously, 'The New Proprietor'. A quarter of a century later, on July 21st, 1954, there was another announcement: 'Lord Beaverbrook has given a block of shares in the Express to the Beaverbrook Foundation, which has been established as a British Empire Educational Trust. The newspapers have therefore passed out of his control.' Nobody seems to have noticed any discrepancy between these two announcements. Nobody, at any rate, seems to have tried to find out the explanation, which was simple: at some time in the years between the two announcements, Beaverbrook had bought back the controlling shares from his son.

Such announcements now excite relatively little interest, even in Fleet Street, mainly because, over the years, there have been so many of them, merely punctuating periods when he is obviously running the newspapers very actively indeed. The

formula has become meaningless: a Beaverbrook disclaimer
of responsibility and control is rather like a routine summer
weather forecast on the BBC—something that people only
half-listen to and nobody believes. Everybody knows that, on
the very day after one of these disclaimers, Beaverbrook will
be at his telephones and his dictaphones as busily as ever.
Nor has any editor or columnist ever been known, after one
of the disclaimers, to say coldly, when given an instruction:
'I'm sorry, sir, but—er—I understand that you no longer
control this newspaper'.

Why has he so often restated a fiction that can hardly still
be intended to deceive? (That it is a fiction, in substance if it
has not always been so technically, is shown by his perfectly
open evidence before the Royal Commission on the Press.[1])
No one explanation is sufficient. It is not enough that the
fiction has often saved him social and political embarrassment: a newspaper proprietor is constantly dunned for free
publicity on behalf of all sorts of worthy and unworthy
causes, from campaigns for the preservation of historic
buildings to charity film galas, or reproached by indignant
and influential acquaintances who have been attacked in his
papers; and it is a convenient face-saver if he can say,
credibly or not, 'I leave all that to the Editor—I never interfere'. A more serious motive may be suggested by the rough
treatment that Beaverbrook received from the House of
Commons in 1918: at many times during the past thirty
years it may have seemed to him possible that he would
shortly be called on to take ministerial office (as he did again
in 1940); and the more often he had told the world that he
had nothing to do with the *Express*, the more convincing, so
he might suppose, his dissociation from it on taking office—
which was indeed real enough—would appear to be.

Whatever his main motive for these gestures of disengagement, it may be guessed that in the mid-1920s, in these years

[1] See pp. 140 and 151.

of Baldwin's ascendancy in the Conservative Party, he was beginning to feel—not, indeed, bored with his newspapers themselves, but that the first intensive struggle to save and to create them was victoriously ended. He still nursed and bullied them assiduously, but they no longer represented quite so fierce a daily challenge to his ingenuity and courage as the newly-acquired *Daily Express* once had. This slight easing of pressure at one point combined with bereavement and consequent loneliness to plunge him into a prolonged *cafard*.

That this is not too fanciful an analysis of his mood at that time is shown by a remarkable article by Mr C. F. G. Masterman which appeared in the *Sunday Express* ten days after Beaverbrook had founded the Manchester edition of the *Express*. The subject of the article was Beaverbrook himself, and it was the fourth in a series entitled 'Splendid Failures'. Masterman was a distinguished and intelligent Liberal who had been, in turn, Beaverbrook's victim and his beneficiary; Beaverbrook had succeeded in getting him out of Parliament by running a candidate to split his vote, but had later treated him generously and employed him as a writer. At any rate, Masterman knew Beaverbrook well, and this is what he wrote about him:

He has done everything that he wanted to do, and he cannot see anything else worth doing. At comparatively early middle age, he finds no more worlds to conquer . . . He eats and drinks less than the average artisan.

He could easily have been Minister again in a Conservative Government. But he was so bored in previous experience that he had no desire to repeat it. And in any case he has no fundamental sympathy with the stupidities and squalors and sentimentalities of a Conservative Party.

He is a good speaker—better than he realizes. But he has now immured himself in the House of Lords, in which any live voice merely sounds and scares like Aeneas addressing the spectres of the dead.

He hates and despises 'Socialism'. He is naturally a Liberal, but has little belief in the future of the Liberal Party . . .

Lord Beaverbrook not only sees the gates of all these avenues closed. He is more mournful in not caring whether the gates . . . are open or shut . . .

He talks of success, but he does not believe in success, and success turns to dust and ashes in his mouth.

If Baldwin was ever bored, he could read *John Inglesant* and vegetate in Worcestershire. If Churchill was bored, he could paint. Beaverbrook cared little for serious reading and could neither paint nor vegetate. There was a vacuum in his soul.

Such a vacuum is dangerous. The activities in which Beaverbrook was now engaging, with driving restlessness, may have been an anodyne to his bruised spirit: to Baldwin they seemed mischievous indeed.

*   *   *

By the end of 1924 he had dropped the idea of a centre party—partly, perhaps, because it had involved collaboration with so many whom he regarded as inveterate Free Traders. For more than a decade thereafter he fought a ding-dong battle with Baldwin, seeking to impose his will on him— sometimes wooing, sometimes basking in a brief lull or reconciliation, then attacking again with sharper acrimony. After the *People* interview, Baldwin rarely deigned to reply to him publicly—only once, indeed, with full force; yet Beaverbrook was outpointed in almost every round of the contest.

Five months after the *People* interview, there was another General Election. The Labour Government was thrown out— largely thanks to Rothermere's 'Red Letter' stunt. Perhaps this dubious but useful aid mitigated for a time Baldwin's hostility to the 'coalition gang' and the press lords, or perhaps he felt that the Abbey by-election result had been a warning too serious to disregard; at any rate, Churchill was forgiven his piratical candidature and appointed Chancellor of the Exchequer. Whatever Rothermere felt about the appointment, it did not appease Beaverbrook: he had favoured Sir Robert Horne for Chancellor; Churchill was a Free Trader; the appointment was attacked in the *Express*.

A few months passed. Baldwin's stock was rising; he felt stronger, but knew that there were undependable men, plotters, and enemies in his own Government and Party. He must have grunted with disgust if he noticed an account of a luncheon-party given in London by Mrs William Randolph Hearst: the guests included Balfour, Beaverbrook, Birkenhead, Churchill, and Lloyd George—'an honoured employee of the Hearst Press', as the *Morning Post* observed satirically, adding that the party had been 'almost a fête of the Coalition'.

By May, 1925—just a year after the *People* interview—Beaverbrook was beginning to be impatient with the Government; but his attitude to Baldwin himself was ambiguous. In an article in the *Sunday Express* (headed 'The Government Arraigned') he wrote of Baldwin: 'I never thought that he himself could be so good or his Government so bad'. A few days later the *Express* printed a warning that Independent Conservative candidates would again 'arise' and that it was 'quite likely' that the *Express* would support them.

Soon Baldwin himself was again being attacked. In October, 1925, the *Spectator* remarked: '... the persecution of Mr Baldwin ... has passed beyond reason and decency. Many onlookers are asking: "Can a political party possibly survive when the most popular newspapers which nominally support it are engaged day and night in ridiculing its leader?" [But] the Press is less powerful than it seems to be ... Mr Baldwin passes serenely on his way without paying any attention ...'

At this moment there was a concerted counter-attack by Baldwin's supporters. Mr Ormsby-Gore[1] denounced Beaverbrook

[1] Later Lord Harlech.

for his propaganda against the League of Nations, and said that he and Rothermere were 'determined to do their best to down Mr Baldwin'; he also, significantly, quoted with approval some 'uncomfortable home-truths' from the *People* interview of the previous year—though he was one of Baldwin's junior ministers and the interview, it will be recalled, had been repudiated. Lord Erskine spoke of Beaverbrook's 'personal vendetta' against Baldwin. Mr Cooper Rawson, MP, spoke of his 'venomous spite', *John Bull* of his 'envenomed fury'. Commander Eyres Monsell[1] and the Duke of Portland swelled the chorus of censure—the *Bury Free Press* explaining to its readers that the Duke's attack represented 'the attitude of Society' to Beaverbrook and Rothermere: 'neither peer is *persona grata* with the Upper Ten, whose exclusiveness shudders at the penny Press ... The *Mail* and *Express* are served out to the aristocracy of the kitchen ...' *Truth*, in a more balanced half-term-report style, said: 'Lord Beaverbrook is gaining in experience ... but he still handicaps himself by impetuous and amateurish exhibitions ... He will go far if he is capable of concentration on newspapers and manages to impress upon himself that responsibility goes with power.' Baldwin himself was to echo this sentiment, devastatingly, six years later.

One of the best-known squibs of the moment was a quatrain by some anonymous wit that went the rounds at the Office of Works:

> *When round for public works we look*
> *Two pressing jobs at once appear :*
> *To dam for ever Beaver Brook*
> *And drain the mud from Rother Mere.*[2]

[1] Later Viscount Monsell.

[2] The *Morning Post*, characteristically, published a rendering of this into Latin Sapphics:

> *Herculem quisquis studet aemulari*
> *Purget Augeae Rotheris lacunam*
> *Castorisque infanda premat perenni*
> *Flumina claustro.*

195

Equally lively, if less classical in form, was Mr Herbert Morrison's contribution to the row—an open letter to Beaverbrook and Rothermere in *London News*:

My Lords,
You're a bright pair of lads, aren't you?
Has it ever dawned on you that nobody in Great Britain is doing more to destroy the influence of the Press than you two specimens of the Lloyd-Georgian aristocracy? . . .
I am, My Lords,
Yours for Socialism . . .

Strongest of all the criticisms was by a Liberal—the Editor of the *Weekly Westminster*, who wrote, of *Politicians and the Press*: 'This trivial little book . . . displays the working, at the heart of our national life, of a dangerous, irresponsible, and corrupting power.'

Perhaps surprisingly, this counter-attack seems to have had some effect. For a time Beaverbrook's direct attacks on Baldwin were fewer and milder, and mostly in the form of editorials rather than in challenging signed statements. He wrote articles on subjects outside the immediate party quarrel: he advocated the 'trustification' of coal, he published his reminiscences of H. G. Wells. He was grooming Castlerosse as a columnist. ('I predict confidently that Viscount Castlerosse will have the most brilliant journalistic career of his age.') He started the *Daily Express* community-singing stunt, which caught on well. It was at this time, too, that he began his short career on the Turf.[1] Moreover, Conservatives of all sorts—feudalists, industrialists, small middle-class men—were united, in 1926, by an unprecedented and immense demonstration of the power of the organized workers, the General Strike. To help run Churchill's official news-sheet, the *British Gazette*, Beaverbrook lent several key-men from the *Express* —the night superintendent, the head machine-room overseer,

[1] See p. 16.

the chief mechanical engineer. The *Morning Post* praised his 'instant, unstinted, and uncalculating aid'. In the face of this external enemy, the Tories called a truce to their civil war.

Beaverbrook melted into an almost genial mood: one Monday the *Daily Express* published a letter from him which ran, in part, 'Sir, I wish that every reader of the *Daily Express* had seen the splendid issue of this week's *Sunday Express* . . . a completely fresh standard for Sunday reading of clean and wholesome literature. My compliments to the staff of the *Sunday Express* . . .'; and he found time to send a 'Christmas' message to the shopkeepers of Leatherhead. ('It is salesmanship which counts.') A week or two later he was indulging in optimistic prophecy: 'The whole economic position points towards a big boom'. This was not very long before the great American depression, and in Britain there were already nearly a million and a half unemployed. The big stores, however, whose advertisements were so important to the *Express*, were probably grateful for anything that might tend to give trade a boost just after Christmas.

Two years later, at the end of 1928, he was fairly cooing at Baldwin. A curious diary-note, signed by him, appeared in the *Sunday Express* under the guise of a news-story: it described the twenty-first birthday party of Birkenhead's son, Lord Furneaux, and was lavish in its praise of Baldwin's speech on that occasion. 'I am astonished . . .', he wrote. 'A turn of wit, a fine humour, an excellent address, a voice more than good for oratorical purposes. I have had to revise my whole conception of Mr Baldwin's speaking.'

A little later he was involved in a serious car accident. As a thank-offering for his escape, he sent £25,000 to Baldwin, asking him to distribute it to institutions engaged in medical education. A few months after this he gave a still more substantial gift—£63,000 spread over seven years—to the medical school of St Mary's Hospital, Paddington.

All this was only the lull before a new and more violent storm, that was to rage, almost without a break, until Baldwin's final and victorious retirement. The storm's first rumblings accompanied the General Election of 1929. Again Labour came to office without a clear majority; again there were recriminations on the losing side, the *Morning Post* publishing editorials, attacking Beaverbrook and Rothermere, under such titles as 'Enemies in Disguise' and 'The Kisses of an Enemy'. By now he was used to such terms of abuse; they did not distress him at all. What did disturb him more seriously—stinging him, indeed, into action—was the suggestion which the *Morning Post* was also able to make, that Beaverbrook himself had, for once, been as negligent as all the other politicians in not keeping the Empire in the forefront of his election campaign propaganda. The charge was just: Beaverbrook and the *Express*, almost ignoring bigger issues, had made a demand for larger railway goods-trucks their main campaign policy. It was 'a bit thick', said the *Morning Post*, that he should now presume to rebuke anyone else for not being keen enough on the Empire.

He rose to this taunt with an extravagantly penitent and rhetorical article headed 'Who Is For the Empire?' (the answer being 'All men and no one'). The European manager of the Canadian Pacific Railway hailed the article as 'a first advance in a great crusade'. Beaverbrook picked the word up with zest. A historian might have thought the metaphor somewhat strained; no matter—it was a dramatic word, a militant word. A crusader he would be.

This was the start of his long campaign for what he was soon calling Empire Free Trade—a campaign conducted with every circumstance of strident publicity, with that repetitiveness which is said to be one secret of success in advertising, and with, ultimately, the most insignificant effect on British political life and thought. Up and down the country Beaverbrook and his mercenaries stamped and roared, banging the drum of Empire, lashing themselves into a frenzy of economic xenophobia, interfering in some by-elections, fighting others with their own candidates.

Of course they got big audiences. It was a vivid, brassy show. Beaverbrook was an effective revivalist orator. In his retinue travelled a few big-businessmen (mostly as ignorant as he of the character of the English people), a number of prospective Parliamentary candidates, Conservative and Liberal, and a host of lesser stooges. He seems to have genuinely believed that this touring circus was a potent new political movement; this kind of self-deception is an occupational risk among millionaires who throw their money around in an attempt to buy power, and is, naturally, encouraged by the numerous parasites who profit from it incidentally. Thus, the Editor of the *Daily Express* was telling his readers (including 'the chief reader', as Beaverbrook was sometimes called in the office) that they had 'literally made history' by supporting the Empire Crusade. At the same time he appealed to them to fill in the membership form, which involved no financial obligation. He hoped that the 'great majority' of them would do so. This appeal, with the membership form, appeared in full-page advertisements not only in the *Express* but in all the principal newspapers in Britain; so that it may be assumed to have been seen by practically the entire adult electorate. The response was said by Beaverbrook to be 'immediate and overwhelming'. He was, perhaps, too easily overwhelmed; for it took ten weeks of barking and breast-beating to work the membership up to 200,000—which was less than one per cent of the adult electorate and nowhere near a 'great majority' of the 2,686,093 readers of the *Daily* and *Sunday Express*.

There is a certain period quaintness now in the shrill, ingenuous headlines with which this campaign was boosted so desperately. It may be surmised that the reaction to it of most Conservatives—indeed, of most Englishmen—was not

unlike that of Stalky and his friends, in Kipling's story, to
the visiting Conservative MP's address on Patriotism:

> He plunged into his speech with a long-drawn, rasping 'Well,
> boys', that, though they were not conscious of it, set every
> young nerve ajar. He supposed they knew—hey?—what he had
> come down for? It was not often that he had an opportunity to
> talk to boys. He supposed that boys were very much the same
> kind of persons—some people thought them rather funny
> persons—as they had been in his youth. . . .
> But they must remember that they would not always be boys.
> They would grow up into men, because the boys of to-day made
> the men of to-morrow, and upon the men of to-morrow the fair
> fame of their glorious native land depended . . .
> In a raucous voice he cried aloud little matters, like the hope of
> Honour and the dream of Glory, that boys do not discuss even
> with their most intimate equals; cheerfully assuming that, till
> he spoke, they had never considered these possibilities. He
> pointed them to shining goals, with fingers which smudged out
> all radiance on all horizons. He profaned the most secret places
> of their souls with outcries and gesticulations. He bade them
> consider the deeds of their ancestors in such fashion that they
> were flushed to their tingling ears. Some of them—the rending
> voice cut a frozen stillness—might have had relatives who
> perished in defence of their country. (They thought, not a few
> of them, of an old sword in a passage, or above a breakfast-
> room table, seen and fingered by stealth since they could walk.)
> He adjured them to emulate those illustrious examples; and
> they looked all ways in their extreme discomfort.

As had been shown,[1] Kipling was an even more inflexible
imperialist than Beaverbrook. It is an interesting coincidence
that he, who had once been Beaverbrook's friend, was also
Baldwin's cousin; and he fiercely supported Baldwin when
his leadership was challenged.

Neither Kipling nor Baldwin could have built up the *Daily
Express* into the immensely successful popular newspaper

[1] See pp. 10–11.

that it became; yet both of them knew better than Beaverbrook how to speak to the British people—one as a statesman,
the other as a story-teller—in an acceptable accent.

For the first six months of the Empire Crusade, however,
there was still a watchful truce between Beaverbrook and
Baldwin. Beaverbrook seems to have been confident that the
momentum of his campaign was irresistible, that the Tory
Jericho would fall at a mere trumpet-blast; he refrained for
a time from using more lethal weapons. He chose to publish
'A Plea to Mr Baldwin' not in one of his own newspapers but
in Rothermere's *Sunday Dispatch*. In this he said that,
though the Crusade was a success, there were 'certain individuals' who had a similar vision of a united Empire, 'and
it is their support that we most uncomfortably miss'. The
Morning Post, for instance, 'thinks the policy is a good one,
but in advocating it, *I* am in some queer way supposed
to be acting in opposition to Mr Baldwin. I have, in short,
blunt words, failed to take off my hat to him when I
should have done, and I am told, in consequence, that I
am indulging a private vendetta against him. . . . I will
stand aside and obliterate myself from the movement if
the Conservative leader will announce at the approaching
Party Conference that he adopts our programme of Empire
Free Trade.'

The note of pained, puzzled humility was no doubt sincere;
the offer was handsome enough; and Beaverbrook supplemented it by initiating a debate on Empire Free Trade in the
House of Lords. It is not easy, after this lapse of time, to
recapture the atmosphere of the debate from the varying
newspaper accounts of it. According to the *Daily Express*,
'Lord Beaverbrook was warmly cheered from all sides of the
House. . . .' The *Daily Telegraph* reported 'Opposition from
all sides', the *Liverpool Post and Mercury* that 'the audience
was cold'. The *Star*, alluding unkindly to the offer of self-
obliteration, said: 'He finds himself among the obliterati

without having succeeded in persuading any older Parliamentary hand to hold the baby'.

A few days after this debate, Baldwin was speaking to a Conservative gathering at the Albert Hall. He included in his speech some of the usual platitudes about the Empire and one particular reference: 'We owe a word of gratitude to one not always a supporter of our party, Lord Beaverbrook, for bringing before the country once more that idea ... of a united Empire. I pay tribute to his courage—rare in one of his profession—in offering a subject he believes in to criticism in its proper place—the Houses of Parliament.'

This tepid tribute, with its implied condemnation of political campaigns carried on elsewhere than in the 'proper place', sent the *Daily Express* into a paroxysm of joy and praise. Its headlines howled:

Mr Baldwin's Great Empire Speech.

New Conservative Policy.

Strong Tribute to Lord Beaverbrook.

Mr Baldwin's Pledge.

Vision of a United Commonwealth ...

Baldwin's square head was not turned by all this. He had taken Beaverbrook's wistful overtures, and offer of self-obliteration, at rather less than their face-value; for he was aware of another and more surprising campaign which had started, almost at the same time as the Empire Crusade, in two newspapers belonging to Beaverbrook's friend Rothermere—the *Daily Mail* and the *Sunday Pictorial*. This other campaign had begun with an article by Mr G. Ward Price openly attacking Baldwin and proposing drastic action indeed: the forthcoming National Conference of Conservative Associations, he suggested, should depose Baldwin—and elect Beaverbrook leader of the Party in his place!

That this was not a mere midsummer whim of the individual contributor was shown by the fact that the *Mail* gave its editorial blessing to his 'interesting' suggestion. Justly or not, Baldwin must have assumed that the article had not been printed without Beaverbrook's consent, particularly since it dealt, not too deftly, with the cross that he had carried ever since those days of confusion and suspense in December, 1916 —his peerage. 'His peerage could be only a temporary handicap,' wrote Ward Price, 'since the reconstruction of the Upper House, with the abolition of the hereditary principle, must soon make it possible for all peers to sit in the House of Commons.'

The words 'must soon' were surely written, by so well-informed a journalist as Ward Price, in a moment of aberration or perhaps merely to order: so sweeping a reform of the House of Lords was even less likely in 1929 than it is today. The proposal was greeted with an explosion of almost universal mirth. It was, so to speak, a sitter for the sardonic leader-writers of the *Morning Post*. 'Here, indeed,' they sneered, 'is an argument which might reconcile the Conservative Party to the abolition of the hereditary principle—that it might set free Lord Beaverbrook from the only obstacle—the obligations of his caste—which prevents him from becoming their leader. At last we have an adequate reason for reconstructing the House of Lords!'

Undeterred by this heavy irony, and by the fact that the Conservatives had failed to take his advice, Ward Price persisted in his mission. In the *Sunday Pictorial* on January 5th, 1930, he attacked Baldwin for having 'made costly but futile bids for popularity by adding to the country's burden of pensions and doles', for having given the vote to 'millions of flappers who promptly helped to put the Socialists in office', and for his 'unforgiveable blunder' of encouraging the idea of Dominion Home Rule for India. He added:

> The conviction is . . . fast spreading among Conservatives that their next leader must be found outside the established

hierarchy . . . the name of Lord Beaverbrook becomes steadily more prominent . . . *There is no man living in this country today with more likelihood of succeeding to the Premiership of Great Britain than Lord Beaverbrook.*

This is an extreme example of wishful writing. Years later, it seems almost inconceivable that such words could have been printed, even in a Rothermere newspaper, of a party whose prominent members at that time included Neville Chamberlain and Winston Churchill himself. Yet the changes and chances of the high game of politics may baffle prophets wiser than Ward Price: it is only fair to him to reflect that his forecast would have seemed, to most of his Conservative readers, just as grotesque and distasteful if he had substituted Churchill's name for Beaverbrook's.

Rothermere himself endorsed his employee's nomination at a public dinner. Beaverbrook was present at this dinner, and it is not recorded that, when he spoke, he asked to be spared the honour of leadership. On the contrary, he obliquely accepted the call—by extolling Rothermere's influence and judgement: Rothermere was 'the great master of popular opinion' and 'the greatest trustee of public opinion that we have ever seen in the history of journalism'. ('Really,' remarked *Truth*, 'these barons of the press are making themselves ridiculous.')

Despite all this, Beaverbrook felt able with a straight face to deny yet another *Morning Post* charge of 'bitter and persistent attacks on the Conservative leadership'. He was deeply wounded that such a thing should be said: 'This is not so. I have deliberately refrained from attacking Mr Baldwin . . . I have offered loyally to serve under him—subject, of course, to his adoption of the policy in which I so earnestly believe.' He added a threat which must have seemed to Baldwin and his friends more heinous than any mere personal attack: 'We shall oppose every Parliamentary candidate, no matter of which party, who does not adopt and further the

204

policy of Empire Free Trade as defined by the Provisional Committee of the Empire Crusade'.

Such threats became more frequent and more violent. At Gloucester he said: 'It is essential to save the country even at the expense of wrecking every political party'. The word 'wrecking' carries with it a whiff of sabotage and irresponsibility, the suggestion of a wild man running amok. It is generally reserved by controversialists for their opponents. Here was one coolly proclaiming it as, if necessary, part of his policy.

Nor were these empty threats. In February, 1930, it became evident that they were going to be put into effect. The *Daily Mail* announced the formation of the United Empire Party. Rothermere proclaimed that at the next election the party would 'contest half the seats in the country'. The *Morning Post* refused to publish an advertisement of the new party, because the only alternatives logically to be foreseen were 'the disruption of the Conservative Party or the failure of the United Empire Party'. A fighting fund was started: in two days it raised £40,000.

It may be that Beaverbrook felt from the first that the new party, sponsored by what was, after all, still a rival newspaper, might dim in some way the splendour of his Crusade or divert it from its main purposes. His partnership with Rothermere was always a trifle uneasy: for one thing, they did not really agree on all aspects of Empire policy; Rothermere was less of a whole-hogging food-taxer than Beaverbrook. At any rate, less than three weeks after the formation of the United Empire Party, Beaverbrook dropped out of it. The occasion of his doing so was a speech on March 4th by Baldwin which Beaverbrook professed to find 'perfectly satisfactory'. He wrote that he was 'profoundly grateful' to Baldwin: 'my friends and I are all delighted'—and there would now be no need to run candidates against the Conservatives. People who sent money to the United Empire Party would get it back.

All his friends were not, in fact, unanimously delighted. His principal friend, Rothermere, was distinctly sour. Beaverbrook's change of tactics seems to have taken him by surprise: he must have felt that this was an undependable ally to go tiger-hunting with. The work of the United Empire Party, he announced, 'will by no means cease'. There were all sorts of other causes to fight for: no more surrenders in India, no diplomatic relations with Moscow. Beaverbrook said, glumly, that this was 'a complete departure from the original aims of the United Empire Party'. Rothermere announced that more than half of those whose subscriptions to the Party had been returned had sent the money back again: the good work must go on.

Baldwin may well have permitted himself a grim smile at this point. His stratagem, if that is what it was, had succeeded: Beaverbrook had walked straight into the trap, his two main enemies were now separated. He thanked Beaverbrook for his public-spirited attitude.

It was not to last. A month after Baldwin's tribute to him, Beaverbrook was criticizing a leaflet put out by the Conservative Central Office because it seemed to him to misrepresent, by understating, Baldwin's 'perfectly satisfactory' assurances of March 4th. The publication of the leaflet, he said, was '. . . one in a chain of events which have gradually made the present position extremely difficult'.

What Baldwin had actually said on March 4th was this: he had proposed that, after the next election, an Imperial Conference should 'meet in an atmosphere of perfect freedom, and if . . . there should emerge any form of agreement, arrangement, treaty . . . that does give us great benefits and that demands in return a tax on some articles of food from a foreign country—that whole issue could be put clearly before our people' (by means of the unusual device of a referendum).

It is hard to imagine a 'commitment' less securely binding, more vague and conditional, more riddled with emergency exits. Why Beaverbrook fell for it can only be surmised: either he still had not taken the full measure of Baldwin's cunning, or the mere mention of a possible tax on foreign food blinded him to the qualifications in which it was wrapped, or, more probably, he was glad of an excuse to show Rothermere that he was not irrevocably dedicated to their partnership. At any rate, the Conservative leaflet came as a genuine shock to him: it seemed slightly to shift the emphasis of Baldwin's remarks and to put on the Dominions the onus of taking the desired initiative. He was very cross indeed: the leaflet, he said, must be withdrawn—indeed, only if it were withdrawn would he appear with Baldwin at a Crystal Palace rally which had been organized to celebrate their *détente*. (The rally was cancelled.) The *Manchester Guardian* may have analysed his distemper correctly when it said: 'The true explanation . . . is that Lord Rothermere has at long last succeeded in opening Lord Beaverbrook's eyes to the fact that March 4th marked a Baldwin, not a Beaverbrook, victory.'

Things were now as bad as ever. The *Daily Express* itself said that relations between Beaverbrook and Baldwin were reaching a 'climax', that the 'clash' was 'acute and . . . openly acknowledged'. Beaverbrook asked his readers for more money for the Crusade, claiming to have £100,000 in hand. He announced that he was giving up racing 'on account of his duties in connection with the Empire Crusade'. He rushed from by-election to by-election, backing candidates who challenged the official Conservative line: at South Paddington his candidate (Vice-Admiral Taylor) was actually elected; at East Islington his candidate (Brigadier-General Critchley) merely succeeded in letting the Socialist win by splitting the Conservative vote. Both results seemed equally deplorable to the Party managers—and they observed with anxiety that Critchley, while not winning, had got more votes than the official Tory candidate. They shuddered when they read Beaverbrook's latest challenge: 'If the Conservative

Party does not adopt Empire Free Trade, it is my purpose to break up the Party'. This was stated in even more definite and personal terms in the *Daily Express*: 'The United Empire Party's programme is to run between sixty and a hundred candidates to fight Socialist members and members of the Conservative Party in the South of England who have not formally and expressly adhered to Lord Beaverbrook's leadership'.

Mr A. J. Cummings, describing in the *News Chronicle* Beaverbrook's demeanour at East Islington, said that he 'attacked Mr Baldwin with dramatic force and with an all-embracing look of contemptuous fury'. Tempers were rising to boiling-point. It was at East Islington, too, that so eminent a lawyer as Lord Hailsham permitted himself to say: 'Lord Beaverbrook . . . is compared to an elephant trumpeting in the jungle . . . I am inclined to compare him to a mad dog running along the streets and yapping and barking, and I would remind his Lordship that the best way to treat a mad dog, if you can't muzzle him, is to shoot him.' (He later explained that he had not meant 'physical shooting'.)

In May, being 'disappointed' with the Conservative leaders, Beaverbrook suddenly said that they must 'scrap the referendum' which he had hailed so warmly when Baldwin had announced it in March. Questioned about this apparent inconsistency, he explained that he had accepted the referendum reluctantly, as the only means available of achieving his aim of taxing foreign food. But it was recalled that, a few days after Baldwin's offer, Beaverbrook had boasted, in a speech at Norwich, that it was he who had 'suggested' the referendum. The *Morning Post* remarked: 'Here we see the difficulty of playing cricket with a crusader. He proposes a policy; Mr Baldwin accepts the policy; he then repudiates the policy, and accuses Mr Baldwin of proposing it.' Beaverbrook growled: 'I have no use for word-spinning'.

Baldwin himself was now by no means indolent. So forceful and naked a bid to depose him could hardly be met by a grunt and a shrug of the shoulders. In a single month, in preparation for a meeting of Conservative MPs and candidates which was to be held at the Caxton Hall on June 24th, 1930, he spoke at about a dozen big meetings all over the country, paying particular attention to the North. Among the messages wishing him luck at the Caxton Hall was one from an outstanding Socialist, Harold Laski ('. . . there are those on the other side in politics whose respect for you is angered by the insolent challenge to your leadership.').

He had all the luck he needed. Apart from his own qualities, his enemies had played into his hands by over-reaching themselves. He was rough with them in his speech: 'There is nothing more curious in modern evolution than the effect of an enormous fortune rapidly made and the control of newspapers of your own'. He cited three men by name—Hearst in America, Rothermere and Beaverbrook. 'We are told that unless we make peace with these noblemen'—he put a ring of ironic contempt into the word—'candidates are to be run all over the country. The Lloyd George candidates at the last election smelt; these will stink.' The two strong Saxon monosyllables, uttered with steely emphasis, sent a *frisson* of half-shocked amusement and sympathy through the audience. Some may well have felt abashed, too; many of them had been restive under Baldwin's often apathetic leadership, many were readers of the *Express* and the *Mail*, some had no doubt toyed with temptation . . . This was a stern recall indeed, and Baldwin could afford to be severe; for in his pocket he had a letter, which he fumbled for and now produced and proceeded to read, pausing for a moment, amid tense silence, to adjust his glasses. 'Here,' he said, 'is a letter from Lord Rothermere.' There was another buzz of excitement. In a pregnant stillness, punctuated gradually by muffled exclamations of anger, he read:

. . . I cannot make it too abundantly clear that, under no circumstances whatsoever, will I support Mr Baldwin unless I know exactly what his policy is going to be, unless I have complete guarantees that such policy will be carried out if his Party achieves office, and unless I am acquainted with the names of at least eight, or ten, of his most prominent colleagues in the next Ministry.

The *folie de grandeur* has rarely been displayed so crudely. Indeed the kindest interpretation of Rothermere's letter is that his mind was infected by a touch of that mania which had destroyed his brother Northcliffe. That third 'unless' convulsed the meeting: this was blackmail. 'In his last years,' Mr. G. M. Young has recorded,[1] 'I noticed that Baldwin was fond of living through this moment again: "the Lord had delivered him into my hands".' It was hardly necessary for him to say more, but he rubbed it well in: 'A more preposterous and insolent demand was never made on the leader of any political party. I repudiate it with contempt, and I will fight that attempt at domination to the end.' The audience rose to him, and so did both sides of the House of Commons that afternoon. Yet that morning's *Daily Mail* had forecast that his speech at that day's meeting would be 'Mr Baldwin's swan-song', and had gone on exultantly to proclaim: 'The hour has come, and it has produced the Man'—Beaverbrook.

The man of the hour was, indisputably, Baldwin. Beaverbrook was especially enraged, for he knew that it was the insane indiscretion of his partner that had presented their enemy with so easy a triumph. He himself would never have been so foolish as to put these menacing conditions on paper. If he had demands to make, he had always made them by word of mouth, either in person or by messenger. Baldwin enjoyed an anecdote of Asquith refusing to see such an envoy, charged to offer the support of Beaverbrook's newspapers on certain conditions; pressed for an answer, Asquith had said 'Tell him I will give him half-a-crown for the lot'—and returned to a discussion of Jane Austen.

[1] *Stanley Baldwin*, p. 152.

Beaverbrook was, however, a resilient fighter. Four days after the Caxton Hall meeting, he reaffirmed his determination to convert or to oust Baldwin: 'I will never falter until Empire Free Trade is the adopted policy of this country. And if the Conservative Party will not have Empire Free Trade now and here, and without me, if it pleases the leaders, then the country must have it with me, but without those Conservative Party leaders.'

Nor, though Caxton Hall must have shaken many supporters, was his campaign without some effect. Mr Young testifies that 'the contrast between ardour and placidity was making itself felt on younger minds and more militant spirits . . . Beaverbrook seemed to offer them . . . something clear, tangible, visible: here, it seemed, was a Cause . . . and a man who knew very precisely what he was after and where he was going, which Baldwin did not.' According to Churchill, 'Strong currents of feeling and even of passion are moving under the stagnant surface of our affairs'.

There were to be two further critical engagements in this struggle for power. In October, 1930, at the same time as the South Paddington by-election, a party meeting was demanded, and it was realized that dissatisfaction with Baldwin's leadership could not be dismissed merely as a newspaper vendetta. Beaverbrook, indeed, kept up his nagging from outside, using a metaphor from revivalist evangelism: 'Mr Baldwin is the champion of all backsliders. We believe we have brought him to grace; we lift up our voices in the hymn of rejoicing; and we have hardly got through the first line of it before we see him crawling down the aisle again.' The scene he pictured would be an unfamiliar one to the solid Church of England folk who were the backbone of the Conservative Party in the country; but the comic expressiveness of his voice and gestures, the long-drawn-out harsh '*cra-a-ahling*'—all this was a novelty in political campaigning which still tickled them. Moreover, though he seemed sinister enough to the Tory aristocrats, to the public he was a much less unpalatable figure than Rothermere: he did at least come out and fight in the open, he did not merely lurk in the cowardly immunity of a Fleet Street office, despatching poisonous bullying letters. Another tactical error, which won Baldwin some sympathy—the circulation, on the eve of the party meeting, of a false rumour that forty-four MPs had signed a memorandum demanding Baldwin's resignation—smelt more like Rothermere's work than Beaverbrook's.

Mr Young says that Neville Chamberlain was always inclined 'to seek at least a tactical co-operation with Beaverbrook' and that he would have viewed Baldwin's departure 'with immense relief'. Yet he behaved, at this difficult moment, with perfect loyalty to Baldwin. He drafted the resolutions on which the party meeting voted—at Baldwin's own request, by secret ballot. Baldwin's leadership was confirmed by 462 to 116. Harold Laski wrote to Baldwin again, saying that this was a victory 'for the forces of sheer decency in public life'.

The press lords were undeterred; perhaps they were becoming desperate; or perhaps they had sufficient inside information to realize that Baldwin's position was less stable than it looked and hoped that a hard push might still upset him. Baldwin's own apprehensions were similar—and in February, 1931, they were confirmed by a demand from the Chief Agent of his own party that he should 'reconsider his position'. He was on the verge of resigning: had he done so, Beaverbrook would not have been elected leader, but Neville Chamberlain might have been, and he might well have offered Beaverbrook office or helped in other ways to promote his cause. Baldwin's resignation was delayed. India became the subject of intense controversy: Baldwin, against Churchill and the press lords and the right wing of his party, supported the Labour Government and 'the progressive realization of responsible government in India'. A by-election at St George's, Westminster, was being fought with unexampled virulence: Duff

Cooper was defending Baldwin against an Independent candidate, financed by the press lords, who used the momentous slogan, 'Gandhi is watching St George's'.

Party leaders do not, as a rule, take part personally in by-elections. But Baldwin had, at last, had enough of it. He was, moreover, fortified by the ovation which had greeted his masterly speech on India in the House. On March 18th, 1931, he went to speak for Duff Cooper at the Queen's Hall, and there voiced, without restraint or mercy, the passionate resentment and indignation that had been pent up and accumulating within him during the long years of his ordeal by newspaper persecution. 'I have said little,' he began. 'It is not worth it. I am going to say something today.' He went on to say that the papers attacking him were not newspapers in the ordinary sense, but 'engines of propaganda for the constantly changing policies, desires, personal wishes, personal likes and dislikes of two men'. He developed his theme relentlessly, to the fascination of the audience:

> What are their methods? Their methods are direct falsehood, misrepresentation, half-truths, the alteration of the speaker's meaning by publishing a sentence apart from the context, such as you see in these leaflets handed out outside the doors of this hall; suppression and editorial criticism of speeches which are not reported in the paper. These are methods hated alike by the public and by the whole of the rest of the Press.

> I have used an expression about an 'insolent plutocracy'. These words appeared in the *Daily Mail* of yesterday week: 'These expressions come ill from Mr Baldwin, since his father left him an immense fortune which, so far as may be learned from his own speeches, has almost disappeared. It is difficult to see how the leader of a party who has lost his own fortune can hope to restore that of anyone else, or of his country.'

> I have one observation to make about that. It is signed, 'Editor, *Daily Mail*'. I have no idea of the name of that gentleman. I would only observe that he is well qualified for the post which he holds. The first part of that statement is a lie, and the

second part of that statement by its implication is untrue. The paragraph itself could only have been written by a cad. I have consulted a very high legal authority, and I am advised that an action for libel would lie. I shall not move in the matter, and for this reason: I should get an apology and heavy damages. The first is of no value, and the second I would not touch with a barge-pole. What the proprietorship of these papers is aiming at is power, and power without responsibility—the prerogative of the harlot throughout the ages.

He had indeed said 'something'. In a century in which so many billions of words of oratory have gone with the wind, this speech—'the "harlot" speech', as it is called—is still remembered; and when, some years later, Mr Aneurin Bevan referred to the British press as 'the most prostituted press in the world', one of his friends gently reminded him that he was merely borrowing a metaphor from Mr Baldwin and using it rather less vigorously.

Politics have always been a struggle for power between the 'ins' and 'outs', both between parties and within parties. It is possible after a lapse of time to survey these ancient agonies with more detachment and less moral indignation than those involved in them. Some of those, too, who praised Baldwin as the paramount champion of 'sheer decency in public life' were to be aghast, only a few years later, at his frank admission that he had deliberately deceived the electorate, on the vital issue of rearmament, for fear of losing a General Election— an admission that earned him almost universal execration. Nevertheless, the historian is bound to judge that, in the long war of words that culminated in the Queen's Hall speech, the sense of most of the British people, of all classes and parties, was with him rather than with his enemies. Nor did these ever fully recover from the *coup de grâce* that he delivered on that occasion; and, as the sales of their newspapers soared, their real influence steadily declined. Millions of Britons buy the newspapers of Beaverbrook and Rothermere, as millions of

Americans buy the Hearst newspapers, for their technical competence and their entertainment value; but it is one of the more hopeful aspects of western democracy that so many of the people have so often refused to be guided politically by the newspapers which they prefer to read. Human motives—especially the motives of those seeking political office—are notoriously difficult to disentangle, and Beaverbrook's quest was inspired by genuine, indeed obsessive, devotion to a cause greater than himself, as well as by the vision of supreme power in his own hands; but the popular intuition is often, ultimately, sound in its assessment of character. 'I sometimes think that *character* is what these people most dislike', wrote Geoffrey Dawson, editor of *The Times*, to Baldwin. Like Laski, Dawson was to become in later years a favourite target for attack by the Beaverbrook press.

One more possibly significant factor may be mentioned incidentally. When the full history of techniques of communication in the twentieth century is written, it may be judged that the popular newspaper proprietors were right in feeling acute alarm when the BBC first came into existence and began to broadcast news and comment. They were wrong in supposing that its rivalry would cause people to stop buying newspapers. It was more subtly and fundamentally dangerous than that: by seeking steadily to maintain certain standards of impartiality and objectivity, it has gradually, over the years, helped to teach people to stop *believing* newspapers—newspapers, at any rate, of the more garish sort. This, in the long run, can only be in the interests of decent journalism as well as of the public.

The Queen's Hall denunciation might have been expected, then, to put an end for ever to the pretensions and ambitions of the press lords. Of course it did no such thing; they were not weaklings. Next day Beaverbrook was demanding a withdrawal by Baldwin of one of his secondary charges, that Mrs Baldwin's motherhood welfare campaign had not been publicized by the *Express*—'the newspaper', said Beaverbrook, to nobody's surprise (despite all those disclaimers), 'over which I have control'. None the less, it was a shattering blow to their prestige. Yet—so unfathomable is the maelstrom of politics—within ten days an amicable settlement between the contending parties was officially announced by the Conservative Central Office! It was clear that the Party had felt weaker than Baldwin's brave words had suggested; for it was openly stated that Neville Chamberlain, as the intermediary, had 'asked Lord Beaverbrook to state his terms of support'. A month later, Beaverbrook still felt able to say, with angelic innocence: 'I deprecate and deplore the appearance of dissension in Conservative quarters'. In that year the economic crisis broke upon Britain, and Ramsay MacDonald's 'National' Government was formed[1]; so the truce lasted for a while. It could not, of course, be permanent, while Baldwin lived. It lasted until Beaverbrook next felt restless and moody: next year he was at it again, saying of Baldwin, 'He is really at heart a Socialist. He really is. He is our enemy.' And again: 'Mr Baldwin . . . has the power. I haven't. I wish I had.' (Cheers) And so it went on.

However, he found time to turn aside from the battle to reply to a questionnaire in a Salvation Army periodical, *The Life-saving Scout and Guard*. The hero of his youth, he said, had been John Knox. The book that had helped him most? Samuel I and II.

His answer to 'What is the motto of your life?' was, perhaps, more unexpected. In his firm, quick, forward-sloping hand, he wrote: 'Do justly, love mercy, and walk humbly'.

---

[1] On September 28th, 1931, Beaverbrook published a manifesto, in terms more glowing than he had ever applied to Baldwin: 'I ask you to give . . . your confidence to Mr Ramsay MacDonald and his colleagues . . . Ask no questions. Seek no pledges . . . Trust in Mr MacDonald's leadership. Rely on Mr Neville Chamberlain . . .' (who succeeded Philip Snowden as Chancellor of the Exchequer in November, 1931, three months after MacDonald's National Government had been formed and after a General Election).

CHAPTER TEN

KING AS PAWN

*As Cleopatra . . . Sarah Bernhardt stabbed the slave
who bore to her the tidings of Mark Antony's defeat
at Actium; she stormed, raved, wrecked some of the
scenery in her frenzy and finally, as the curtain fell,
dropped in a shuddering, convulsive heap. As the
applause died, a middle-aged British matron was heard
to say to her neighbours: 'How different, how very
different from the home life of our own dear Queen!'*

IRVIN S. COBB

ONE MORE clash with Baldwin—the final, the most sensational, and the most historic—was yet to engage Beaverbrook.
It is unnecessary to trace in detail the further progress of
their feud in the years that preceded this clash. Ramsay Mac-
Donald, the 'boneless wonder' of Low's cartoons, vanished
from power; a more horrific portent was arising in Germany.
Beaverbrook found institutions other than Baldwin equally
meet for his attacks, and less potent in retaliation: the League
of Nations, the Peace Ballot, the Co-operative Movement.

His newspapers, too, continued to keep him busy. From this
period dates what has been described as the 'Americanization'
of the *Express* technique of news-presentation. Beaverbrook
had been struck by the new (yet, in some respects, quasi-
Homeric) formulae with which *Time* magazine was experi-
menting. Characteristic of this clipped, highly stylized
language were portmanteau neologisms (*cinemagnate, journal-
issimo*), the frequent omission of definite articles, tricks of
dramatic inversion in the construction of sentences, and the
insertion before persons' names of strings of often disrespect-
ful descriptive adjectives as well as professional labels of
identification. ('To Eastbourne's balding, myopic, Edinburgh-
trained physiotherapist William John Snooks, 53, came

217

last week news that . . .') *Time* became obligatory reading
in the *Express* office; and Beaverbrook, abolishing an older-
fashioned column of social gossip with which he had long
been impatient, instituted a new column signed with the
pseudonym 'William Hickey' (after the eighteenth-century
diarist, to whose entertaining memoirs Castlerosse had introduced him).

At first this column was meant to be modelled closely on
Time (from which its title, 'These Names Make News', was
lifted directly). Day after day Beaverbrook used to dictate to
the columnist paragraphs commenting on persons whom he
considered of topical interest (i.e., mainly Canadian and
American business 'tycoons', relieved by a few 'socialites')
in what he supposed to be *Time*style; and the columnist,
being young and nervous, had the stuff printed exactly as it
was dictated. The column was at first intensely monotonous
and jagged. Beaverbrook persevered in his tuition, and the
columnist gradually ventured to interpret his instructions less
literally. Beaverbrook's vigilance relaxed; whole weeks went
by without a summons to Stornoway House, the large ugly
house in Cleveland Row (later blitzed) which was then his
London residence. The column developed as an original
feature, evolving and maturing through the years, and was
found readable by many; but this might well not have happened if it had not been for the initial shock treatment, the
drastic break with the older feature, the exaggerated discipline
of the artificial style.

This experience may be taken as typical of Beaverbrook's
relations with his writing staffs. He wants something new
(perhaps based on a transatlantic idea). He doesn't quite
know how to define and present it. He experiments. He nags.
He gives a writer no peace until what he wants is produced.
Then, but for occasional incursions and reminders, he will
leave him to get on with the job—unless he is a writer of
leading articles expressing policy or a directly political

columnist such as 'Cross-bencher' of the *Sunday Express*, in which case, as may be guessed from Mr Peter Howard's description[1] of his apprenticeship to this post, he can expect neither peace nor independence. (He must not, however, rattle his chains too ostentatiously. An *Express* columnist once referred to himself in print as a 'wage-slave'. Early that morning Beaverbrook was on the telephone to the editor. 'If we have any slaves on the newspaper,' he said, with a sinister chuckle, '*set them free.*')

Typical also of his shrewdness—but showing some insensitiveness to the *nuances* of personality—is the extensive use by the *Express* of such pseudonyms as 'William Hickey', 'Beachcomber', 'Cross-bencher', and 'Ephraim Hardcastle', and their retention, as the newspaper's 'property', on contributions by many different journalists of varying views and styles. The point of this is that, if a successful columnist leaves the newspaper, he cannot take elsewhere the 'goodwill', and the readership, attaching to the pseudonym. It is not possible, in fact, to copyright a name or pseudonym; but the *Express* took the precaution, in the earliest days of the 'Hickey' column, of extracting from the columnist a signed agreement that the pseudonym belonged to the newspaper, not to him. In the absence of any such agreement, journalists are free to challenge a practice less beneficial to them than to their employers; and it has been challenged successfully at least twice—by Mr Jonah Barrington, formerly of the *Express*, who adopted this pseudonym as his own name by deed-poll, and

---

[1] In *Innocent Men*, p. 17: 'Beaverbrook took immense trouble over me. His instruction in the art of journalistic writing was unflagging, vivid, and beyond price. For my part I make no bones in recording my debt to Beaverbrook for the long hours of toil and instruction which he gave me over those years. He drove me on unceasingly, illuminating the dark days with a ray of sunshine and stirring up the easy summer weather with a thunderbolt or two. And I shall always be grateful ... Did I conduct feuds and vendettas? Certainly I did. If I heard that anyone had criticized my employer or my newspaper, I would wait patiently for weeks, maybe months, until the moment arrived to hang my victim's hide on the fence and take vengeance on him ...'

by Mrs Muriel Forbes, who took the *Sunday Times* to court and stopped the use by a successor of the pseudonym ('Mary Delane') by which she had become professionally well known.

It was in the mid-1930s that the 'Hickey' column began, by Beaverbrook's orders, to apply to Baldwin the superficially apt *Time* epithet, 'bumbling': 'Bumbling Stanley Baldwin' became a stock figure of fun.

In 1936 Baldwin's position, even among his most faithful supporters, was shaken by two events. There was his admission that he had concealed the truth about the defences of the country in order to win the Election of 1935; and there were the repercussions of the Hoare-Laval Pact, which had shocked public opinion deeply. Baldwin, 'feeble, toneless, and unhappy', as Mr Young pictures him, gave way to public opinion and sacrificed Sir Samuel Hoare.[1] Describing the episode in a Canadian magazine, Mr Beverley Baxter wrote of Baldwin: 'They say that he will never recover from this blow, that he will never regain his mastery over the House or his prestige in the country . . .' The prophecy might have been fulfilled but for the domestic problem that now began so to obsess the rulers of Britain that, for a time, Mussolini and Hitler and the statistics of unemployment almost faded from their minds—the problem which Dr Lang, Archbishop of Canterbury, referred to in his diary, with neutral distaste, as 'The King's Matter'. None was more worried about it than Baldwin himself: here was an issue demanding that prompt, decisive action which he found so uncongenial; it was an issue with profound, possibly catastrophic, constitutional implications, an issue necessitating also his interference in the private and sexual life of persons, a generation younger than

[1] Then Foreign Secretary; later Viscount Templewood. 'There is a case for a scapegoat', the Editor of *The Times* wrote privately to a colleague. At this time Hoare was a frequent visitor to Beaverbrook at Stornoway House, and constantly consulted him by telephone (using an alias to conceal his identity from switchboard-operators and secretaries). The scrapping of the pact plunged Beaverbrook into a fit of gloom.

he, with whom he had nothing in common[1]; and he was already, in the summer of 1936, breaking down under the intense pressure of Cabinet work. Yet, when the moment of crisis came, his handling of the affair was so masterly that Hoare and the deception of the electorate were alike forgotten, his enemies were confounded, and the most popular King for centuries was deposed and exiled with a convulsion deeper indeed but scarcely more lasting than had attended the replacement of Asquith by Lloyd George in 1916.

The main facts of the Abdication crisis are familiar to millions of British and American readers of Sunday newspapers and illustrated magazines, to whom they have been repeatedly retailed with a wealth of romantic embellishment, more or less authentic. Already, indeed, a considerable literature has grown up around this crisis; this literature was surveyed cursorily in an article in the *Spectator* of July 30th, 1954, by Mr George Curry, a British historian working at the University of South Carolina, who has made a special study of the subject. Many sources of study—state papers, overseas Dominion as well as United Kingdom Government documents, the official biography of King George VI, the private diaries or memoirs of Sir Walter Monckton, Lord Hardinge of Penshurst, and others closely concerned—will not be available for some time. There are differences of emphasis and interpretation in the various existing accounts; but so much is now known that it is unlikely—as Mr John Connell remarked in an unsympathetic comment on Mr Curry's article —that future publication of official papers 'can add much to our knowledge'.

The three most important full accounts of the Abdication crisis now extant are: the Duke of Windsor's own account, originally published in *Life* magazine and expanded for

---

[1] Dr Thomas Jones, in *A Diary with Letters*, records that Baldwin said to him: 'When I was a little boy in Worcestershire reading history books I never thought I should have to interfere between a King and his Mistress'.

inclusion in his book, *A King's Story*; the account by Mr Stanley Morison in an appendix to his final volume of *The History of The Times*; and the account by Mr Geoffrey Bocca in his popular biography of the Duchess of Windsor, called in America *The Woman Who Would Be Queen* and in Britain (no doubt for legal reasons) *She Might Have Been Queen*. Mr Curry seems to be unaware of a significant fact about these three accounts: two of them, at least, owe much to a single source of information—Beaverbrook; and the third was serialized in the *Sunday Express*.

This may seem particularly surprising in the case of the Duke of Windsor's own account; but the Duke's recollections of an incident so acutely painful to him and his wife may well have been confused and would necessarily be partial. It is known, at any rate, that when the Duke was preparing his story (in collaboration with the distinguished American journalist, Mr Charles Murphy, who actually wrote a good deal of the text for him), Beaverbrook provided much detailed information and diary extracts. Mr Morison, again, is a personal friend of Beaverbrook,[1] and consulted him on a number of occasions when he was preparing his Appendix. Much of Mr Bocca's lively journalistic prose, and his frequent flashes of obviously 'inside' information, might have come straight from the discs of Beaverbrook's recording-machine. The publication of the first serial instalment of his book in the *Sunday Express* provoked a sharp repudiation, alleging inaccuracy, from the Duke. As this instalment consisted largely of a description of a ball in New York, it is hard to see that any inaccuracies in it can have been substantial or important. A public challenge to the Duke to identify them, with a promise to pay £1,000 to charity if they were proved, was not taken up. The incident was trivial in itself, but may

---

[1] They once sang 'The Red Flag' together at Beaverbrook's dinner-table, to the consternation of some earnest transatlantic industrialists who were also of the company.

be taken as an indication that relations between the Duke and Beaverbrook are cooler than they once were.

Beaverbrook's principal direct contribution to the history of the Abdication crisis was contained in a review of *The Times* book which he broadcast in the Home Service of the BBC on May 25th, 1952. (On May 14th he had also reviewed the book on television, concentrating chiefly, on that occasion, on the character and career of Northcliffe.) In this broadcast he said:

These are the facts which the book sets forth:

(1) That the editor of *The Times*, Geoffrey Dawson, was the most important factor—with the sole exception of the Prime Minister, Stanley Baldwin—in compelling the King to abdicate.

(2) That he did it by methods which many would condemn.

(3) That he pursued his quest with a vigour that seemed more like venom.

Then, after a personal description and assessment of Dawson, Beaverbrook went on:

Now here is the factual account of the constitutional crisis taken from *The Times* Appendix. That Dawson was of more importance than any of the Prime Minister's Cabinet colleagues, is made abundantly clear in Mr Morison's narrative. Dawson was almost invariably consulted first. The crisis was launched by a letter written by Major Hardinge to his master, the King. Dawson saw that letter in draft and approved it. Thereupon Dawson set out on a propaganda canvass of public men.

Then, when the King put forward to Baldwin the project of a morganatic marriage—that is, that he should take a wife but not a queen—Dawson was consulted by Baldwin. Only after this consultation was the project submitted to the Cabinet and the Dominion Governments. When the replies came in, Baldwin conveyed the information to Dawson before he took it to the King. Dawson sat with Baldwin, comforting and encouraging him, when the Prime Minister lost his nerve. Then editor Dawson conducted a campaign in *The Times* advocating the

importance of keeping the Crown and its representatives remote
from glaring personal scandal. Dawson was intimidating the
King in code. He succeeded in terrifying His Majesty.

About this time I was in New York. The King telegraphed
and telephoned me to come to London. It is stated in *The Times*
book that when Dawson knew that I was due to arrive he
threatened to print a leading article attacking His Majesty himself in order to block any help that I might be able to give. And
on arriving at Fort Belvedere, where the King was in residence,
I found him in terror of Dawson. He had sent Mr Walter
Monckton to the editor, asking that he might have a promise
that the so-called 'Full Life' of Mrs Simpson would not be
published. He received an assurance that publication would not
take place in the next issue. Cold comfort.

When Dawson set out to mobilize opinion against the King
in the columns of *The Times*, he deliberately suppressed all
letters which were in favour of the King—and at the outset,
as is stated in *The Times* book, they were overwhelmingly so.
Then, at the end, he made three disreputable assertions in his
leading articles. He wrote that all would have thought Edward
fit to rule, if he had never ascended the Throne. He branded
Mrs Simpson personally in the severest language. And he
declared that King George V's last days had been clouded with
anxiety for the future. This information was supplied by the
Archbishop of Canterbury, who told Dawson that King George's
death had been hastened by his son's infatuation.

All the foregoing facts I take from the exciting Appendix of
Stanley Morison's 'History of *The Times*'. No doubt I put a
different interpretation upon some of these events, but the
accuracy of the narrative cannot be disputed. There is one
notable omission. Stanley Morison does not tell that editor
Dawson published one piece of journalism which was innocent
on the surface, but which carried wounding and malicious
innuendo. He does tell that public opinion was heavily on the
side of the King and the King's proposal for a morganatic
marriage. *The Times* successfully swayed public opinion in the
opposite direction. The King, now the Duke of Windsor, went
into exile when he boarded the destroyer *Fury* that foggy

December night, and put out to sea for France. He has not yet returned.

One day shortly after the abdication, President Roosevelt asked me to go to Washington. He examined me in every detail of the royal tragedy. He could not understand it. He quoted the old saying that no man should ever resign, but wait to be sacked. I replied that I never could discern any real purpose or steady policy in the conduct of the King. It seemed to me that he just allowed himself to be pushed out. President Roosevelt was not convinced. Years after, when the President was dead, I was given an explanation of the conduct of the King in a single sentence. When the Duke of Windsor disembarked from *Fury* at Boulogne and bade farewell to the friends that had come with him, he turned to one of them and said, 'I always thought I could get away with a morganatic marriage'.

So the King had a policy after all. Clearly it had been his intention to barter the threat of abdication against government acknowledgment of the morganatic marriage. The game was played to the end, and *The Times* and Mr Baldwin won the last trick. If I had known of this conversation before the death of President Roosevelt, I could have given him the answer to his question in the words of a King: 'I always thought I could get away with a morganatic marriage'.

As Beaverbrook must have foreseen—without too much dismay—this broadcast stirred up a storm of protest and controversy. Newspapers and reviews of all shades of opinion agreed that the BBC had belatedly discovered a broadcasting genius of immense natural force; but, whereas comment on the television talk had been almost wholly favourable, reactions to the sound-radio account of the Abdication were more critical. Writers in the *Daily Telegraph*, the *Manchester Guardian*, the *Yorkshire Post*, the *Spectator*, and *Time and Tide* questioned Beaverbrook's interpretation of what he called the 'facts' as set out in *The Times* book, or the propriety and taste of rubbing open these old sores. Such words as 'mischievous', 'deplorable', and 'glaringly irresponsible'

—familiar enough throughout Beaverbrook's career—were used freely. Mr Wickham Steed, formerly editor of *The Times*, wrote to *The Times* defending Dawson's memory in the strongest terms, calling the broadcast 'a public misdeed of heinous quality' and 'a spiteful diatribe'. Lord Brand supported him. Some critics took special exception to the broadcast because it came only three months after the death of King George VI (while the nation and Commonwealth were 'still mourning the death of this great and good King') and on 'Empire Sunday', too.

The question of the propriety of broadcasting such a talk at all is a subsidiary one. It seems necessary now only to suggest that the BBC is not customarily given to reckless indiscretion in its handling of matters affecting royalty; that the newly published volume of *The Times* history was a legitimate subject for lengthy review, on the air as in the press[1]; and that Beaverbrook, in his twofold review of it, was entitled to select those passages on which he could comment with special knowledge. The good or bad taste of his comments is a matter of opinion; but it would be, in general, of advantage to historians if public men who have been involved in great events would always tell all that they can remember of them, so that their versions may be challenged during their lifetimes and the truth begin to emerge from the consequent arguments.

Certainly Beaverbrook's version was challenged sharply. Of much greater importance than the taste of what he said is the question of its correctness. Wickham Steed, besides protesting against its indecency, called it 'a travesty of the facts'. For instance, he picked on Beaverbrook's accusation:

[1] As Beaverbrook himself wrote: '. . . it was not me who brought up the old story . . . Nor was it me who chose the moment of publication.' He wrote this in an expensively printed and copiously illustrated forty-page pamphlet, containing the texts of his broadcasts and a categorical apologia for them, which the *Express* prepared for sale at a shilling a copy. This pamphlet would undoubtedly have had an immense sale. For some reason it was decided at the last moment not to publish it.

When Dawson set out to mobilise opinion against the King in the columns of *The Times*, he deliberately suppressed all letters which were in favour of the King—and at the outset, as is stated in *The Times* book, they were overwhelmingly so.

This, Steed pointed out, was an interpretation of a sentence and a footnote on pages 1042 and 1043 of *The Times* history. The sentence ran:

Dawson organised an analysis of the vast mass of correspondence that had poured into Printing House Square ... in order to have the basis for the following day's leader.

The footnote ran:

None of these letters to the Editor was ever published but they were studied for the indication they gave of the progress of public opinion. The earliest letters, following the shock of the first newspaper comments, mainly reflected an unquestioning loyalty to the occupant of the Throne, which gradually wavered and gave way to a more critical approach with much legal argument. Mingled with moral doubts, this attitude ended in marked hostility to the King: he was judged as one who had failed to put his public duty before his private inclinations.

Steed added:

Geoffrey Dawson, as I knew him, and as the History recognises, was disposed to reflect and follow, rather than to lead and guide, public opinion. In deciding to print none of the letters that reached him, and to use them for his own guidance—and doubtless for that of the Prime Minister who wisely consulted him—he truly reflected public opinion.

Every reader can judge for himself of the fairness of Beaverbrook's gloss on the sentence in the book and its footnote. It must at least be agreed that his interpretation—with the change of emphasis from studying the letters for guidance to the mobilizing of opinion, the suggestion that only those letters favourable to the King were 'suppressed', whereas the book says plainly that *none* of the letters was published, and

227

the tendentious substitution of 'overwhelmingly' for 'mainly' —was straining to the extreme one possible meaning of the passage.

His defence of other passages in the broadcast is more convincing, especially if he was relying to some extent on private knowledge (though the argument in the unpublished pamphlet was based entirely on quotations from *The Times* book, set beside the relevant extracts from the broadcast). But his charge that Dawson made 'three disreputable assertions' in leading articles seems far-fetched if the 'assertions' are examined in their context. The article that hurt the King himself most deeply was the one discussing the proposal for a morganatic marriage, in which, said Beaverbrook, Dawson 'branded Mrs Simpson personally in the severest language'; and the words in it which caused special offence were: 'The Constitution is to be amended in order that she may carry in solitary prominence the brand of unfitness for the Queen's Throne'. These seem harsh words indeed; but the King, his nerves raw and frayed, failed to notice that they were the logical climax of an argument tending, in effect, not so much to 'smear' Mrs Simpson as to protect her from the likely consequences of her friends' ineptitude. If—this argument ran—you succeeded in reviving the stale device of a morganatic marriage, *you*, her friends, will be branding Mrs Simpson as unfit to be Queen. The argument is sophistical, in view of the Editor's own obvious disapproval of the lady, and the language is strong (though not unduly so, in so important a constitutional crisis); but argument and language hardly deserve to be dismissed as 'disreputable'.

Beaverbrook was unquestionably justified, however, in his condemnation of 'one piece of journalism . . . innocent on the surface, which carried wounding and malicious innuendo'. He did not identify the item to which he was referring; but it must almost certainly have been an unimportant item of social news which the Editor of *The Times* chose to print immediately next to Mrs Simpson's desperate and pathetic statement offering 'to withdraw forthwith from a situation that has been rendered both unhappy and untenable'. The item read: 'Thelma Viscountess Furness arrived at Southampton in the liner *Queen Mary* yesterday from New York'. As Lady Furness was well known, among those informed on such matters, to have been one of the King's most intimate friends, this juxtaposition was an instance of feline malice and vulgar frivolity, at a moment of grave crisis, that can scarcely have been paralleled in the worst of the gutter press. So Dawson himself must have realized; for after the first edition the item about Lady Furness was moved to another page.

It is as unthinkable today as it would have been in the latter years of Queen Victoria's reign that scandalous gossip about the private life of the Monarch should be current among quite a wide circle of people. It is hard for those used only to the impeccable *mœurs* of the courts of King George VI and Queen Elizabeth to recapture the almost Restoration or Regency atmosphere of the eleven-month reign of Edward VIII, whose ways, as Archbishop Lang said with a sigh, were so 'strained and wayward'. The Prime Minister and Mrs Baldwin, for instance, were invited to a formal dinner-party at St James's Palace: 'My wife was well-placed,' he said, 'but I own it surprised me to see Mrs Simpson at one end of the table and Lady Cunard[1] at the other'.

For some months, however, the British public as a whole knew nothing of what was going on—though readers of American news-magazines who bought them at local bookstalls and not direct by mail from America were surprised to find passages cut out of some issues with scissors. The silence of the British newspapers astonished Americans, who were fully informed about the King's 'romance'; they attributed

---

[1] One of the least staid of Mayfair's rich hostesses and social climbers in inter-war years.

the silence to royal censorship. There is, of course, no such thing in England (as the King found when he asked Baldwin to stop *The Times* from printing an article criticizing Mrs Simpson). There was, however, a 'gentlemen's agreement' between the newspapers—largely organized by Beaverbrook and the present Lord Rothermere, then Mr Esmond Harmsworth—to report baldly and unsensationally the hearing of Mrs Simpson's divorce petition at Ipswich. In addition, though the Newspaper Proprietors' Association as such took no action to secure reticence, there was a general sense among editors that the story was too delicate, too grave, 'too hot to touch', until it became absolutely necessary to do so; and there were some informal consultations as the crisis developed. The stringent laws of libel were also present in editors' minds (and were the cause of the mutilation of the magazines by the distributors, who are as vulnerable as editors and printers to proceedings for libel). There was thus a voluntary censorship, as effective as the technically voluntary censorship that operated in the Second World War; but it could not have been imposed by the King.

Still curtained from the public, this high drama was approaching its climax in mid-November, 1936. For some reason—asthma was the reason given—Beaverbrook chose to leave England at this moment and to cross the Atlantic, in the German liner *Bremen*, on his way to the dry air and sunshine of Arizona. The King, disturbed by a warning that the newspapers were about to break their silence, cabled to Beaverbrook asking him to return at once. Beaverbrook received the message in mid-ocean. Castlerosse, who was with him, thought little of the King. 'Go on to Arizona,' he said. 'He's not worth it.'

Beaverbrook arrived in New York at 8.30 a.m. on November 20th. The reporters buzzed around him, full of questions about the King and Mrs Simpson and about the 'censorship' of the British press and his part in arranging it. 'Who? Me?'

he cried. 'I know nothing about any censorship. I know nothing about Mrs Simpson.' He preferred to talk to them about international politics: the League of Nations was dead, 'there will be peace in Europe for years to come', Russia was not a menace and, being 'locked up now by ice and snow', could 'afford to say all the saucy things she likes'.

Despite Castlerosse's advice, he had practically committed himself to returning to England at once to stand by and advise the King. The *Bremen* was due to turn round and start back to Europe late the same night. Beaverbrook had reserved a stateroom provisionally; but his mind was not completely made up. He disliked London's winter fogs; he was not greatly interested in the King, as man or as monarch. Still . . .

He went to lunch with his friend Mr Joe Patterson, chairman of the New York *Daily News*, a newspaper beside which the London *Daily Mirror* would look prim and quiet. While he was at the *Daily News* office, a telephone message came: 'London calling Lord Beaverbrook'. Beaverbrook was alarmed: he guessed who the caller was, and tried to dodge the call, partly because he was still hankering for Arizona, partly because he was appalled by the thought that the transatlantic telephone conversation might be overheard or tapped—in the *Daily News* office, of all places! New York was agog with curiosity about the King and Mrs Simpson. There would be a row, and he would be blamed, if there were a leak.

The operators were insistent. The call was put through to Beaverbrook in Patterson's office. The King came on the line immediately. Patterson left the room. The conversation could hardly have been more indiscreet: the King spoke with the utmost candour of his plans and hopes. He was in dogmatic and confident mood: it did not seem to be in his mind that he would be obliged to abdicate. Beaverbrook agreed to return at once to London. Patterson, coming back into the room, found him mopping his brow as though after an acute physical ordeal. No word of the telephone conversation ever found its way into the *Daily News*.

One minor difficulty was to devise some plausible public explanation of his immediate return. He told the reporters that the ocean crossing had done his asthma so much good that he proposed to continue the same treatment: he might even cross the Atlantic four or five times running. The explanation was accepted, the newspapers commenting merrily on this millionaire caprice. Back in London, those in power were better informed: by one means or another, they had learned that the King had recalled Beaverbrook, and that the *Bremen* would soon land him in England. 'This news,' says Mr Morison, 'inclined Dawson ... to think that the leading article held in storage would be required ...'

On Friday, November 26th, Beaverbrook landed at Southampton. He drove straight to the King's country home, Fort Belvedere. The Duke records that he greeted Beaverbrook cordially, grasping his hand and saying: 'You have done a fine thing for me, and I shall always remember it'. Beaverbrook was on a diet; at luncheon there were special dishes for him. The two men had a long and intimate talk. Beaverbrook was horrified to learn that the King had put the morganatic marriage proposal formally to Baldwin. He realized at once that, sprung on them without a preliminary 'softening-up' campaign, in the terms in which Baldwin would present it to them, it would be unacceptable to Cabinet, Dominion Governments, Church and public. He must have had some inkling, too, that the King, by naïvely telling Baldwin that if he could not, as King, marry Mrs Simpson, he 'was prepared to go', had put himself in Baldwin's power—that his threat of abdication might be, in Mr Bocca's vivid phrase, a 'grenade ... stuck in his hand'. Beaverbrook hurried off to London, found out what had taken place at that day's Cabinet meeting, and urged the King by telephone to try to stop the

232

cables consulting the Dominions about the morganatic marriage proposal. It was too late to do so.

Moreover, the King, as he has himself recorded, was 'impatient for the answer from the Dominions'. This impatience was to be his downfall. It is part of the irony of the whole episode that Beaverbrook and Churchill—usually, by temperament, men of quick, decisive action—were all the time pressing on the King a policy of delay, while Baldwin, the procrastinator, was moving, as he had moved in the St George's by-election, with force and speed; and that the King, by rejecting his friends' advice, was helping his enemy. 'Leave it over', Beaverbrook would say to him. 'Next week, next month will be time enough to consider abdication.'

By next week, however, the news had broken, some remarks by the Bishop of Bradford at his diocesan conference being made the occasion for its release. The shock to the public was staggering. The King's private life and future prospects became, in an American phrase which Beaverbrook liked to use, 'Topic A'. No one talked of anything else. 'The situation is unhappy and untenable'—a phrase adapted from Mrs Simpson's statement of would-be withdrawal—became the first line of an extempore blues in a Soho night-club. The respectably married Bishop of Kensington happened to bear the not uncommon name of Simpson: when a stentorian flunkey at a reception announced 'The Bishop of Kensington *and Mrs Simpson*', a nervous hush fell on the room. The clamorous and universal publicity itself made a policy of delay more impracticable; an emotional crisis in which the whole nation was involved could not be allowed to continue; Neville Chamberlain, characteristically, observed that the Christmas trade was already suffering. Baldwin, too, was alarmed by Mrs Simpson's statement and by the *Daily Express* headline next day: END OF THE CRISIS; for he was by now determined that, Mrs Simpson or no Mrs Simpson, the King must go. (Constitutionalists had been perturbed by the King's

233

remark 'Something must be done' when confronted by the misery of mass-unemployment in the Welsh coalfields, and by the *Daily Mail*'s exploitation of it to embarrass the Government.) After one of Baldwin's difficult talks with the King, in the course of which he felt bound to say how earnestly the Cabinet hoped that he might yet forswear marriage and so remain King, he confided to a friend that he had for a moment felt some alarm: 'I thought he might change his mind'.

The Duke's account shows that Beaverbrook's advice weighed with him considerably, but came too late, not only because of the publicity but because he had made proposals to Baldwin that were really irrevocable. It is just possible to toy with the fancy that, if Beaverbrook had not gone to America in mid-November—or if it had been possible, in 1936, for him to return by air instead of by sea—Edward VIII might still be on the Throne. But Mrs Simpson could not in that case have been his wife, either as Queen or morganatically, and Mrs Simpson and the King were bent on marriage. It is true that at one moment, under extreme pressure (partly organized by Beaverbrook), she made her gesture of renunciation; but the King was able, by long-distance telephone, to talk her out of it. 'She wanted a ring', is Beaverbrook's terse summing-up of the story—a wedding-ring from the man she loved, as King or as ex-King.

There is a significant passage in *A King's Story* in which the Duke, analysing the attitude of the Prime Minister and the Archbishop of Canterbury, shows that he only partly understands the Archbishop's opposition to his marriage to a woman who had been divorced, 'albeit the innocent party'; for, in the Archbishop's eyes, the fact that she had been the 'innocent' or the 'guilty' party was irrelevant: a former spouse still living was the insuperable obstacle. The Duke adds:

No idea would have been further from Mr Baldwin's wholly respectable mind. Yet it seemed to me that if his argument were carried to its logical conclusion, then I should have taken a mistress. A discreet house near by, a key to a garden door, decorous associations—the relationship might be privately deplored, but it had had notable precedents.

Such an arrangement would not have shocked the more worldly of the King's advisers, and it may be that when they were counselling delay, there was in their minds the unspoken hope either that Mrs Simpson might consent to an informal association or that the King's ardent affection for her might cool, as his affection for other women had cooled. The unobtrusive establishment of Mrs Simpson as the King's mistress might have been, as the Duke says, more shocking to Baldwin; yet in the most harassing moments of the crisis, at least in its earlier stages, this distasteful alternative may have flitted through even his mind as a lesser, because less conspicuous, evil. But the King was obstinately set on the one project—marriage to Mrs Simpson, and at the earliest possible moment.

Some commentators at the time tended to overestimate the influence and activity of Archbishop Lang. In fact, though his views were clear, he withdrew deliberately from active intervention. Far more important was the reaction of the Dominions, and in particular that of Mr (later Lord) Bruce, a Roman Catholic, who was Australian High Commissioner in London. Special obloquy was heaped on the Archbishop for his broadcast after the affair was over and George VI had been proclaimed King. Like Dawson's valedictory article in *The Times*, which discussed the ex-King's failings and the 'exotic society' that he preferred, this was denounced as 'hitting a man when he's down'. The charge was embodied in a scathing four-line verse epigram which gained wide currency; its author was said to be Mr Gerald Bullett. Such a charge cannot be seriously sustained. As Mr Morison points out, the ex-King's 'overwhelming personal popularity' made it all the more necessary to destroy the notion of him as 'a romantic figure, who might . . . inspire a party bent on his restoration'. For his part, the Archbishop, as senior prelate of the Established Church, with close official and personal relations with the Court, could hardly have ignored altogether an event that had shaken the nation and the monarchy; but, if he had spoken publicly before the abdication, he might more justly have been accused of seeking to influence and prejudge the issue. He was entitled to point the moral as he saw it; indeed, it was his duty to do so; and it would have been cowardly merely to indulge in amiable platitudes.

One man throughout this crisis was really the master of events—Baldwin. As the Duke has written, 'he manœuvred with a swiftness and directness that astonished even his colleagues'. Here was the Fabian striking hard indeed. Every proposal by which the King sought to wriggle out of his dilemma—the morganatic marriage, a broadcast to test the feeling of the nation—was turned down ruthlessly. Both Beaverbrook and Churchill worked on the script of this never-delivered broadcast, Churchill going to see it at Stornoway House late at night after an Albert Hall meeting at which a friendly reference to the King had excited loud applause. 'Don't show Baldwin or the BBC what you are going to say,' Beaverbrook warned the King. Of course Baldwin and the Cabinet had to see it; and of course they refused to allow the King to deliver it.

The Act of Abdication was announced and signed on Thursday, December 10th, but the King had taken his final decision on the previous Saturday. Beaverbrook, 'sensing the favourable upsurge in public opinion', says the Duke, 'had steadily hammered away on the theme of delay'. But the King was 'wearied to the point of exhaustion', oppressed by his 'loneliness and isolation'. The few whom he would see found him almost in a state of collapse. On the Monday—when there was no more point in fighting and there were

merely financial and other practical details to negotiate with
Baldwin—the King sent Beaverbrook a friendly but firm
message, by Walter Monckton, saying that he would for a
time have no further communication with him. Three days
before the Abdication, therefore, Beaverbrook passes out of
the Abdication story.

Despite this message, there was one further communication
from the King. Beaverbrook was in the dentist's chair when
word was brought that the Palace wanted him on the telephone. 'I can't go,' said he. The dentist laid down his instruments. 'I'll do no more work on your teeth till you take that
call,' he said. The call was a brief one: in the last moments of
his reign, the King was calling to say good-bye to the friend
whose efforts and advice had been of so little avail.

Save for Churchill (who was shouted down in the House)
and the Beaverbrook and Rothermere newspapers, Baldwin
had the support, throughout the crisis, of the Labour and
Liberal parties as well as almost all the Conservatives, and of
the overwhelming majority of the national and provincial
newspapers. Mr Morison says bluntly that they 'realized that
it was the supremacy of Parliament over Monarchy that was
being challenged'. There was little in the immediately subsequent conduct of the Duke and Duchess of Windsor to prove
their critics wrong: one of Beaverbrook's last services to the
Windsors was to fly to Paris to try to deter them from their
foolish and ill-fated tour of Hitler's Germany and to advise
them against visiting America under the auspices of the
notorious Charles Bedaux.

Like his enemy Geoffrey Dawson, Beaverbrook was himself a staunch supporter, in the years that followed, of
Chamberlain's policy of appeasement; but it was not for any
ideological consideration that he sided with the King. Nor,
despite the friendliness with which the Duke has written of
him, did he care much about the King for his own sake or for
that of his hereditary office. He has spoken of the monarchy

as 'a useful institution'; but his concern for it has already been seen to be lukewarm. The constitutional argument about a King who showed some tendency to speak and act independently of his ministers was a matter of indifference to him. Human motives are usually mixed, not least in a character so complex as Beaverbrook's. As the Duke of Windsor himself observes, one of Beaverbrook's motives in supporting him was, no doubt, to keep on the Throne a King who had 'tramped the outer marches of the Empire he had loved'; but 'an additional impulse was furnished by his long-standing enmity for Mr Baldwin'. In the early stages of this crisis it must have seemed that the King had at least a sporting chance of winning his battle against Baldwin; had he won, Baldwin's prestige would have been damaged irretrievably. Both these considerations probably influenced Beaverbrook in his decision to return from New York.

As it turned out, he failed yet again, as he always did in his direct encounters with Baldwin. The Abdication represented the final triumph of a premier who seems to have satisfied more perfectly than any other, before or since his time, the standard English taste for amateurism in public life. He was not, in fact, an amateur; he was a highly competent professional; but he was a professional superbly disguised as an amateur. This was the mask, this the sturdy, sublime hypocrisy, that foxed so many of those who seemed, on the surface, far smarter than he.

Mr Bocca clearly thinks that Beaverbrook misjudged the probable Commonwealth reactions; he remarks that Beaverbrook's antagonism to Baldwin was so intense that he was apparently willing even to endanger, by his campaign for the King, the imperial cause to which he owes allegiance. 'Victory for Lord Beaverbrook's man,' he writes, 'would have meant . . . an Empire that might have cut its ties rather than pay homage to Wallis Warfield Simpson Windsor as Queen or even as First Lady. Baldwin in fact was fighting Beaverbrook's

fight. Yet Baldwin, even today, . . . is the one man Beaverbrook seems unable to recall with magnanimity.' Here there
may have been some conflict between two beliefs both held
passionately by Beaverbrook; for a secondary motive in the
affair was provided by his steady championship of the right
to remarriage of those who have been divorced. The true
Presbyterian doctrine of marriage, he has often insisted, is
that it is a contract—not, as with the Episcopalians and the
Romanists, a sacrament.[1] 'There are some scoundrels in the
Presbyterian Church now,' he will grumble, 'who are trying
to introduce the notion that it is a sacrament. They are
wrong.' So maximum publicity is given in his newspapers,
especially in the *Standard* Diary, to the remarriage of the
divorced, and to the various marital mishaps of persons in
the public eye; and so it did not seem to strike him that there
could be any incongruity in the marriage to a divorcee of a
King who was shortly to become 'Supreme Governor on
Earth', and to nominate the bishops, of a Church that would
be theoretically bound, in the event of such a marriage, to
excommunicate him.

His last defeat at Baldwin's hands, however, did not leave
Beaverbrook feeling particularly sore. For one thing, age and
ill health, aggravated by the strain of the crisis, obliged Baldwin to retire very soon. Moreover, Beaverbrook had not
found any cause to regret his decision to reject Castlerosse's
advice and respond to the King's appeal. He had been for ten
days at the heart of the tornado: 'Tornado', indeed, was the
code-name by which the King and Mrs Simpson agreed to

[1] 'Although marriage be no sacrament . . .' (*The Directory for the Publick
Worship of God*, 1654); but the *Westminster Confession* itself (Chapter XXIV,
V) uses 'contract' only of an engagement between persons not yet married.
Nor does it seem to envisage the remarriage of a guilty party: 'In the case of
adultery after marriage, it is lawful for the innocent party to sue out a divorce,
and, after the divorce, to marry another, as if the offending party were dead'.
This is clearly quite different, however, from the Catholic concept of marriage
as a sacrament which, if validly performed, not merely may not but cannot be
dissolved except by death.

refer to him in long-distance telephone conversations. It had been an exhilarating experience: his asthma was forgotten. 'I wouldn't have missed it for worlds,' he said afterwards, 'because of the fun I got out of it.' He is perhaps the only one of those intimately involved in the crisis of December, 1936, who could have used the word 'fun' in this context.

Rather more than a year after these events, Beaverbrook and Churchill were dining together in a gay party on the French Riviera. They started recalling the many battles in which they had been engaged in the past quarter of a century of their public life. Churchill observed that, though they had often been wrong, one of the two of them had always been right.

'That's easy,' cried Beaverbrook. 'We always differed!'

'Except once,' Churchill reminded him.

'Perhaps we were both wrong that time,' said Beaverbrook.

CHAPTER ELEVEN

ODD MAN IN AND OUT

*Power, for the sake of lording it over fellow-creatures
or adding to personal pomp, is rightly judged base. But
power in a national crisis, when a man believes he knows
what orders should be given, is a blessing.*

WINSTON CHURCHILL

'SHOT 32. Plymouth Jetty. Floating at the edge of the dock
water we see the front page of the *Daily Express* bearing the
headline: "THERE WILL BE NO WAR".' Such was an early
shot in Mr Noël Coward's wartime film of the Royal Navy,
In Which We Serve.

Despite his jingoism, Beaverbrook has never cared overmuch
for British films. They are either too slow or too finicky for
his taste. Moreover, with a few associates, Canadian and
British, he had at one time a good deal of money—some four
or five million pounds—invested in that section of the cinema
industry which prospered chiefly by the showing of Holly-
wood films. It was in the early 1920s that he bought control
of the Provincial Cinematograph Theatre Company: in 1929,
shortly before the slump, he sold out to the Ostrer group, at
a profit of two million pounds.

Coming at the height of the war, when so many other
public men had been allowed to forget their pre-war records
of appeasement—and when he himself had rendered notable
service to the nation—this shot in the Coward film may well,
if he saw it, have struck Beaverbrook as a most unjust and
woundingly satirical reminder of an ill-starred campaign.

It was in September, 1938, that the *Daily Express* began
to print the slogan: 'THERE WILL BE NO WAR THIS
YEAR OR NEXT YEAR EITHER'. The slogan was
splashed right across the front page on September 19th, and
appeared frequently until August 7th, 1939. Long and earnest

editorial conferences preceded its publication; there were those in the *Express* office who opposed it because they thought it false, others because they felt it wrong to lull the British public into careless cheerfulness. Beaverbrook overrode them with one reiterated argument: 'If we're right, everyone will praise our foresight. If we're wrong—nobody will remember.' Unfortunately for him, the latter part of this forecast proved as false as the slogan itself: Mr Coward was not the only man to reflect in later years that such propaganda as this, appearing day after day, month after month, in the most widely circulated British daily newspaper, must have reinforced substantially Ribbentrop's assurances to Hitler that Britain would not fight, and so, indirectly, have encouraged the invasion of Poland. Eventually, as usual, he had his way: the Editor of the *Daily Express*, Arthur Christiansen, is believed to have drafted the first part of the slogan; Beaverbrook himself added the characteristically cocky last four words, crying: 'We must nail our colours *high* to the mast!'

The campaign was not confined to the mere repetition of a slogan. The most casual glance at the files of the *Express* during 1938 and 1939 discovers innumerable expressions of the policy of optimism and appeasement. On March 10th, 1938, a leading article gushed: 'Welcome Herr von Ribbentrop, Hitler's Foreign Minister. You have the right to believe that he comes here as an Ambassador of peace, sincerely seeking it.' A month earlier (on February 12th) an article headed 'Don't Talk War' had ventured into the realm of logic: 'The present worries of Europe only make war more unlikely'. Three days after the Ribbentrop welcome: 'Why All This Gloom? Lord Beaverbrook Predicts Years of Peace for Us'. On August 15th, 1938, Beaverbrook was quoted by Mr William Hillman of Hearst's International News Service as saying: 'Germany cannot and will not march into Czechoslovakia . . . The Germans are not in a position to fight . . .

When war does come, British interests will not be involved
and Britain will not be in it.' (This was one of the few occasions on which he did envisage the possibility of an early war,
though one not involving Britain.)

In November, 1938, *Time* magazine, in a not altogether
friendly 'cover-story' on Beaverbrook, noted that in September and October the *Daily Express* circulation had risen to
over two-and-a-half million ('Crowed the *Express:* "Peace
. . . met the demand"'). The same story assessed Beaverbrook's 'personal fortune' at 'some $40 millions'[1]; and re-
ported that, when he had polled the *Express* staff to ascertain
if they agreed with his policies, the answer was 'almost unanimously NO'.

One of Beaverbrook's personal friends among American
newspapermen is Mr Roy Howard, of the Scripps-Howard
group. In April, 1939, interviewed by him, Beaverbrook seems
to have talked about the prospect of war more seriously than
he was talking to his British readers. On April 11th Howard
quoted him as saying:

> So far, the menace to Britain depends upon the threat to
> bomb London. Now London is in a position to meet and
> delay that menace.
>
> Our output of planes has been stepped up very rapidly. It
> has been reported to me from reliable sources that our output
> last month [March] approximated a thousand first-line planes.
> That figure does not include training planes.
>
> . . . it is believed that we divide our strength fifty-fifty—half
> bombers and half fighters. Germany is supposed to divide on
> a basis of three-quarters bombers and one-quarter fighters . . .
> It is said now that the German first-line airplane strength
> amounts to approximately five thousand ships, and the British
> front-line strength to three thousand.
>
> If these figures are correct, then London is safe.
>
> There is no doubt that for two or three days German bombers
> would do great damage. But the possible amount of damage has

[1] But cf. p. 17.

243

been exaggerated . . . More than nine-tenths of the London area
is represented by open spaces—streets, parks, etc., which mini-
mises the danger from blind bombing . . . It has been demon-
strated [in Spain] that a war cannot be concluded through
bombing attacks.

. . . England is faced with the necessity that airplane production be tremendous . . .

I believe that war in Europe depends ultimately upon the
attitude of the British people. They will not put up indefinitely
with threats and menaces.

The war spirit may finally possess the people. If this spirit
does arise, it may force the Government to take drastic
measures.

I hope very much that the day is far removed, but the English
people won't stand indefinitely the injustices, persecution and
abuses now being perpetrated in Europe.

In the light of later experience, Beaverbrook's apparent
assumptions that aircraft production was then fairly satisfactory, and that a bomb falling in a street would do little
damage, seem complacent. None the less, the comparative
realism of this interview is in striking contrast with his con-
tinuous efforts to soothe the British people into acquiescence
in those 'injustices, persecution, and abuses' which his newspapers had for six years so pointedly ignored. Mr Howard's
capacity to draw him out was not shared by other American
interviewers; a month later he was telling one of them, by
transatlantic telephone, that, though there was 'still great
anxiety', the situation was 'even better' than before the
March crisis (when Hitler had broken the Munich agreement
and overwhelmed Czechoslovakia), that he was confident that
a major war had been postponed for some time, and that
Danzig, in any case, was not worth a major war.

Beaverbrook has defended this campaign simply as an
expression of his unvarying policy of Isolation: Empire
unity, friendship with the United States, no European en-
tanglements. 'Let foreigners fight their own battles. Leave

the Europeans to their dunghill.' The slogan, as amplified, insisted that there would be no war *involving Britain*. Beaver-brook believed this, or managed to convince himself that he did; he has also argued that the sheer repetition of the slogan helped, like a hypnotic incantation, to 'lower the tempera-ture', and that in any case he was calling at the same time for greatly strengthened defences for Britain. His critics point out that, while these two policies might not be absolutely inconsistent with each other, it was rather too much to expect the British people to rearm energetically, paying heavy taxes to do so, if he was also assuring them—not merely as a hope but as a definite prophecy of the future, which they were only too desperately glad to believe—that the arms would not be needed. He himself was to learn in 1940 that his pre-war advocacy of rearmament had indeed been as futile as his fore-cast had been mistaken.

He may have been influenced towards his 'no-war' policy partly by his French contacts. For several years before the war he went fairly often to Paris, where he would meet M Jean Prouvost, owner of the newspaper *Paris-Soir*,[1] and members of the '*deux cent familles*' who said among them-selves 'Better the German Right than the French Left'. He became, accordingly, one of those who said: 'The French, anyway, won't fight'; and this was one element in his assess-ment of the European situation.

Nor were his newspapers alone in their support for Cham-berlain and his policy. Apart from the general clamour of relief which hailed the Munich agreement, the most influen-tial of all British newspapers, *The Times*, was itself the most definite in advocating appeasement; its misjudgements are candidly admitted in its own History.

Less than a month before war actually broke out, Beaver-brook went to Canada for a holiday. Arriving in Quebec on

[1] Pre-war *Express* columnists often described M Prouvost as 'the Beaver-brook of France'. The *cliché* was scrapped in June, 1940.

August 11th, he said: 'I would not be out here if I did believe that war was imminent'. He added that if war should come, the British people were psychologically prepared for it; it is not recorded that he took any credit for having shared in that preparation. Three days later an *Express* leader-writer, faithfully echoing his master's voice, wrote: 'The storm has not yet broken. And the *Daily Express* believes that Hitler will keep the peace this year.' The note was not quite so unshakenly confident as it had been. Senior members of the *Express* staff were gravely perturbed. E. J. Robertson himself took the responsibility of removing the 'no-war' slogan from the paper, and communicated with Beaverbrook urging him to come home at once. Beaverbrook told him that he was bringing him back 'on a fool's errand', but had sufficient faith in his judgement to return.

He reached Southampton late on the evening of August 31st. A message was awaiting him: he was to go at once to see Sir Samuel Hoare. (Hoare at that time was the 'line of communication' between Beaverbrook and the Prime Minister, Neville Chamberlain.) He drove through the rain to Hoare's house. What he learned there brought home to him the bitter realization that war was inevitable.

For a day or two, none the less, both he and Chamberlain struggled to resist the inevitable. Beaverbrook argued that Poland was 'no friend of ours'. Chamberlain—reluctant to admit the ruin of his own work, and still not fully aware of Hitler's true character—insisted on giving him 'one last chance'. Churchill, Simon, Hore-Belisha, almost all the leading members of Chamberlain's Government, were for declaring war: as late as Saturday, September 2nd, when German troops had crossed the Polish frontier and bombs were falling on Warsaw, his hesitation exasperated them. On the Sunday morning he could hesitate no longer: Hitler had not replied to his message. 'Chamberlain,' Beaverbrook has said, 'declared war to save his Government.'

Beaverbrook met Hoare three times during the following week. His first war mission was a strange one: he was sent to Washington to find out, by indirect means if possible, what President Roosevelt really thought about the war, a matter on which Chamberlain did not feel fully informed. On arrival in America he gave a newspaper interview which was intended to pique Roosevelt's curiosity: he wanted Roosevelt to send for him and ask him about the war without realizing that he himself was in search of information. The ruse worked, and the mission was successful: he ascertained that Roosevelt would give general support to Britain's war effort, though he was not yet prepared for actual intervention. But the choice of Beaverbrook as an envoy may well have caused offence to the Foreign Secretary, Lord Halifax: official diplomacy is apt to deprecate the employment of unusual channels. (Some time later Beaverbrook learned that Halifax had been angered also by the Gollancz booklet, *Guilty Men*, with its devastating exposure of the pre-war appeasement of Hitler by most of the prominent Conservative leaders. Its pseudonymous author, 'Cato', was in fact three of Beaverbrook's own employees, Michael Foot, Frank Owen, and Peter Howard; and Halifax believed that Beaverbrook, with his usual *penchant* for making trouble, had provided them with material. One day Beaverbrook—by now a Cabinet Minister, and officially divorced from the *Express*—met Halifax, who said to him jocularly: 'You must find it hard to live on £5,000 a year'. 'Ah!', said Beaverbrook, 'but I've always got my royalties from *Guilty Men*!')

For the greater part of the 'phoney war' period, however, he was lethargic and despondent. He was not convinced of the wisdom or necessity of the war itself; it still seemed to him folly to have given a guarantee to Poland that could not now be implemented. On his return from America late in October, he had seen Chamberlain, and Chamberlain had hinted at the possibility of his joining the Government, perhaps as Minister of Information—an appointment also advocated, 'For the nation's sake', by the *Daily Sketch*. Had Chamberlain pressed this strongly on him, he might have accepted, in the hope that a new job might help to dispel his depression; but Chamberlain's offer was as half-hearted as Beaverbrook's refusal of it. In November an attack of asthma sent him to the south of France; and friends who saw him there found him in as sullen a temper as he had ever shown. It seems likely that this mood was the underlying cause of an *Express* campaign whose irresponsibility shocked people of all parties —a campaign against the rationing scheme that wartime perils and shortages had obliged even the Chamberlain Government to introduce.

An editorial on November 21st, 1939, urged the public to 'revolt against the food rationing system, that dreadful and terrible iniquity which some of the Ministers want to adopt'. It alleged that there was 'no necessity for the trouble and expense of rationing merely because there may be shortages of this or that inessential commodity'. At least as unhelpful was an editorial on an even graver issue which appeared on January 2nd, 1940:

MILLIONS WHAT FOR?

The Government plan a mighty army. Millions of men in khaki. What for? To please the French . . .

There is no need for such a big army. The Maginot Line is already sufficiently armed and manned . . . The Line is so well constructed that it gives plenty of security to the French on land . . . At sea, and in the air, Britain is already taking her part in the war to an immense degree. We should concentrate on these two spheres . . . A large army will damage our manufacturers and general business life irreparably . . .

What is to happen? All is not lost. The will of the people can prevail. Let the public show their determination to resist the proposal to build up this enormous army. Then registration may take place, but calling up will be postponed.

Among all the false predictions in which newspapers of various political colours have at times indulged, among the myriad words of wrong counsel addressed to newspaper-readers, these two *Express* editorials stand out with unenviable singularity. As usual, however, the readers took practically no notice of the policies advocated by their favourite newspaper: there was no perceptible mass-movement of 'revolt' against rationing, and nobody but a few earnest pacifists and Communists, who had nothing else in common with the *Express*, opposed the war effort in any of its military aspects. It may therefore be said, in mitigation, that such outbursts did no positive harm.

To this period belongs a possibly apocryphal incident no echo of which reached the public until more than a year later, when Beaverbrook was a Minister. In June, 1941, a question was asked in the House of Commons about a leaflet distributed by Communists during the Greenock by-election: the leaflet contained extracts from a speech made in Glasgow by Mr John McGovern, MP, in which he had stated that in April, 1940, he and his colleague James Maxton had met Beaverbrook privately, and that Beaverbrook, because 'he saw no sign of Britain beating Germany', had offered to join with these pacifists of the Independent Labour Party in backing 'independent peace candidates' for Parliament. Churchill answered the question: he repudiated the allegation utterly, referring with contempt to 'malicious vapourings', and read the following letter dated March 8th, 1940, from Beaverbrook to the pacifist Lord Tavistock (later Duke of Bedford):

> Very many thanks for your letter.
>
> I have never felt any anxiety in regard to the wisdom and the certainty of continuing the war.
>
> I am a supporter of Mr Chamberlain, and I believe in his war policy. If peace becomes a possibility, I feel sure he will do everything in his power to promote it.
>
> At the same time I am much obliged to you for writing me about your negotiations.

Mr McGovern got up, however, and said that the statements in his speech and in the leaflet were 'completely true'; and Maxton, more cautiously, added that, while the matter did not seem to him of public importance then, McGovern's word 'would not go unsupported'. After this brief exchange at question-time, no more was heard of the matter.

There is evidence from another eye-witness of Beaverbrook's mood and conduct in this month. On April 30th Lord Reith recorded in his diary: 'Beaverbrook fulminated against the Government; he would overthrow them as soon as this evacuation [of Norway] was over; till then his papers would keep quiet'.[1] This testimony could, however, fairly be interpreted as portraying impatience with inefficiency in the prosecution of the war as much as desire for a negotiated peace.

From these and other symptoms of a renewed zest for mischief, it may be supposed that Beaverbrook was beginning once more to find inactivity galling. He permitted one of his leader-writers, Mr Alan Wood, to publish in the *Daily Express* a signed attack on him and his policies:

> He spends his time sending out continual messages of contempt and derision against his victims, with the impish delight of a small boy squashing flies on a window-pane. And the Government pay far too much attention to him . . .

Why did this attack appear at this time? No doubt it was a safety-valve for a talented employee sickened by much that he had been ordered to write. It is just possible also that Beaverbrook, if he did not inspire, was not displeased by one passage in the article:

> But I have a high opinion of him as an administrator. Give him a job to do in the Government and he would get things done with . . . energy and drive.

[1] *Into the Wind*, p. 379.

ODD MAN IN AND OUT

Beaverbrook himself, the writer added, was completely opposed to any such proposal.

By May, 1940, he was seeing a good deal of Churchill, dining with him often at the Admiralty. On May 10th, after the debate on the Norway disaster, Chamberlain resigned. Churchill became Prime Minister, amid general acclamation. He immediately invited Beaverbrook to be Minister of Aircraft Production. Beaverbrook refused: he feared that the job might be too difficult because his enemies in high places would now revenge themselves on him and put obstructions in his way; this, he told Churchill, might bring discredit on the Government as well as on himself. The suspicion may not have been as far-fetched as it seems. Besides Beaverbrook's own reluctance, Churchill has recorded[1] that 'there were other resistances to his appointment'. However: 'I felt sure that our life depended on the flow of new aircraft; I needed his vital and vibrant energy'. Churchill therefore persisted in his offer. Public considerations apart, there was an intense personal—almost sentimental—satisfaction to Beaverbrook in his solicitations: it was the first time since the death of Bonar Law that a Prime Minister had *needed* him.

'To his personal secretaries,' Mr David Farrer, who was one of them, has recorded,[2] 'Beaverbrook protested with increasing vehemence that he would not take office, and with each protest the secretaries became more certain that he would.' His appointment to the post was eventually announced on May 14th. Next day the German break-through on the Meuse began—foreshadowing inexorably the fall of France and the Battle of Britain. When Churchill went on his eleventh-hour mission to Tours, seeking to inspire the French to continued resistance, he took Beaverbrook with him; and Beaverbrook reinforced his rejection of the plausible and desperate French appeal for the commitment to a lost cause

---

[1] In *The Second World War*, volume II, p. 12.
[2] In *The Sky's the Limit*, p. 7.

of Britain's entire air strength. In his *Second World War* Churchill has written: 'I took Edward Halifax and General Ismay with me, and Max Beaverbrook volunteered to come too. In trouble he is always buoyant.' As Churchill had realized many months earlier, 'It was vital that our metropolitan fighter air force should not be drawn out of Britain on any account. Our existence turned on this.'

Much of the story of Beaverbrook's work at the Ministry of Aircraft Production is well known; it is an essential part of the story of Allied victory in the Second World War. Even his critics concede that this is the most creditable episode in Beaverbrook's long life. One Labour Minister who served with him in Churchill's Government—and often opposed him—has said: 'It was his finest hour. He saved us. Nobody else could have done it.' Churchill's own considered judgement is in his book: 'All his remarkable qualities fitted the need. His personal buoyancy and vigour were a tonic. I was glad to be able sometimes to lean on him. He did not fail. This was his hour. His personal force and genius, combined with so much persuasion and contrivance, swept aside many obstacles . . .' At the time, Churchill told the House of Commons: 'Lord Beaverbrook is at his very best when things are at their very worst'.

Things were certainly at their worst when he took office. Behind the front line of aircraft there were in immediate reserve only five Spitfires and Hurricanes; in a few minutes of battle five pilots might have to bale out, and that whole immediate reserve would be exhausted. In the three months before the Battle of Britain, Beaverbrook had to revolutionize an aircraft industry organized for steady expansion towards maximum production three *years* later. Such had been the leisurely timetable under Chamberlain's leadership. Now speed was essential.

It was both an advantage and a disadvantage that the Ministry of Aircraft Production was a new creation, hacked out of one part—the production departments—of the Air Ministry. This meant that Beaverbrook was less hampered by tradition and precedent than most new ministers; but it also meant that he had no ready-made 'machine', few senior staff, no premises. Such staff as he had were working at Harrogate, where they had gone when Whitehall was evacuated in 1939. Beaverbrook brought them back to London; set up his office in his own home, Stornoway House, until he could move into proper ministerial quarters in Millbank; and proceeded to recruit the most able men he could find in industry, in the Royal Air Force, and in the Civil Service, to work with him—men like Mr (later Sir) Patrick Hennessy of Ford's, Sir Charles Craven of Vickers-Armstrongs, Air-Marshal Sir Wilfred Freeman, Group-Captain Grahame Dawson, and Mr Trevor Westbrook. At the head of the civilian side of the new Ministry was Mr (later Sir) Archibald Rowlands. He and Beaverbrook at first regarded each other with some antipathy: Rowlands—though Beaverbrook could not question his ability and energy—was a man trained in the orderly ways of the Civil Service. Three weeks after the Ministry was formed, they had their first, fierce row. Beaverbrook, knowing how valuable a man Rowlands was, sent him a case of wine as a jocular peace-offering. Thereafter there was harmony between them, and their mutual respect grew steadily.

The words invariably applied to Beaverbrook's methods as Minister are 'dynamic' and 'unorthodox'. His brief term of office has become a legend in the Civil Service. Lord Reith quotes him as saying: 'Wherever I find organization, I break it'. Over his desk hung three slogans:

COMMITTEES TAKE THE PUNCH OUT OF WAR.

ORGANIZATION IS THE ENEMY OF
IMPROVISATION.

ALL THINGS IN WAR ARE SIMPLE, BUT THE
SIMPLE IS ALWAYS DIFFICULT.

At last he had something to do which engaged to the full his intuition and initiative, his passionate industry, his taste for piracy, and his gifts of personal combat and persuasion; and at last all these attributes were concentrated on a task of the highest national importance. He was no longer the odd man out: he was the odd man in—and many who had reviled him were thankful to have him at their side. There was now no need for him to worry about the wider issues of the war: this technical, practical job was completely satisfying to him.

Inevitably, he made some powerful new enemies as well as millions of new friends. He was always at odds with 'the Air-Marshals', as he called the senior officials of the Air Ministry; they had been from the start, he thought, jealously suspicious of the new Ministry, and they resented his intrusions on their preserves and his habit of rewarding enterprise by promotion —Wing-Commanders becoming Air Vice-Marshals overnight at his insistence, so that it was said that MAP stood for Ministry of Accelerated Promotion. They opposed almost all the ideas that Beaverbrook thought his brightest. They opposed his Atlantic Ferry (ATFERO)—the imaginative scheme under which hundreds of bombers were delivered from California to Britain, carrying incidentally important supplies and priority passengers. One of the worst rows concerned aircraft storage units: here again Beaverbrook was trying to impinge on what the Air Ministry regarded as their property. The dispute was so sharp that Churchill set up a committee to look into it, under Mr Attlee's chairmanship. Beaverbrook, alone, faced a bevy of hostile air-marshals. The committee seemed disposed to decide for the air-marshals. 'All right,' said Beaverbrook. 'I'll go to the public.' He did not have to do so.

In his first few days as Minister, he had a violent—and successful—tussle with another formidable opponent, Lord Nuffield. Nuffield had a big shadow factory for the production of Spitfires, and controlled an organization for the repair of damaged aircraft; he was himself Director-General of Maintenance at the Air Ministry. Beaverbrook seized the shadow factory and transferred its control and management to another firm; and himself claimed jurisdiction over all repair organizations throughout the country. Nuffield appealed to Churchill: Churchill backed Beaverbrook.

The most intractable of all his antagonists, however, was Ernest Bevin, the Minister of Labour. Bevin instinctively distrusted Beaverbrook; he was a man of rock-like obstinacy; he was a man whom—unlike Nuffield—Churchill could not afford to lose; and he was determined to control and to mobilize all manpower. Beaverbrook demanded an absolute priority on manpower for aircraft factories: Bevin said that it was his job to arbitrate between the rival claims of the various departments. Beaverbrook said: 'We won't be arbitrated on'—and took prompt unilateral action. Only four days after taking office, without consulting Bevin, he issued a public appeal, by radio and through the press, inviting garagemen to become fitters in aircraft factories: 'Go at once to the nearest aircraft factory or . . . apply to the nearest Labour exchange.' There was a rush of garagemen in response to this appeal; chaos at the exchanges, which had not been warned how to handle this sudden influx of war-workers; and—it may be surmised—an almighty explosion in the Cabinet. Soon after this incident, Bevin said to Beaverbrook, grimly: 'D'you mean to work with us or not?' Beaverbrook replied: 'I certainly mean to get everything I need'. For the short period of extreme emergency, he did; but Bevin had his way later. What he resented most of all was Beaverbrook's habit of addressing mass-meetings of shop stewards. He told Beaverbrook that regular Trade Union officials should always be present on such occasions; and he told some of his Labour colleagues that he suspected Beaverbrook of trying to capture (or to disrupt) the Trade Union movement.

Mr Farrer's little book, written from close personal observation, is still the best outline of Beaverbrook's achievement as a Minister, in its three phases: 'the first three months, dominated by the need to put airplanes into the air; the long succeeding winter, when the blitz was beaten by a mingling of expedients, with the policy of dispersal of aircraft plants as the key factor; and the short final period of relatively calm waters'.

Typical of Beaverbrook's fresh approach was his cult of 'cannibalism'. In May, 1940, the sight of wrecked aircraft lying uselessly in southern and eastern England filled many with despair: Beaverbrook rejoiced at it. This was an untapped source of supply: parts from three or four damaged aircraft could be made into one aircraft fit for service. Within weeks of his taking office, the output of repaired aircraft, which had been negligible, was growing steadily. By June 3rd, Churchill could write to the Secretary of State for Air, Sir Archibald Sinclair: 'Lord Beaverbrook has made a surprising improvement in the supply and repair of aeroplanes, and in clearing up the muddle and scandal of the aircraft production branch . . .'

One Sunday, despite the protests of other ministries, he commandeered all the transport aircraft that could fly and sent them to Bordeaux to bring back a great load of engines and spare parts which he had somehow had collected there during the collapse of France. Again, he sent 'action squads', led by three civilians and one RAF officer, to bring in from all over Britain every spare instrument they could find. 'These men,' writes Mr Farrer, 'descended on RAF depots, breaking ruthlessly into stores held on operational stations against future needs, snatching from bewildered storekeepers their little hoards of instruments . . . together with obsolete spares which could be remade for present use.' Everyone has heard tales—some true, some apocryphal—of what was later described as Beaverbrook's 'inspired brigandage': how, learning of the arrival at the docks of consignments of valuable material destined for other ministries, he would send trucks very early in the morning, with orders signed personally by him, to requisition them. Such conduct was found intolerable by other members of the Government: it was justified only by the acuteness of the emergency with which he had to grapple—and, later, by the fact that he had not failed in his main task.

Throughout this time the strain of overwork was aggravated by anxiety for his son Max[1]; but anxiety was swallowed up in pride when a New Brunswick newspaper remarked that the Aitkens were busy 'reducing the disparity between the British and the German air forces: the father builds British machines, while the son destroys the German ones'.

Seven days a week he worked; nor was Sunday a rest-day for any of those near him. Crises always seemed to occur at week-ends. One Friday evening a shortage of fabric for barrage balloons was discovered. The managers of the north-country factories concerned were summoned to London overnight; by the Saturday afternoon they were on their way back to work, with orders to get busy that night; all Saturday the police were rounding up foremen and workers from their homes and from parks and pubs and clubs; urgent messages were flashed on to the cinema screens calling them to work at once.

On May 21st Beaverbrook announced that all factories were to work all through Saturday and Sunday, day and night, for the next four week-ends: 'Any firm unable to follow this advice . . . should send me a telegram explaining the difficulties, and I will do what I can to smooth them out.' 'Cassandra' wrote in the *Daily Mirror*: 'A new spirit has swept into our aircraft factories'. *Time* said: 'A Canadian village bumpkin who all his life has outsmarted city slickers . . . ripped out orders which brought aircraft factory heads scrambling for lightning interviews'.

[1] See p. 11.

In all these operations Beaverbrook was unlike almost every other minister in one respect particularly: he made his presence felt, and his voice heard, personally; he disdained the usual departmental channels. Every night Air Vice-Marshal Park[1]—in command of No. 11 Fighter Group, which defended London throughout August and September, 1940—had to let Beaverbrook know personally how many Spitfires and Hurricanes would be needed next day. Every day the demand was met—often only by ingenious expedients and furious bullying, for the margin between losses and production-plus-repair was terrifyingly narrow. Again and again the Minister himself would write or telephone to upbraid or to congratulate the people in the industry, almost as if they were his own Fleet Street employees: at two o'clock in the morning some modest Nottingham lace-maker, whose six-man workshop had been turned over to the production of small parts for aircraft, would be roused from bed by a worried wife to speak to 'somebody from London who says he's Lord Beaverbrook'—and the rough Canadian voice from Stornoway House would bellow that he had done 'fine work, fine . . . And we want even more from you next month. Goodbye to you.'

His public announcements, too, and his notices to workers, were free from pompous, colourless jargon—and he never forgot gratitude as well as exhortation. One factory notice, at the end of June, 1940, began 'Thanks, a thousand times, thanks!'; went on to say that those who had worked seven shifts a week since mid-May were now entitled to one day off; and ended 'Here is a health to you on your brief holiday, and long life and happiness to Merrie England!' In other notices there were biblical echoes—'Many are they that rise against us', and 'You have sought out many inventions'. He coined slangy phrases that caught on: 'the boys in the back room' (from his favourite Dietrich film), 'high, wide

[1] Later Air Chief Marshal Sir Keith Park.

258

and handsome', 'beautiful bombs'. A broadcast started: 'That good man, John Calvin . . .'

This personal approach was one aspect of his gift for public relations in general. His achievement was solid; but the least important parts of it, in a directly practical sense, were those which appealed most vividly to the public imagination. The ordinary citizen, asked a year or two later what he remembered of Beaverbrook's Ministry, would probably have recalled two items—the appeal for domestic pots and pans to provide aluminium, and the Spitfire Funds. Neither of these campaigns was of major practical importance: as critics pointed out at the time, there was plenty of aluminium left in the shops when Beaverbrook was taking the housewife's buckets; and the production of Spitfires was not limited by want of money, any amount of which could not have bought any extra materials or manpower. Nevertheless, each of these 'stunts', in its way, enabled ordinary civilians to feel that they were taking a fuller part in the war effort; and the Spitfire Funds in particular—which totalled £13 millions by the end of April, 1941—provided a unique emotional link between the RAF, the aircraft factories, and countless contributors in Britain and overseas. They were also, like 'war savings weeks', anti-inflationary. In this side of the work, Beaverbrook was helped immeasurably by Mr J. B. Wilson, a shrewd and imperturbable newsman whom he had brought from the *Express* office.

A more important contribution to the production of aluminium—illustrative, too, of Beaverbrook's flexibility of mind—was made by a German-Jewish refugee named Loew. He was an aluminium expert of world renown, but, in the panic round-up of aliens that followed Dunkirk, he was threatened with internment. In the face of considerable 'security' opposition, Beaverbrook insisted on using him in his Ministry. Moreover, he ransacked the internment-camps for other alien experts to work with Loew. The experiment was so successful that Beaverbrook repeated it a few months later. He provided a doctor of his acquaintance—a man capable of talking to the internees in their own languages and of evaluating them psychologically—with the dossiers of nearly two thousand craftsmen whose skills were being wasted in the camps of the Isle of Man, and sent him there to screen them. Among them were precision-engineers, lens-grinders, clock-makers. Nearly all of them were set free for war-work. The Commandant of one camp complained: 'It really is the limit. To start with, you print in your ruddy papers, "Intern the lot". Now you want to get 'em all out again!'

What was the real effect of all this uproar and striving? Was there any justification for the barbed gibe of a Cabinet colleague who, when Churchill referred to Beaverbrook's 'magic', retorted that the chief stock-in-trade of magicians was illusion? Was Beaverbrook merely a showman, useful perhaps in boosting the morale of airmen and workers, and would aircraft production have expanded as rapidly without his Ministry? Obviously some speeding-up and expansion must have begun before he took over: even his superhuman pushfulness could hardly have doubled, within three weeks of his taking office, as did happen, the production of Hurricanes. His tribute to those who had worked on the job before him may have been slightly more than the conventional courtesy. Nevertheless, the figures remain impressive: four days before he took office, the metropolitan Air Force had 782 serviceable Hurricanes and Spitfires; four months later, after weeks of intensive battle and bombing, there were 1228 serviceable Hurricanes and Spitfires. By the end of September, 1940, there was a shortage of pilots, not of aircraft. It may still be argued by some that this improvement would have occurred in any case: to that argument Beaverbrook can retort that in the first four months of 1940 output was 199 aircraft (fighter and bomber) *behind* schedule; but that in the next six months, under his direction, output was 1134 *ahead* of schedule. Moreover, the narrowness of the margin between losses and output has already been shown: the extra impetus that he certainly gave to a tendency that may already have begun—with the additional resources derived from 'cannibalism' and his various piratical forays—may have been just enough to keep that narrow margin in being.

At any rate, those who worked closely with him at the time have no doubt that the main credit is his. Rowlands, that hard-headed Civil Servant, said: 'The Royal Air Force won the Battle of Britain ... but it would never have had a chance to do so but for the activities of one man—and that man was Lord Beaverbrook'. Colonel W. C. Devereux, managing director of High Duty Alloys, recalled later that Beaverbrook had sent for him two days after becoming Minister, and had said: 'Devereux, they tell me the bottleneck of production is aluminium alloys. I want certain selected machines to have all the alloys which can be put into them ... Draw up a programme ...' Devereux added: 'It was done, and if it had not been done there would not have been the reserves to hand over to the pilots who fought the Battle of Britain'. Churchill, when depreciatory rumours began to be current, wrote to him: 'they [the Air Ministry] resent having had the MAP functions carved out of their show, and I have no doubt they pour out their detraction by every channel open'. One of the treasured items in Beaverbrook's personal collection in the University Library at Fredericton is a Christmas card sent to him in 1941 by Air Vice-Marshal Park (the man who reported to him nightly his requirements for the next day). The card is inscribed: 'Grateful thanks for not allowing my squadrons ever to go short of fighter aircraft throughout the Battle of Britain'. *Experto crede.*

Even Mr Farrer's book, however, though it is in the main a tribute, admits that Beaverbrook as a Minister had his defects: 'He never took any steps to retain the goodwill of Parliament ... he left himself wide open to criticism on

BEAVERBROOK

several grounds—of intolerance, hastiness, inability to compromise, lack of political balance . . . His natural desire for power was conditioned always by his unwillingness to exercise it otherwise than as he personally thought best . . . Everywhere it had operated, MAP had created conditions of storm and stress.' While the emergency was at its worst, few criticized. When the worst was over, accumulated resentments began to be heard. On March 11th, 1941, there was a debate on the Air Estimates in the House of Commons: Beaverbrook was handled less roughly than he had been as Minister of Information, twenty-three years before; but some members showed that they were aware of the disagreements between the Air Ministry and the Ministry of Aircraft Production, and Dr A. V. Hill, MP for Cambridge University, made a powerful and learned speech deploring an alleged neglect of research and the rumoured resignation of Sir Henry Tizard, who had been in charge of research and development. Mr Austin Hopkinson, MP for Mossley, said that the 'break-up of the scientific committee' had been 'totally unnecessary and . . . due to the interference of a certain person who shall be nameless, but who made the conditions under which the committee had to work absolutely impossible'. Sir Henry Tizard, he said, had 'found it . . . quite impossible to work at the Ministry of Aircraft Production'.

Beaverbrook must have regretted once more his relegation to the House of Lords: how he could have pummelled these carpers if he had been able to get at them in their own House! However, his second-in-command, Colonel Llewellin,[1] Parliamentary Secretary to the Ministry of Aircraft Production, dealt faithfully with them, saying that Tizard had not definitely resigned but was ill, and that rumours of other resignations were 'a great deal of rubbish'. He also entertained the House with an account of the suggestions received from amateur inventors, which had numbered forty thousand in December, 1940: one proposed that the clouds should be

[1] Later Lord Llewellin.

frozen and anti-aircraft guns mounted on them, another that a cat should be taken up in every fighter aircraft, since the cat could see in the dark and 'wherever it was looking you could aim your gun'.

There had indeed been a few political discomforts and disturbances before this, mostly arising out of Beaverbrook's quarrels with his colleagues in the Government on the priorities to which he thought his Ministry entitled and on his continued 'poaching'. On August 30th, 1940, for instance—at the height of the Battle of Britain—the *Railway Review* published a strong attack on him by Mr John Marchbank, General Secretary of the National Union of Railwaymen. Marchbank went so far as to say that Arthur Greenwood, Ernest Bevin, and Herbert Morrison had 'made possible his Lordship's success, sometimes in spite of himself, when his impulsiveness and lack of knowledge on technical matters ran him into precipitate action which could not be carried through'. Indeed, he added, 'the work of the Aircraft Production Department owes more to the patience of three Labour ministers than to Lord Beaverbrook's impatience and impetuosity'. Beaverbrook should remember that 'political intrigue is a different matter when practised in the Labour and Trade Union Movement from what it was when practised with Tory and Liberal parties in the last war'.

Simultaneously the *National Review* was sniping from the Right. Beaverbrook, it sniffed, was 'the Sir Horace Wilson of the present régime'[1]; and 'Prime Ministers, it seems, must have their favourites'. There might be 'harm to the country'. Beaverbrook was in the War Cabinet (he had been promoted to it a few weeks earlier): 'he may go Still Higher'. Meanwhile, attacks on such sound men as Duff Cooper were led by Beaverbrook's 'jackals'.

[1] A few years earlier public opinion had been disturbed by the versatility of Sir Horace Wilson, Head of the Civil Service, whose advice Neville Chamberlain had sought on matters, such as foreign policy, outside his normal scope.

These ungrateful outbursts may have had their effect on Beaverbrook. Victory in the Battle of Britain—which was assured by the destruction of 185 German aircraft over south-east England on September 15th—must also have eased slightly the strain under which he was working (even though the problems of the blitz at once claimed his attention). Any relaxation, any sense that a job is done, or half-done, is apt to stir anew his spiritual wanderlust. On October 1st, this significant note appeared in the Londoner's Diary of his own *Evening Standard*: 'Today asthma has laid its harsh hand as firmly on [Beaverbrook] as a gaoler receiving an old prisoner back after a brief release'. A month later the same paper said that he could not go abroad to a more suitable climate until he had resigned from the Government—a clear hint that resignation was already a possibility in his mind. It has been shown repeatedly that Beaverbrook's bouts of asthma are related to his states of mind; but the physical symptoms have been genuine enough. Colleagues who slept near him in the Cabinet shelter found the sounds that emanated from him more distressing than the distant noise of the bombs; and Churchill, rather unkindly, recalls that he once said, during an important conference, 'Let someone go out and stop that cat mewing'—on which 'a silence fell on the company, and I realized that this was the asthma of my poor friend'. Relief from this affliction was found only at a great height: at one time Beaverbrook seriously thought of spending several hours a night flying ten thousand feet or more above the earth, in order to get some peaceful sleep.

Few ministers had more flying to do, in the way of duty, than he. Two of his trips abroad were especially notable—his visit to Moscow in September, 1941, when he and Mr Averell Harriman led the Anglo-American Supply Mission, and his visit to Washington with Churchill in December, 1941. He was freer to undertake these overseas assignments because he had ceased to be Minister of Aircraft Production on May 1st,

ODD MAN IN AND OUT

1941. Early that year he had undergone a painful eye operation. Mr Farrer records: 'Frictions in his dealings with others, which previously he had welcomed, had become now a tax both on his temper and on his health ... During April he was engaged on various controversies with the Air Marshals ...' He resigned not only because of these but 'much more because of his temperamental reluctance to remain long in any one post. The excitement and the stimulus had left him ... it is part of his character to lose interest once the crisis is over'. Churchill did, however, succeed in persuading him to remain in the Government, with the then unfamiliar title of Minister of State; this he held until the end of June, 1941, when he became Minister of Supply. (In October, 1940, when Mr Herbert Morrison had left the Ministry of Supply for the Home Office, Churchill had tried to persuade Beaverbrook to take on Supply as well as Aircraft Production: but his struggles with the Air Marshals had induced a sobering diffidence in him. He seriously doubted if he could do both jobs without making mistakes—'and if I made one mistake', he told his friends, 'the Air Marshals would tear me limb from limb'.)

The decisive events of 1941 were Hitler's attack on Russia and the Japanese attack on Pearl Harbour: the two most powerful nations in the world were forced by Axis folly into a shot-gun alliance with Britain. The news of the attack on Russia came through early on Sunday morning, June 22nd. Michael Foot was one of Beaverbrook's week-end guests at Cherkley: he woke the household by playing at full blast a record of the 'Internationale'. Beaverbrook went off to see Churchill at Chequers. Eden and Lord Cranborne[1] were there; also Sir Stafford Cripps, home on leave from Moscow, where he was Ambassador. There was some difference of opinion on the line that Churchill should take in his broadcast that evening. At that time Cripps shared the official Foreign

[1] Later the Marquess of Salisbury.

Office view that Russian resistance could not last very long. Beaverbrook argued that Soviet manpower was almost inexhaustible; that in any case some of them had always wanted the Russians to fight the Germans, and here it was happening; and that the broadcast should therefore be positive in character, welcoming the Russians as allies and encouraging them to resist the Nazi invaders. This was, in fact, the line that Churchill took: he reiterated his hatred of Communism, but his broadcast swept aside many old prejudices and suspicions, and carried the nation, including most of the Conservative Party, into enthusiastic collaboration with the Soviet Union. The Cherkley house party listened to the broadcast; Beaverbrook got home late from Chequers, having been delayed on the way by a car breakdown, and there was much jubilation.

According to Churchill, it was a month or two after this that Beaverbrook 'became the champion in the War Cabinet of Aid to Russia'. Before his actual visit to Russia, however, there was an interesting event in the western world to attend to: though America was not yet in the war, Churchill and President Roosevelt met on board ship off the coast of Newfoundland to agree and to sign the declaration of general principles known as the Atlantic Charter. Churchill wrote the first draft which contained the clause: 'Fourth, they [the two nations] will strive to bring about a fair and equitable distribution of essential produce, not only within their territorial boundaries, but between the nations of the world'. Roosevelt suggested the insertion of the phrase 'without discrimination and on equal terms'. Churchill, recalling the Ottawa agreements, resisted this. Mr Sumner Welles said that this was 'the core of the matter': this phrase expressed the State Department's 'ideal'. Churchill observed sardonically that Britain had sought for eighty years to adhere to Free Trade 'in the face of ever-mounting American tariffs'. Welles was 'a little taken aback'.

Churchill, in touch by cable with the War Cabinet, was sending Attlee, the Deputy Prime Minister, comprehensive summaries of the discussions. Roosevelt's proposed amendment of the fourth point caused some concern at home, and Churchill does not record that the War Cabinet agreed to the compromise that he and Roosevelt reached—the omission of Roosevelt's 'without discrimination' and the insertion of the words 'with due respect for their existing obligations'. Various possible amendments—and many other matters—were discussed for most of August 11th. Early the next morning Beaverbrook arrived at the conference, having flown the Atlantic: he had been delayed by fog, and had come on by train; he took part vigorously in the last stages of the discussion.

The Charter, at last agreed, was signed at about noon. The disputed clause contained the protective phrase; in its final form it read: 'Fourth, they will endeavour, with due respect to their existing obligations, to further the enjoyment by all peoples of access, on equal terms, to the trade and to the raw materials of the world which are needed for their economic prosperity'. In later years it was realized gradually that the signatories, in reaching agreement, had fallen into an ambiguity which could be used by either of the powers concerned to nullify the principle of the whole clause; it might indeed have been used by Britain in and after 1947—as Beaverbrook earnestly hoped that it would be—to cushion the imperial economy from the effects of the General Agreement on Tariffs and Trade. It has been supposed by his friends—though the chronology in Churchill's account does not seem to support this view—that the qualifying words were inserted largely at Beaverbrook's insistence. His succinct, colloquial summary of the final phase of this incident was: 'Sumner Welles kicked up hell. Roosevelt supported him, but preferred lunch.' On his return from this outing, the *Manchester Guardian* observed that he was looking 'more thaumaturgic than ever'.

So he was in a brighter frame of mind, enjoying the relief from ministerial routine, the discomfiture of Mr Welles, and the prospect of adventure ahead, when he set off for Russia on September 22nd. He and Harriman sailed in the cruiser *London* through the Arctic Sea to Archangel, and flew thence to Moscow. Beaverbrook carried a personal letter to Stalin from Churchill, explaining that he had the 'fullest confidence of the Cabinet' and was one of Churchill's 'oldest and most intimate friends'. None the less, the result of the expedition was unpredictable. Stalin, indeed, needed much that the western powers could send him, and had just begun his pressure on Churchill for the opening of a Second Front 'somewhere in the Balkans or France'; but there was the record of long years of mutual hostility, which had not been completely wiped out by Churchill's broadcast of June 22nd, and Soviet Russia seemed to these rich men from the west more alien than any other country they had done business in.

Beaverbrook had been to Moscow ten years before, as a tourist, with Arnold Bennett, Lady Louis Mountbatten, Mrs Edwin Montagu, and other friends. On that occasion, he told Harriman as they sailed north-eastwards, he had seen Stalin alone, with Litvinov as interpreter. They had not got on very well: Stalin had accused various British ministers of being implicated dishonestly in certain oil deals, and had asked Beaverbrook to expose the matter in Britain. Also, Beaverbrook had lost his passport—stolen, he supposed, by the GPU. Also, the Russians had kept a rather closer eye on the party than was comfortable because they believed, or pretended to believe, that Lady Louis Mountbatten was a sister of the late Tsar.

Now again, despite the changed circumstances and the character of their mission, the Russians' first reception of Beaverbrook and Harriman was, as Churchill puts it, 'bleak'. Beaverbrook worked hard to thaw the frost. Believing, rightly or wrongly, that his and Harriman's rooms would be wired and all they said recorded, he took care when they were alone to talk loudly and often in praise of Stalin. He also created a good impression on the Russians by saying that he was perfectly satisfied with their interpreters and refusing to take British interpreters with him to the discussions.

According to diplomatic observers then in Moscow, one conversation that Beaverbrook had with Stalin marked the turning-point in their relations. Stalin now disclosed for the first time the reason for his coolness. If the western allies were sincere in their professions, he said, why did they keep open a line of communication with the enemy? For a moment Beaverbrook did not understand what he meant. Stalin explained: he meant Rudolf Hess, whose sensational flight to Britain had taken place four months before. Beaverbrook denied that Stalin's suspicions were justified: there was no question, on the British side, of using Hess as a messenger to Hitler. On the contrary, the proposal put to the British by Hess, that they should make peace with Hitler and leave him free to attack Russia, had been rejected unhesitatingly. Why then, asked Stalin, was Hess kept alive? Why not simply shoot him? That, said Beaverbrook, was not the sort of thing that could be done in England.

The atmosphere was better after this, and when they got down to the business of the mission, an affinity seems to have developed between the two men, so unlike in their ideologies and origins, yet alike in their understanding of the realities of power, in contempt for woolliness or weakness, in practical competence, and in off-duty conviviality. Beaverbrook was much impressed by Stalin's detailed technical knowledge. Stalin was asking for a large number of Spitfires. Beaverbrook said that some of the fighters sent to him would have to be Hurricanes. 'They've got 1,450 h.p. engines,' he added, by way of explanation. 'No,' said Stalin, '1,250.' Beaverbrook enjoyed this exchange so much that he released it to the press through the British Embassy. The Soviet censors killed the story—because they thought that it might make Beaverbrook look foolish.

In the end, they reached a friendly agreement, largely because Stalin was able to demonstrate to Beaverbrook the extent and urgency of Soviet needs and to convince him of the strategic importance—to the west as well as to Russia—of meeting them; and because Beaverbrook, with Harriman at his side, was able to assure Stalin that almost all the supplies that he asked for would be forthcoming. When they left Moscow, Stalin embraced Beaverbrook warmly. He was believed to be the only British statesman who had been so honoured. Stalin remarked that Beaverbrook and Harriman were the only men he had ever met who worked as hard as he did himself. Some time later, back in London, Churchill telephoned to Beaverbrook one day to complain that Stalin was being seriously troublesome—referring to him, as was customary, as 'Joe'. Beaverbrook said: 'You leave him to me—I'll sack him'; for he had misheard the name as 'Low'. They talked at cross-purposes for several minutes; four or five private secretaries who were listening in to the conversation had some difficulty in stifling their laughter.

Ever since this mission Beaverbrook has shown admiration for Stalin as a man, and an understanding of the problems that faced him after the war. As is his way, when his respect has once been won, he is remarkably little affected by fashion or by propaganda: even quite recently, after all the years of cold war, he has startled visiting American business men and journalists by giving a realistic appreciation of the position of the Soviet Union in 1945, in a sense highly favourable to the Russians. A student of the policy of his newspapers in the post-war years would find that, while they were bitterly hostile to the British Labour Government, they were involved less whole-heartedly than other popular newspapers in the anti-Soviet *Gleischaltung* of the western press; one recent example is their opposition to western German rearmament—

though this may also be regarded as a modern application of
Beaverbrook's perennial isolationism, since such rearmament
is presented as a 'contribution' to a continental defence
system in which Britain is involved.

Churchill learned of the agreement with delight, and cabled
to Beaverbrook on October 3rd: 'Heartiest congratulations
... No-one could have done it but you. Now come home and
make the [one group undecipherable] stuff...'

He went home, and went on making the stuff; but another
mission soon took him abroad again. A few weeks after
Pearl Harbour he and Churchill went to Washington, arriving
there on December 22nd. The purpose of this mission was at
least as crucial as that of the mission to Moscow; for America
was, and must increasingly become, the great source of supply
for all the allied powers. Nor, since the Japanese attack, were
any restraints imposed by domestic politics: even the most
isolationist Americans had been converted, almost unanimously, to support of the war effort (though among these
there was still more emphasis, for reasons of geography and
of economic interest, on Asia than on Europe). What this
would mean, they had not yet fully realized. In the course of
his first talks with the Washington experts on production,
two facts became more and more apparent to Beaverbrook:
one was that the effective direction of the war was now passing
from Britain to America; the other was that even the most
able and responsible Americans had a complete misunderstanding of the needs of their own, and the Allied, war
machine.

There is independent American evidence of the impact of
Beaverbrook on Washington. Mr Donald M. Nelson wrote
at the time:

Lord Beaverbrook emphasized the fact that we must set our
production sites [sic] much higher than we have for the year
1942... He pointed out that we had yet had no experience in
the losses of matériel incidental to a war of the kind we are now

271

fighting. He also felt we had very little conception of the productive facilities of the Axis powers. He said that . . . Stalin told him that Germany had thrown 30,000 tanks into the fight with Russia, and in starting from scratch as we were we had to build up a reserve in addition to supplying our forces . . . He made the statement that if an invasion of America was attempted we had no conception of the number of tanks we should have to cope with. He emphasized over and over again the fact that we should set our sites [*sic*] higher . . . For instance, he thinks we should plan for the production of 45,000 tanks in 1942 against Mr Knudsen's estimate of 30,000 . . .[1]

President Roosevelt himself was not present at the meeting thus described by Mr Nelson. But he also was subjected to a Beaverbrook bombardment. In a note to him, Beaverbrook 'set the expected 1942 production of the United States, the United Kingdom, and Canada against British, Russian, and American requirements . . . The comparison exposed tremendous deficits . . .' He insisted that they should budget for far greater production, quoting actual figures—saying, for instance, that they should 'double the quantity of anti-aircraft guns then programmed'. He took Canadian estimates of production for 1942 as a basis: 'the excess of American over Canadian resources should permit the United States to produce fifteen times as much'. At this point in his note he engaged the President's sympathy by a candid admission: 'This last was an argument that could be torn to bits'. Nevertheless, 'it was one which he thought the President should consider'.

The immediate result of these exchanges was dramatic. Roosevelt decided for a $50 billion war programme for 1942

[1] Memorandum, ' Notes on a meeting held in the office of the Vice-President in the Capitol, with Jesse Jones, James Forrestal, Robert P. Patterson, W. S. Knudsen, William L. Batt, Harry Hopkins, Leon Henderson, Robert Lovett, W. Averell Harriman, E. R. Stettinius, Sidney Hillman, Lord Beaverbrook, Vice-President Wallace, Donald M. Nelson, on Monday, December 29th, at 2.30 p.m.', quoted in volume I of *Industrial Mobilisation for War*, the official *History of the War Production Board and Predecessor Agencies, 1940–1945* (whence also are derived other data quoted).

5 With Group-Captain Max Aitken, DSO: Buckingham Palace investiture (1942)

6 With Sir Winston Churchill: the garden of 10 Downing Street (May 1954)

'that would tax to the utmost the productive capacity of the United States'. The official American *History of the War Production Board* states: 'The immensity of the specific production objectives for planes, ships, tanks, and anti-aircraft guns that the President announced on January 6 made men gasp. Even to experts they appeared unattainable'.

In the event they were not all attained. They were modified to some extent in the spring of 1942. By August 8th Mr Nelson was saying: 'The total objectives for 1942 and 1943 are beyond attainment'. There were complaints of 'chaotic scheduling'. The official history shows that '. . . only about one-third of [fifty selected munitions] items had a record in which actual output was within ten per cent of scheduled production. The proportion of items whose production was seriously overestimated . . . increased from quarter to quarter . . .' Mr Knudsen, it will be recalled, had estimated that 30,000 tanks could be produced in 1942; President Roosevelt had accepted Beaverbrook's figure of 45,000. Actual production for the year was about 25,000.

None the less, Beaverbrook had once more shown that his *métier* was to stir things up, to persuade men not to be content with the reasonably adequate but to make a bid for the unreasonable and excessive, to galvanize them into quicker and bigger achievements than they had thought possible. Orderly production schedules may have been dislocated in that year; but he had set in being a new momentum, whose long-term effects on the whole course of the war were probably even more important than his better-known work at the Ministry of Aircraft Production. As in the case of the agreement with Stalin, probably nobody but he, with his North American big-business background—certainly no conventional, conservative Englishman—could have talked round the hardest-headed and highest-powered industrialists in the United States. It was a feat that may stand for ever to his credit.

273

Churchill and Beaverbrook returned to England by flying-boat, via Bermuda. The flight from Bermuda to Plymouth took eighteen hours. The pilot noted that 'all passengers had gone to bed during the night excepting Lord Beaverbrook, who sat up reading the whole time'.

CHAPTER TWELVE

THE WORM IN THE BUD

I asked no other thing,
No other was denied.
I offered Being for it;
The mighty merchant smiled.

Brazil? He twirled a button,
Without a glance my way:
'But, madam, is there nothing else
That we can show to-day?'

EMILY DICKINSON

HE WAS, indeed, entitled to look back over 1941 with some
satisfaction. He had put a girdle about the earth. As Churchill
notes, he 'had the confidence both of the Russians and of the
Americans'. Churchill therefore revived the proposal that
Beaverbrook should undertake the 'single directing authority'
over both the Ministry of Supply and the Ministry of Aircraft
Production, thus becoming an 'opposite number' to Mr Donald Nelson in Washington.

But it was just at this moment of outward success that new
tensions were increasing within him and, consequently, in his
relations with his colleagues. In the autumn, shortly before
the American visit, he was again troubled by asthma, and
several newspapers printed rumours that he was contemplat-
ing resignation. The *Express* neither printed nor contradicted
these rumours. Hannen Swaffer—who saw Beaverbrook from
time to time—remarked: 'If he resigned, it would be with
disgust, not asthma'. An *Evening News* diarist reported that
Churchill was 'having to mediate between Lord Beaverbrook
and Mr Bevin'. *Time* magazine said, on November 10th:
'The testy, growling Beaver ... was stirring up a Cabinet

crisis that might bring about a drastic reorganization ... [he] approached open battle with Bevin on the question of woman-power.'

Churchill's own book indicates with some frankness the acuteness of these difficulties, which must have aggravated the already immense burden of his own responsibility—particularly as they coincided with some of the worst external anxieties of the whole war. There was growing press clamour against the 'old gang' still numerously represented in the Government. *The Economist* was 'not very happy about the leadership', and was disappointed that Churchill had been 'captured' by the 'Conservative machine' instead of leading the Party 'away from the Brummagem neo-feudalism of its recent years to the Disraelian tradition of constructive, popular, and progressive realism'. At the end of January, 1942, the House of Commons went into secret session for two days to debate a motion of confidence. 'Churchill and the Government generally,' remarks Lord Reith (then Minister of Works and Buildings), 'were in an unhappy state ... Beaverbrook had been put on to broadcast. Much disquiet, even among Ministers.' Churchill promised 'some major changes in the Government'.

One of these changes, in the minds of Churchill and of Beaverbrook, was the concentration of power on the home front in Beaverbrook's hands. This proposal was strongly resisted: Bevin was not the only minister to threaten resignation if it was carried out to the full; and opposition to it came from both Conservative and Labour ministers. There was indeed agreement that there should be a Ministry of Production, with consolidated powers; the dispute was on the extent and nature of these powers. 'Every point,' says Churchill, 'had to be fought for as in a battle'—and Beaverbrook, like his antagonists, was constantly threatening to resign if he did not get the powers that he no doubt genuinely believed necessary to the efficient performance of the task.

'At last,' Churchill records, 'I reached the end of my patience';
and on February 10th—a week after the creation of the new
Ministry had been announced in Parliament in general terms
('a new tremendous sphere')—Churchill wrote to Beaverbrook a letter in which exasperation is hardly disguised:

> I have lavished my time and strength during the last week in
> trying to make arrangements which are satisfactory to you and to
> the public interest and to allay the anxieties of the departments
> with whom you will be brought in contact. I can do no more.
>
> I am sure it is your duty to undertake this work . . . and that
> you have ample powers for the purpose . . . If after all else has
> been settled you break on this point [power to determine types
> of merchant vessels] or indeed on any other in connection with
> the great office I have shaped for you, . . . you will be harshly
> judged by the nation and in the United States, having regard to
> the extreme emergency in which we stand . . . I hope therefore
> that you will not fall below the high level of events and strike
> so wounding a blow at your country, at your friend, and above
> all at your reputation . . .

It was a strong and moving appeal; but it failed in its
purpose. There had been one specific reservation in the
announcement of the transfer to the new Ministry of the
duties of the Production Executive: all duties were to be
handed over 'excepting only those relating to manpower and
labour'. This of course, as Churchill has explained, 'trenched
upon the very strong personal antagonisms which had developed between Lord Beaverbrook and Mr Ernest Bevin'.
The clash between them may be said to provide an answer
to a classic problem: what happens when an irresistible force
meets an immovable object. Bevin was the immovable object:
he would not budge. It was Beaverbrook who went, sulkily
refusing a consolatory Viscountcy: his resignation was announced a fortnight after the creation of the 'new tremendous
sphere', the 'great office . . . shaped' for him personally by
his friend and leader.

Churchill's letter of February 10th shows how keenly he must for a time have resented this apparent defection at a moment of national danger; but he seems to have realized even then, against his own inclination, that it was inevitable, and he was able, on reflection, to excuse it as the vagary of a sick man:

> His health had completely broken down, and he did not feel he could face the new and great responsibilities . . . the long and harassing discussions which took place in my presence between him and other principal Ministers convinced me that it was better to press him no further.

Regret, in any case, rather than resentment was dominant in Churchill's mind:

> I felt his loss acutely . . . I always meant to have him back when he was restored to health and poise, but this intention I did not impart to my colleagues at this time.

This reticence was, no doubt, prudent.

The general public and the fighting men, absorbed in the griefs and hardships of war and blitz, heard only muffled echoes of these Cabinet-shaking convulsions. Had the full story been known then, some doubt about the outcome of the war might have been pardonable: as in 1916, the military conflict itself seems to have been almost forgotten in the highest quarters while personal and party feuds raged and were uneasily resolved by this or that concession and rearrangement. Even the public may have been puzzled by two Cabinet reshuffles within three weeks and by the fact that Beaverbrook's resignation 'on grounds of health' was followed at once by a further announcement that he was to go to Washington (with its exacting climate) on important 'special duties' which he was evidently not too ill to undertake. Four days after his resignation he was reported to be in bed with asthma; but the *Manchester Guardian* said that his 'disappearance' would 'astonish the country', and *The*

Economist remarked: 'This is no time for any man of competence to retire to his tent'.

Churchill, writing of Beaverbrook's condition during this distressing episode, uses the term 'nervous breakdown', and sees the origin of the breakdown in the 'physical affliction' of asthma. Medical authorities agree that asthma is almost always psychosomatic in character, and the coincidence of sharp bouts of the disease with Beaverbrook's periods of emotional disturbance has been stressed. He had been moving towards this 'breakdown' for some months. 'I had already,' says Churchill, 'brushed aside an impulsive resignation during our visit to Washington.' Beaverbrook, he adds, 'now developed an unaffected and profound weariness and distaste for office, and while in one mood demanding ever wider and more untrammelled powers, sought in his heart that relief from burdens and anxieties which many others of my colleagues also desired'.

They, however, were men better adjusted to the society in which they had risen to eminence by well-mapped ways, in either of the great parties then in coalition; men, too, who had learned from their early years, at public schools, in the armed forces, or in trade unions, to work as members of a team. Churchill here portrays, torn by inner conflict, a man who had no such training, an individualist *par excellence*, 'self-made', an essentially solitary guerrilla fighter. He was, at a higher and more tragic level, like the child in the famous Victorian advertisement for Pears' soap: 'He won't be happy till he gets it'. But what, in his case, was 'it'?

The recollection of his intimates suggests that Beaverbrook was never in his life more unhappy and restless than in the weeks that preceded his resignation. There are a few clues to what may have been the real cause of his conflict. One is the farewell letter which he wrote to Churchill on his resignation. It is strikingly unlike the somewhat stilted letters customary on such occasions; yet it is no mere informal personal note and ends with what is almost a litany of laudatory phrases, extravagant in their warmth:

26 Feb 42

My dear Winston

I am leaving this office to-day and going to the place I came from. And now I must tell you about twenty-one months of high adventure, the like of which has never been known.

All the time everything that has been done by me has been due to your holding me up.

You took a great chance in putting me in, and you stood to be shot at by a section of Members for keeping me here.

It was little enough I gave you compared with what you gave me. I owe my reputation to you. The confidence of the public really comes from you. And my courage was sustained by you. These benefits give me a right to a place in your list of lieutenants who served you when you brought salvation to our people in the hour of disaster.

In leaving, then, I send this letter of gratitude and devotion to the leader of the nation, the saviour of our people, and the symbol of resistance in the free world.

Yours affectionately,

Max

For some time there had been a tendency in sections of the press, especially in America, to build Beaverbrook up in the public mind as the real 'No. 2' in the Churchill Government, instead of the less 'colourful' Attlee, who in fact deputized for Churchill throughout the period of the coalition. This imaginary picture of the present was often coupled with speculation about a hypothetical future, 'if anything should happen to Churchill'. In that event, said some commentators, Beaverbrook would succeed Churchill as Prime Minister. As early as August 15th, 1940, Beaverbrook's old friend Mr Joe Patterson, publisher of the New York *Daily News*, had reported, after a visit to Britain, 'discontent about the war among the working people of England' and had forecast a shift of power in the Cabinet, adding: 'This shift, if it

280

THE WORM IN THE BUD

happens, will throw out Winston Churchill as Prime Minister and throw Lord Beaverbrook in. Beaverbrook, it is felt, being a business man, will make some sort of compromise with Germany before Britain and Germany wreck each other.' This last sentence, an expression of Patterson's own attitude to international affairs, must have been as embarrassing to Beaverbrook as it was certainly, by this time, untrue in its implications; but the suggestion that preceded it may well have lingered in his mind.

In January, 1941, again, an Associated Press dispatch had nominated Beaverbrook as Churchill's 'probable successor', comparing his wartime career with that of Lloyd George, who had been Minister of Munitions before rising to the highest office. The celebrated novelist Mrs Elinor Glyn interviewed him at 12 Downing Street on behalf of the Hearst press, and found him 'a vivid, enduring symbol of calm certainty' (perhaps the only example on record of the application to him of these singularly unsuitable words); she also described him as 'the Prime Minister's right-hand man' and as 'the only possible successor to Winston Churchill'.

If such a succession seems, now, improbable, and the forecasts of it grotesquely ill-informed, it must be remembered that, just as, in 1930, Mr Ward Price had not had the advantage of seeing Neville Chamberlain and Winston Churchill actually in charge of governments, so in the turmoil of the war's dark middle period, when all was uncertain, these prophets had little chance of assessing accurately the characters of the various men in the British Government. No one writing ten years later would have made their mistake of underestimating Attlee and Bevin; but it was at the time natural that they should be dazzled by the most obviously potent 'personality' among Churchill's ministers—the one, moreover, most accessible to American interviewers. Nor was it only Americans who wrote in such terms: the *National Review*'s apprehension that Beaverbrook might go 'Still

Higher' has already been mentioned; and in September, 1940, Hannen Swaffer, prophesying that Beaverbrook would be succeeded as Minister of Aircraft Production by Lord Ashfield,[1] also thought that Beaverbrook might go 'higher'. He wrote: 'A year ago, Beaverbrook's chance of high office would have been laughed at. Now, it is accepted as natural!'

All these hints cannot have escaped Beaverbrook's eye. He also saw in the *News Chronicle* the results of the various Gallup polls in which, from time to time, the popularity of ministers was canvassed, and he may have been unduly excited by one set of percentages recorded therein. On July 1st, 1941, the figures for Churchill's runners-up had been:

> Eden 37 per cent
> Bevin 7
> Beaverbrook 7
> Attlee 1

By December, 1941, though Eden now had 50 per cent, Beaverbrook, with 14, was well ahead of Bevin, with 9, and Attlee, with 4. Six weeks later—and only three weeks before Beaverbrook's resignation—there was a startling change in the figures. They now read:

> Eden 70 per cent
> Beaverbrook 60
> Bevin 41
> Attlee 21

What he may possibly have overlooked was that these figures were given by the pollsters' clients in answer to different questions. In this poll they had been asked to nominate four men for a small War Cabinet *to assist Churchill*; in previous polls they had been asked to nominate Churchill's successor *if he had to go*. Eden had remained unapproachably

---

[1] Lord Ashfield, formerly Albert Stanley, was the man who had become President of the Board of Trade instead of Beaverbrook in December, 1916. He was now working under Beaverbrook at MAP.

at the top of these other polls. (Later, when Beaverbrook had left the Government, his percentage sank, and a new name rose into the higher percentages: when the question of Churchill's successor, if he had to go, was put in May, 1942, Beaverbrook was tied with Attlee and Bevin at 2 per cent, Eden scored 37—and Stafford Cripps had 34.)

It is one of the diseases and disadvantages of power that those holding it come eventually to believe the propaganda that they have themselves inspired. From whatever sources Beaverbrook's ambition was fed, some of those then close to him remember that at various times in 1941 and 1942 he believed himself to be the coming Prime Minister of Britain. In a nature impatient for power, such a belief or hope is only one stage short of action to secure its fulfilment. Could such action be taken better from within the Government or from outside it—from within, using the apparently less forceful Eden, perhaps, as a mounting-block that could later be kicked aside, or from outside in a newspaper and platform campaign that would be a thousand times more effective than the Empire Crusade had ever been, the more so because millions of people, disturbed by military reverses and disasters, were awaiting just such a focus and rallying-point? This was a tactical reason for hesitation. For a time, therefore, he seemed content to await the call that must come soon, and took no overt action.

It would be superficial, however, to find only in this tactical dilemma the cause of his misery—it is not too strong a word —in the first six weeks of 1942. The true and deeper cause is more to his credit. Bonar Law had always reigned in his heart, and had stirred in him a devotion as truly unselfish as any attachment in his life; but next after Law in his personal hierarchy came Churchill. His feeling of friendship for Churchill was genuine and deep: the exaggerated rhetoric of his letter of resignation, if it betrayed some sense of guilt, expressed also a real affection. Here, surely, is the essence of the conflict that racked him in this supreme nervous crisis of his life: his desire for power was at war with his loyalty to his friend. The two emotions were riding a see-saw on the threshold of his mind, one up one day, the other the next day: his asthmatic groans and snufflings became volcanic, his tears flowed like those of a seventeenth-century evangelical martyr. Resignation from the Government eased this tension in its most torturing form: he was still Churchill's friend, but no longer also bound to him as a colleague. But the canker of ambition—his half-concealed 'worm i' the bud'—was never to be assuaged. The energetic Miss Elsa Maxwell perhaps stumbled on (and simplified) the truth about him when she wrote in her syndicated column, 'Party Line', of his 'three dreams of conquest—(1) Bonar Law, (2) Edward VIII, (3) World War II'.

It took him several weeks partially to recover from his resignation and all that had gone before it. Then he went and had a long, tranquil, and useful talk with Churchill (who has testified that, even just before his resignation, he 'was able to take a coolly detached view of everyone's affairs except his own'). He had been disinclined to accept the Washington assignment; Churchill now talked him into it. There was a special announcement that the Government attached 'high importance' to the visit. On the eve of his departure, Beaverbrook conferred in a suite at the Savoy with some of his employees—E. J. Robertson, Christiansen, Frank Owen, Michael Foot, J. B. Wilson—and with Mr Brendan Bracken, MP, then Minister of Information,[1] and had a 'long and earnest talk' with M Maisky, the Soviet Ambassador in London.

Important as this mission was said to be, it was also mysterious; and Beaverbrook's behaviour in America became increasingly erratic. His status had been defined in the press as that of a 'temporary production envoy'. On arrival in

[1] Later Lord Bracken.

America on March 25th, however, he described himself as 'simply a sick man needing a rest'. Soon, despite this need, he was talking business with President Roosevelt and Mr Harry Hopkins 'till the early hours of the morning'. On April 9th he went to the Bahamas for an 'indefinite rest'; on arrival there he dined with the Duke and Duchess of Windsor. The 'rest' was not, after all, indefinite: he left the Bahamas four days later, spent a week or so at Miami, and was back in Washington, and lunching at the White House, on the 22nd.

Next day the world knew what he had been hatching. He launched a campaign that was to earn him praise from those who had been his political enemies and the most resentful criticism from those who were nominally his political friends —a campaign in support of Stalin's demand for an immediate Second Front.

He chose an occasion for the inauguration of the campaign that was certain to secure maximum publicity for it—a New York gathering, which he had been invited to address, of the Bureau of Advertising of the American Newspaper Publishers' Association. He spoke at length and eloquently to this influential audience. First he described the splendour and endurance of the Battle of Britain. Then he praised the Soviet Union, where 'Communism under Stalin has won the applause and admiration of all the western nations'. He declared that there was neither religious nor racial persecution in Russia. Political purges? Of course—but those purged had been traitors. Beaverbrook goes all the way for any cause that he sponsors. 'Stalin,' he asserted, 'accepts the Atlantic Charter . . . He did so in my presence. He expressed no dissent, but entire agreement. He asked many questions, but then he is a curious man.'

He then developed the main theme to which all this had been an introduction. A Second Front in western Europe would provide 'an opportunity to bring the war to an end here and now'. Sonorously he declaimed: 'Strike out to help Russia! Strike out violently—strike even recklessly!' Speaking with the authority and knowledge that his hearers were entitled to assume in one who had so recently been Minister of Supply, he assured them solemnly that the project was practicable: 'How admirably Britain is now equipped in weapons of war for directing such an attack on Germany, I well know'. Few of them would have known of a broadcast in which, six months earlier, he had warned Britain that 30,000 more tanks were needed for the opening of the offensive against Germany.

He also mentioned to these American publicity experts a rumour which he had found to be widespread: 'Of our own great leader, Mr Churchill, I read in all the newspapers and I am told here and there, wherever I go, that he will fall before the summer is out. You must help me to kill that bad rumour. Such a disaster we cannot contemplate in Great Britain.'

On both sides of the Atlantic this speech excited a furore. The *New York Times* saw in it the 'return of Lord Beaverbrook to politics and opposition politics at that'. Coast-to-coast publicity in the United States was summed up in a *Daily Express* report headlined: 'The Beaver's call sweeps America'. In Britain, most of the Tories were indignant: this was what they called 'rocking the boat'. Lord Kemsley's *Sunday Times* said: 'We will not be hustled by inopportune pressure'. A Communist commentator underlined Beaverbrook's 'revelation' that he had been advocating a Second Front since October (i.e. while he had been in the Government). There were questions in the House (for much, after all, had been made of the importance of Beaverbrook's mission to Washington): Attlee answered, drily, that he was not there officially but on a 'special mission of an informal kind'. On May 5th he returned to England—'bronzed and well', said A. J. Cummings.

Just as he had once stumped the country for his Empire Crusade, and again to inspire the workers to build more aircraft and more tanks, so he now stumped it for the Second Front. The *Daily Express* organized mass-meetings 'to speed the Second Front and sweep out the "men of Munich"' (among whom the proprietor of the *Express* was not now numbered); the speakers at one of them included Mr Shinwell, Lord Strabolgi, Michael Foot, and Frank Owen (who had lately been called up but was writing in *Tribune*, under the pseudonym Thomas Rainborough, articles severely critical of Churchill and his war strategy). A well-known radio-commentator broadcast to America an interview in which he quoted Beaverbrook as saying that the Second Front was coming 'soon'. At a great Anglo-Soviet demonstration at Birmingham, he said: 'The Army is, in my opinion, equipped ready for the job and wanting to do it'.

Unfortunately, this stage of his campaign coincided with severe military reverses in North Africa. Beaverbrook's Birmingham rhetoric did not sound so convincing to a public stunned by the news that, contrary to all expectations, Tobruk had fallen and twenty-five thousand British troops had surrendered—especially when Alan Moorehead, the distinguished war correspondent of the *Express* itself, reported that the Army, in Libya at any rate, was *not* 'equipped for the job', that it was inferior to the Germans in tanks, in guns, and in aircraft (lacking dive-bombers in particular). These revelations of inadequate equipment shook the Government and the prestige of Churchill himself; but Beaverbrook also felt their repercussions, for there were many to recall, as *The Economist* did, that he had been, 'at one time or another, responsible for the ordering and manufacture of all these items of equipment'.

None the less, throughout July, the lobbies and the newspapers were full of rumours that he was going back into the Government: it was said that Churchill had asked him to be

Minister of Defence; it is certain that, if the offer was made, he refused it. He plugged away at his Second Front propaganda; besides the public campaign, dinners were arranged at which he addressed twenty or thirty MPs at a time. Besides the Second Front, he was now urging also an early General Election—a demand that was less widely supported. 'Nothing in a Disraeli novel,' said *Truth*, 'could equal the excitement and the comings and goings.' In the desert of North Africa the men of the Eighth Army sweated and fought and bled.

Soon came news of one of the war's bloodiest incidents— the ambitious raid on Dieppe, which Churchill was later to describe, making the best of it, as 'a costly but not unfruitful reconnaissance in force'. Costly indeed it was: of the 4963 men of the Canadian 2nd Division who landed in France, 3369 became casualties in the nine hours that the raid lasted, more than 900 of these losing their lives.

Ill omens had attended this operation from the first. Rehearsals in June, near Bridport, had been unsatisfactory. Lord Louis Mountbatten,[1] Chief of Combined Operations, had seen them and had said that further rehearsal was essential and that the raid could not take place in June. In July inclement weather caused two postponements: the rugged Canadian troops, trained, briefed, and keyed up, were bitterly disappointed. At this point Lieutenant-General Montgomery[2], then General Officer Commanding in Chief, Southern Command, said that the raid was 'off for all time'. He was against remounting it because he thought that, after two cancellations, it would be increasingly difficult to keep the preparations for it secret.

Nevertheless, it took place, with, of course, the approval of the Chiefs of Staff and the Prime Minister (Mountbatten having taken the responsibility of saying that a leakage of

[1] Later Admiral the Earl Mountbatten of Burma and First Sea Lord.
[2] Later Field-Marshal Viscount Montgomery of Alamein.

7 Cherkley (1953): dictaphone, telephone, paper

8 Nassau (1955): garden engineering

information could be prevented, as in fact it was); and it is clear from various official records which have now appeared[1] that the reasons for pressing on with the project were both military and, in the wider sense of the word, political. The military reason was stated by Churchill in the House of Commons on September 8th, 1942: 'I personally regarded the Dieppe assault, to which I gave my sanction, as an indispensable preliminary to full-scale operations'. So it turned out to have been; for those responsible for its planning became the chief planners of Overlord—the actual invasion of Europe—and in the major task the lessons of Dieppe were decisive. It also misled the Germans into scattering their defences all round the French coast—a strategy more effective against raids than against invasion. The 'political' reasons for Dieppe were: (1) it was desirable to find active employment for the large numbers of Canadian troops who had endured for too long the boredom and frustration of training in Southern England; (2) the authorities were beginning to be rattled by the Second Front campaign still kept up by Beaverbrook and the Communist and other spokesmen of the Left, and felt that some show of action might take the edge off it; and (3) even more serious was the pressure for a Second Front from Stalin himself—and Churchill, who had the ticklish task, about this time, of breaking to him the news that there was to be no Second Front in 1942, might find it useful to be able to represent at least one operation in the west as 'diversionary aid' to Russia.

The tragedy of Dieppe plunged Beaverbrook not merely into one of his periodical fits of gloom but into an absolute paroxysm of rage which even those accustomed to his moods found alarming. His wrath was concentrated against the man whom he held mainly responsible for the revival of the

---

[1] Particularly *The Canadian Army, 1939–1945, an Official Historical Summary*, by Colonel C. P. Stacey.

U

unlucky project—Mountbatten. Some little time after it had taken place, when the grim toll of Canadian lives was still fresh in people's minds, Beaverbrook and Mountbatten were dinner-guests at Mr Averell Harriman's apartment in Mayfair. Beaverbrook was tired. When the conversation turned to Dieppe, there was an angry dispute, and he used language which seemed to imply that he held Mountbatten personally responsible for the heavy casualties. Harriman was shocked by this ugly scene and discussed it with Churchill next day.

Beaverbrook's friends say that he was sorry afterwards that he had gone so far in the expression of his feelings. None the less, his disapproval of the Dieppe assault, and of Mountbatten as the man behind it, was not mitigated in the course of time. When Colonel Stacey's Canadian Army history appeared in 1948, a half-page review in the *Evening Standard* was devoted exclusively to one section of it—that dealing with Dieppe—and to insisting that Dieppe had been a 'strategic blunder', an 'utter failure', and an 'ill-conceived and badly-planned adventure'; and, whereas some might have said, and did in 1942 say, that the failure of Dieppe showed how impossible the full Second Front would have been at that time, the *Standard* reviewer boldly declared that 'It would have been better to have launched the full-scale attack and secured a permanent toe-hold in France. The plan was there, ready . . .' However that may be, Beaverbrook has often explained that Dieppe provided a twofold basis for his antipathy to Mountbatten. He deplored a loss of Canadian lives which he thought should have been avoided; and he deplored it particularly because the lives seemed to him to have been lost in an attempt to damage his own propaganda campaign. This was a grave charge to bring against a senior officer; for it implied, not only that political rather than military considerations were uppermost in Mountbatten's mind, but that nine hundred lives had been sacrificed in an operation deliberately designed, for political reasons, to fail.

In fact, Mountbatten, as a serving officer, had no concern with the political aspects of the raid; and, whatever mistakes were made in its execution, those directly responsible for planning it confirm that neither he nor his staff ever wanted to make a frontal assault on Dieppe. The planners at Combined Operations Headquarters favoured landings on either side of Dieppe, away from strong fixed defences: the town itself, they proposed, should then be entered by land from east and west. Landings actually made at these points were relatively successful; one, by No. 3 Commando under Lord Lovat, was completely so. But the general plan devised by Combined Operations was changed by the Army authorities themselves. All this was explained to Beaverbrook by Mountbatten at Mr Harriman's dinner-table; but he was unwilling to accept the explanation.

Even the most casual reader of the *Express* newspapers must be aware that Mountbatten is not one of their favourite public figures. To most newspapers, and most British people, his character and achievements make a strong appeal: the *Express* has rarely had a good word to say for him. This phenomenon is the clearest illustration available of one of the less agreeable aspects of Beaverbrook's character. If he is tackled about the *Express* vendetta against Mountbatten, he will indignantly deny the existence of a vendetta: the very word is one to whose use the *Express* has taken exception. He will argue, justly enough, that newspapers are entitled to criticize public men of whose policies or performance they disapprove. In the case of Mountbatten, he will cite not only Dieppe but India: as an imperialist of the old school, he was against the handing-over of India, and Mountbatten, the last Viceroy—even though only the agent and emissary of the British Government—was the man who 'threw India away' and was thus, 'by his hasty action and in failing to define boundaries . . . responsible for terrible disasters'.

Many people—including some who at the time opposed the Labour Government's action on India—would now disagree with Beaverbrook's reiterated reproaches to Mountbatten on the subject. None the less, if Dieppe and India were his main concern in this connection, his attitude could be condoned: newspapers are free to state their proprietors' views on public policy, even when those views seem to the majority of their readers eccentric and misguided. It is possible, however, that Beaverbrook's feud against Mountbatten springs from a deeper, earlier, and more personal source. For many years before the war, he was quite friendly with Mountbatten. At some point, for some private reason, this friendship was broken; and Beaverbrook's private summing-up of the Mountbattens now is: 'Mountbatten is vain, not clever. The woman is clever, not vain.' It is to this disagreement that those who have known intimately both Mountbatten and Beaverbrook attribute the origin of the public feud.

Whether this interpretation be correct or not, it is important not to over-simplify the tale of the relations between them. Beaverbrook was well-disposed towards Mountbatten at various times in 1940 and 1941: after the episodes of the *Kelly* and the *Javelin*, he wrote Mountbatten letters of almost extravagant praise. It seems that a little later, when Mountbatten had become, in turn, Chief of Combined Operations and a full member of the Chiefs of Staff Committee, relations between them cooled, possibly because Mountbatten was too busy to respond as warmly as he might have to the overtures that Beaverbrook then made. It is a characteristic of Beaverbrook's temperament, often noted by those concerned, to resent bitterly any sign that those whom he has regarded as his protégés are slipping away from his sphere of influence and rising to power independently of him.

There was a *rapprochement*, however, when Mountbatten was appointed Supreme Commander in South-East Asia.

Mountbatten saw Beaverbrook to ask his advice about his relations with Chiang Kai-shek and about public relations for the South-East Asia Command. Beaverbrook advised him to make friends first with Madame Chiang, and to approach the Generalissimo through her; and went to some slight trouble to procure Frank Owen as editor of the SEAC forces newspaper, and to enable Mountbatten to promote him to field rank. (As Owen was then only an officer cadet at Sandhurst, this promotion was fiercely opposed by the Secretary of State for War, Sir James Grigg. Beaverbrook helped to persuade Churchill to intervene—and he was reluctant to do so, rightly suspecting Owen's hand in some of the *Tribune* attacks on him.) From time to time after this, reasonably cordial letters passed between Beaverbrook and Mountbatten: in April, 1945, for instance, Beaverbrook wrote congratulating him on his KCB and on his 'splendid services'; Mountbatten replied that there was no one from whom he would sooner have received congratulations.

There is thus some evidence in support of Beaverbrook's denial of uninterrupted hostility. It must also be said that, if this hostility is correctly traced to personal resentment rather than to public disagreement, Beaverbrook himself is probably unconscious by now that this is its source and has rationalized his antagonism. Nevertheless, some of those who have examined systematically the numerous references to Mountbatten and his wife that have appeared in the *Express* during recent years, have come to the conclusion that there is truly a feud.

In 1954, Mountbatten's career was crowned by the announcement of his appointment as First Sea Lord, with effect from March 1955. The comment of a serious newspaper, *The Observer*, is worth quoting:

His appointment is particularly to be welcomed because it shows no Tory prejudice against the man whom Mr Attlee chose to transform our relationship with India. It is also pleasant to see the complete ineffectiveness of the boring campaign waged against Mountbatten by the Beaverbrook newspapers for the last ten or twelve years, a vendetta that has borne all the appearances of personal spite.

At least as significant—for there was, after all, a long-standing feud between the Astor and the Beaverbrook newspapers—was a comment in the *News Chronicle* by A. J. Cummings, who has always been one of Beaverbrook's staunchest friends and admirers among those who differ from him politically: under the headline 'STOP SNIPING AT LORD LOUIS', he expressed the hope that Beaverbrook might have 'changed his mind' about 'this brilliant man'. This was too sanguine.

Whichever theory of the origin of this hostility be accepted, therefore, it has clearly been carried on occasion to extreme lengths; and this in itself may tend to confirm the view that there is an emotional basis for it, however unaware of the emotion the instigator of the feud may now be. If this is so, some critics will view with scepticism the claim—endorsed, indeed, by the Royal Commission on the Press—that the British Press is the best in the world. Its system of ownership and control would at any rate be open to abuse, if under it some of the nation's most notable public servants could be subjected to constant criticism in order to satisfy private caprice.

*　　　*　　　*

His activities for the rest of the war were inconsiderable in comparison with the services he had rendered in 1940 and 1941. Early in 1943 he suddenly subjected the House of Lords to a boisterous onslaught. An average active peer will speak perhaps once a month in that decorous chamber: Beaverbrook initiated several major debates within a few weeks. He attacked planning, organization, and the committee system: 'as organization becomes complete, it becomes

rigid'; the war effort was too rigid, 'war is the art of leading
with the unexpected'. He expounded the ministerial strategy
that had indeed been useful both in aircraft and tank production and *vis-à-vis* the Americans: 'Don't give the industry
a safe programme . . . Give the industry a programme that
puts the firms at the stretch and keeps them all out all the
time.'

In another debate he demanded immediate all-out aid to
Russia: 'send supplies in prodigal plenty'. So far Britain and
America had sent only 'parsimonious' supplies—5,800 tanks
and 2,000 aircraft by the end of 1942. 'A swarm of bees in
May . . .' Critics argued that this was a deviation from his
Second Front policy: if most of the tanks were to be sent to
Russia, they would not be available for use in the West.
Churchill, questioned in the House of Commons, referred
blandly to Beaverbrook's 'process of emphatic stimulation'.
One of his debates—on the Ministry of Aircraft Production—
took place in secret session. In another, he attacked bureau-
cracy in agriculture: 'nine inspectors on my tiny little farm!'
The *Manchester Guardian* found his 'sudden resurgence'
interesting: 'he crows again'; his crest, the *Guardian* recalled,
was 'Upon a drum proper a cock gules, wattled, armed, and
legged or'. The *Daily Herald* wrote: 'What is he up to? What
is the game? As often as not . . . Lord Beaverbrook himself
has not known the answers. He has a profound belief in
activity for its own sake. He wants to "go places"—but his
interest is in the motion rather than the destination. If he
cannot be an inspiration to the national mind, he will nevertheless very happily fulfil the rôle of an itch in the body
politic.'

The *New Statesman*, however, praised him for initiating a
debate on the Second Front. Simon, the Lord Chancellor,
had condemned this 'catchpenny phrase' as 'a slogan based
on ill-founded clamour'. Simon, said the *New Statesman*, was
'the most disastrous Foreign Secretary Britain ever had';

and 'once again he could smile and smile and undermine the will to act'. Lord Trenchard supported Simon, and deplored 'the working-up of dangerous feeling among people who cannot possibly be told the facts'. Lord Strabolgi supported Beaverbrook, but was repudiated by the other Labour peers. Tass, the Soviet news-agency, broadcast the full text of Beaverbrook's speech, at dictation speed, to all radio-stations in the Soviet Union. The *Daily Express*, reporting this debate, resorted to a familiar trick of tendentious Parliamentary reporting: remarks by Beaverbrook which excited any applause were reported as exciting 'loud cheers' or 'cheers and laughter'; reports by his opponents which excited any applause were reported as exciting 'some cheers'.

Because he was using it as a platform, the House of Lords, of which he had for so many years thought so little, now began to grow in importance in his mind: the mandate of the House of Commons, he announced, was 'no longer valid'. 'Janus', in the *Spectator*, was curious enough to measure the inches devoted to his speeches by the various newspapers. For two debates the sum was:

> *The Times*, 16½ inches.
> *Daily Telegraph*, 17½.
> *Daily Herald*, 20½.
> *Daily Mail*, 21½.
> *News Chronicle*, 27.
> *Daily Express*, 101.

In April, 1943, the *Manchester Guardian* reported him 'still in eruption', his special target now being alleged discrimination against small distributors of milk in favour of the Co-ops and United Dairies. Soon he was off to Washington again with Churchill, Lord Leathers, Lord Cherwell, and a high-powered staff of experts, ninety strong. A carefully worded announcement indicated, however, that he was an accidental fellow-traveller: he was 'officially stated . . . to be engaged

on a private mission'. The sometimes-well-informed columnist Drew Pearson said that he had come to visit a New York
asthma specialist, Dr Al Brach.

On September 25th, to the general surprise, he took office
in the Government again, as Lord Privy Seal (thus depriving
political columnists of their favourite joke that, whatever the
Lord Privy Seal may be, he is neither a lord nor a privy nor
a seal).

Next time the opportunity occurred in the House of Lords,
Lord Brabazon—who had succeeded him as Minister of Aircraft Production—teased him gently about his Second Front
campaign: 'I should like to know whether, having joined His
Majesty's Government, his conscience is quite clear on this
matter'. Beaverbrook nodded; Brabazon said that he hoped
that the nod would be reported 'throughout the world, up
and down the steppes of Russia and in Moscow', and that
it would 'keep Dr Goebbels awake at nights'. The nod was
indeed significant: Beaverbrook must have known by now
that D Day was only a few months ahead.

Brabazon also at this time reviewed—oddly enough, in
Tribune—Mr Farrer's book on Beaverbrook and MAP. 'If
anyone ever deserved sympathy,' he wrote, 'it was the unfortunate individual who succeeded someone who had
reorganized the aircraft industry, ridden roughshod over all
other departments, made a bitter enemy of the Air Ministry
(its only customer), run publicity with a skill never equalled,
and incidentally helped to save England and the world.'
There had been in Beaverbrook's administration, he said, 'a
lot of ballyhoo . . . but much pure gold'; and he confirmed
that 'Beaverbrook was always a little afraid of Air Marshals'.

As Lord Privy Seal, he had no specific ministerial duties
and therefore 'plenty of opportunity to indulge his tireless
energy' (*News Chronicle*) in all directions. *The Economist*
observed: 'Formally, he is not a member of the War Cabinet;
actually, he has always had access to the highest counsels,

297

whether in office or not'. Mr Claud Cockburn's news-sheet, *The Week*, said that his appointment would increase Moscow's confidence in the West and would be 'a signal to Washington'. Other Left-wing papers viewed it more glumly. The *Manchester Guardian* remarked, with some obviousness: 'he does not thrive on sinecures'. It was supposed that he would be undertaking special overseas missions for Churchill. The *New Yorker*'s London letter compared the Tories discussing his appointment with a 'housewife ... discovering that the family cat was at the cream-bowl again'. The *Express* at once took on a quieter tone, and dropped the Second Front campaign.

The lull was as brief as lulls have always been in this turbulent career. By January, 1944, there were rumours that Beaverbrook was to replace Grigg at the War Office, and more disturbing rumours that he had his eye on Eden's job as Foreign Secretary. These rumours were taken so seriously that the staid and cautious *Yorkshire Post* (with which Eden had a family connection) reported with alarm 'a hint that Lord Beaverbrook would like to take a hand in diplomatic affairs'. *The Economist* also reported 'much talk of Mr Eden's resigning the Foreign Office' and 'an element of pressure', whose source, from 'attacks in the press', it was 'not difficult to guess'. Mr Cockburn declared that 'the struggle around the succession to the Premiership' was 'reaching a new peak of intensity'. Mr E. P. Stacpoole, the experienced lobby correspondent of the Press Association, reported 'extraordinary "whisperings" about Lord Beaverbrook', quoting unnamed Conservative MPs as saying that he intended to put three or four hundred candidates in the field at the next election, and that, if he became Prime Minister, it would be simple to pass a one-sentence Bill permitting him, though a peer, to speak in the House of Commons. This was a new variation of Ward Price's forecast, fourteen years before, of an early reform of the Lords for the same desirable purpose;

it met with as chilly a welcome from MPs generally and the public.

However, he was in fact confined to important, but limited and technical, tasks: post-war civil aviation plans (on which considerable concessions were made to Washington), oil conferences, replies to debates in the Lords. Lord Reith has described one of these speeches: 'I had never seen or heard anything like it in the Lords. He finished in an adulation of Churchill's planning of the war; Churchill, we were informed, was responsible for Rolls-Royce engines being produced in America. Latham mildly described it as a noisy and mostly irrelevant display of pyrotechnics.'

Once the invasion of Europe was fairly launched, those in charge of the war began to feel that it was, in a sense, as good as won; it was now merely a question of time. A few thousand more soldiers had to die, of course, a few thousand more air-raids had to kill civilians on both sides. Increasingly, however, the minds of politicians were preoccupied with post-war problems and the General Election that must follow the war. An egregious suggestion appeared in the *Daily Express*: without regard to the demobilization scheme then being care-fully worked out, on the broadly equitable basis of age plus length of service, Conservative Party agents, as such, should be released from the forces forthwith! Possibly the lack of public enthusiasm for the rumoured promotion of Beaver-brook had temporarily discouraged him; at any rate, it was alleged by Mr Cockburn in *The Week* that his ambition had been deflected in a new direction—the chairmanship of the Conservative Party organization. Mr Cockburn guessed, no doubt correctly, that there were 'a rather large number of young men who would rather enter Parliament under Lord B.'s auspices than not enter it at all'. Mr Sydney Elliott, Socialist editor of the *Evening Standard*, resigned: this was going to be a bitter fight, and the days of some freedom of expression for Socialists in the Beaverbrook press were over.

As early as April, 1945—a month before VE Day—Beaverbrook was trying to persuade his colleagues to agree to a snap General Election. Mr Bracken, falling in with this proposal, began to attack the Socialists, presumably with the object of disintegrating further the already cracked and creaking coalition. Ernest Bevin retorted with an attack on the *Express* for undermining the morale of the troops by agitating against controls at home. Beaverbrook made a speech at Paddington which was, in some respects, unflattering to the electors, but handsome in its references to those on whose offices he had been said to have cast envious eyes:

> It is no use supposing the electorate, after ten years of political truce, is informed on public issues . . . We have to show them that our Prime Minister, Mr Churchill, must lead us through the days that lie before us. We must explain that his colleague, Mr Eden, is also essential to the rebuilding of Britain's influence . . . We have to make it plain that the third member of that triumvirate is Mr Brendan Bracken. I have no doubt that we will have a great Conservative majority in the country.

When the war in Europe was won, and the Coalition dissolved, and the General Election in progress, such sentiments as these were reiterated (except for the heroic status accorded to Bracken) from thousands of Conservative platforms. Churchill and Beaverbrook in particular were absolutely confident of victory. No heed was paid to such hints of disaster as came, for instance, from General Slim, who lunched at Downing Street one day fresh from Burma. 'How are your soldiers going to vote?' Churchill asked him. 'Ninety per cent Labour,' said Slim. Churchill grunted. 'What about the other ten per cent, then?', he asked. 'They won't vote at all,' said Slim.

The campaign was fought fiercely indeed, and Beaverbrook was in the thick of it. Still faithful to Bracken—who had been First Lord of the Admiralty, in the 'Caretaker' Government, for just two weeks—he went to Chatham to describe him, to

an audience of astonished sailors, as the greatest First Lord
since Churchill ('since Noah', the wags parodied it). Bevin,
able now to give back some of what he had had to take from
Beaverbrook during the past five years, called him the 'most
dangerous man in British public life' (to which Bracken retorted that Lord Dowding, who had praised Beaverbrook's
achievement at MAP, knew more about danger than Bevin).
Beaverbrook, heckled at a meeting in the Harrow Road,
said sorrowfully: 'Everybody knows the trouble I've seen.
If ever a man has been maligned, misinterpreted, misreported
and attacked, I am that man.'

Others could have made the same complaint, with less
certainty of publicity for it. The *Express* in particular concentrated its attack on Harold Laski, then chairman of the
Labour Party Executive. He was not, as the *Express* omitted
to point out, leader of the Labour Party; but then Attlee,
who was, had an unalarmingly English-sounding name. It
was easier to work up prejudice with such 'scare' headlines
as 'Shall the Laski "25"[1] Rule Great Britain?' Possibly the
most discreditable headline of the whole campaign, however,
was that printed by the *Express* above the report of a broadcast in which Attlee had stressed that Labour people—as
their war record showed—were as patriotic as Conservatives.
This was headed 'THE NATIONAL SOCIALISTS'—a clear
suggestion that British Labour was essentially akin to German 'National Socialism', whose horrors were fresh in the
electors' minds. This theme was also featured in Churchill's
'Gestapo' broadcast, which shocked millions of people in
all parties and may well have cost the Conservatives many
seats.

As polling-day drew near, the propaganda became ever
wilder. The *Daily Express* did not scruple to prophesy—a
forecast that no responsible newspaper could have made,

[1] The twenty-five members of the National Executive Committee of the
Labour Party.

301

and that no one but a still-unknown Chancellor could even have considered privately—that, if the Conservatives were elected, income-tax would be reduced by half-a-crown in the pound. Even Low vanished from the *Evening Standard* (to get some 'sea-air'). Mr Charles Fenby wrote, in *Leader* magazine: 'The tactics employed by Lord Beaverbrook seem to be based on one idea—that, by marshalling all that is ignorant, prejudiced, and irrational in the country, it is possible to sail to victory on a stream of impenetrable muddiness'. The *Manchester Guardian* drew a parallel with the 'notorious and scandalous' Election of 1918. According to Mr Kingsley Martin,[1] this was because Churchill had 'accepted as an ally and counsellor in electoral tactics the same evil genius who had then so ill-advised Lloyd George'. (Lloyd George, however, did at least win.)

The same charge against Beaverbrook was often repeated in Conservative circles during the prolonged and angry post-mortem which followed the overwhelming Labour victory. At a Conservative candidates' conference in London on October 5th, Mr Spencer Summers and Mr Ian Harvey were among those who sought to pin some of the blame on him. Mr Whiteside (Wembley South) called for his expulsion. Sir Derrick Gunston said: 'I believe there is no man more detested throughout the political world than Lord Beaverbrook'.

This charge does not seem to be altogether well-founded. Beaverbrook himself denied vigorously and categorically that he was responsible for the Conservatives' election strategy and tactics; and his denial was not contradicted by the Conservative Central Office. In particular, he had nothing to do, he said, with the 'Gestapo' broadcast: it was approved by Mr James Stuart (the Chief Whip) and Mr Ralph Assheton (the Party chairman), and the only people with Churchill at Chequers on the day of its delivery, when the finishing

[1] In *Harold Laski*, p. 168.

touches were put to it, were his son Randolph and Mr Stuart. Private enquiries of those who should know confirm these statements; the most that can be said is that the tone of the broadcast was in harmony with the general campaign that the *Express* was running, presumably with Beaverbrook's approval. Never in modern times had an election campaign been conducted at so low a level; and the British people could not have shown more decisively their resentment at this cynical underestimate of their intelligence and sense of fair play.

The precise responsibility for the Conservative tactics is of secondary importance. It is sufficient to note that, whereas on many previous occasions Beaverbrook, while disapproved of on all sides, had at least been able to claim some share in electoral victories, in 1945 he shared most conspicuously in the general discredit. There were many, not only in the Labour Party, to echo Attlee's cutting judgement on him: he was 'the man in public life ... most widely distrusted by decent men of all parties'; and he had 'a long record of political intrigue and political instability, with an insatiable appetite for power'.

The appetite was never to be sated: the power remained a mirage.

PREPARING FOR JUDGEMENT

It is time for the destruction of error,
The chairs are being brought in from the garden . . .
This is the dragon's day, the devourer's . . .

W. H. AUDEN

WINTER stands hard about Cherkley Court. The giant yew-trees mourn, the stucco is peeling, the blinds are drawn: the master is four thousand miles away in the perpetual summer of Nassau, planting more and more flowering trees and shrubs—jacaranda, poinciana, African tulip, pride of Barbados—and supervising the pumping of water for them, through great lengths of hose, from the rain-water tanks below. He will point with pride to these tanks, and his big compost-heaps, and the plants that he has brought here experimentally from his gardens in the other hemisphere, and the fountains that play gently on them. 'This is better than producing newspapers,' he says—and feels, if only for a few moments, that this is truly so.

As if by telepathy, his servants scattered about the world are conscious that life goes on in Nassau, for him and those about him, pretty much as it does when he is at Arlington House or La Capponcina or Cherkley. The physical disabilities of asthma are relieved by the Bahamian climate: the inner restlessness is as compulsive as ever. He himself, in a letter to a friend, once gave a vivid picture of one side of his own character:

> I am the victim of the Furies. On the rockbound coast of New Brunswick the waves break incessantly. Every now and then comes a particularly dangerous wave smashing viciously against the rock. It is called The Rage.
> That's me.

Whatever Beaverbrook's faults and failings may be, he is at least aware of many of them himself; and hypocrisy is not usually one of them. It may even be said that he is apt to exaggerate, to over-dramatize some of the more sombre aspects of his career: there is a certain unreality in the release through a news-agency and publication on the front page of the *Daily Express* of a statement by him that his 'joy has turned to ashes' and that 'rewards are but shadows' because 'miserable and wretched Governments—Liberal, Socialist and Tory—have brought us to a disintegrating Empire . . .' Such protests are almost too self-consciously in his Old Testament prophetic manner.

Truisms about the Jekyll-and-Hyde nature of man apply with particular force to Beaverbrook. There are a few people —not, indeed, so very few: old pensioners and employees, holders of the hundreds of scholarships generously endowed by him, young children of the large Aitken clan, a fair proportion of the population of New Brunswick—to whom he is a figure of godlike power and beneficence, the great and good man in their lives. To more, probably, of those whose paths have crossed his in the past half-century, he is a perplexing but, on the whole, sinister figure: at worst, evil; at best, mischievous.

Sometimes a devil seems to enter into him when he is with friends dear to him and something quite remote from them has made him fretful. Then he will take a delight in contradicting whatever they say, in chaffing them cruelly, in exposing them to the ridicule of the company—exposing also, in the process, his own raw resentment against the hollow parody of power that his life has become.

Then indeed he seems 'the victim of the Furies': it is only strange that the same man, in other moods, can without affectation be called, as many have called him, 'lovable'. Anecdotes of these milder moods are at least as numerous as those of his moods of demonic blackness. Often he is at his most engaging in his relations with erring employees. Castlerosse, who took all his troubles to him, whose debts he paid again and again—not always without a few growls—called him 'my never-ending lord of appeal'. Hearing that another journalist, for whom he had a great affection, had just suffered a domestic tragedy, he abandoned all his engagements, ran bareheaded into the street, jumped into a taxi, and drove straight to the man's house to comfort him; nor did he leave him, by night or day, until the worst was over. Yet another of his journalists, by no means senior in the firm, urgently needed £1,000: he asked Beaverbrook if he might borrow this sum from him, or from the firm, and repay it gradually out of his salary. Beaverbrook gave a noncommittal reply, and said he would let him know. Next day E. J. Robertson sent for him and said that Beaverbrook had discussed the matter with him. 'We have a strict office rule against such advances,' he said, and the journalist's heart sank. 'But,' he added, 'Lord Beaverbrook has instructed me to make you a free gift of £1,000. Here is a cheque . . .' Such kindness goes far beyond the shrewd self-interest which cynics detect in the largesse of rich employers.

In this category belongs a pleasant and typical fragment once recorded by Mr Guy C. Pollock. An editor or leaderwriter who had been in some way contumacious received one of the dreaded telephone-calls. Beaverbrook blazed at him for some minutes—and then wound up the conversation by saying: 'You've thwarted me once, you've thwarted me twice. Next time you thwart me . . . I shall have to go back to Canada. Dine with me tonight. Good-bye to you.'

This whimsical streak in him is unpredictable. Sometimes an encounter that starts well will end badly; sometimes it is the other way about. An elderly couple whom he has known for many years had been visiting him; as they left, the wife asked if he still had any copies of his book, *Success*: if so, might she have one, as she had always wanted to read it? Next day he

gave the book to a servant, to wrap and send to her. Someone suggested that he should inscribe it for her. 'Not at all!',
he said, quite gruffly. 'If she wants me to, she can ask me.'

Unpredictable, too, are his reactions to public attacks on
him. He pretends that he is indifferent to them all. This is
not so: some still wound or anger him, particularly if achievements of which he has some right to be proud, such as his
work as Minister of Aircraft Production, are denigrated.
(He has never learned that there is no merit in not resenting
just attacks only.) On two successive days, early in 1954,
he read the *Daily Mirror* with some care. On the first day,
two pages were devoted to a serious, constructive, candid
analysis of Anglo-American relations, a subject in which he
has professed a lifelong interest. 'Poor stuff, isn't it?', he
grumbled. 'This paper's going off. It's getting dull.' Next day
there was a review by 'Cassandra' of Beaverbrook's book,
Don't Trust to Luck—a review of the most savage and searing
nature, ridiculing Beaverbrook, tearing his book to shreds.
'Good stuff this, eh?', he beamed as he scanned the abusive
epithets. 'Great! ... It's a fine paper, a fine paper ...'

It is by the accumulation of anecdotes that his character can
chiefly be displayed, for one simple reason, essential to the
understanding of his career and personality: he is primarily
concerned not with ideas but with persons—with persons as
companions or as enemies, as subjects for journalistic or
political manipulation, or, empirically, for their usefulness.
His habitual indifference to abstract ideas has already been
mentioned; it is, indeed, not merely indifference but positive
antipathy. This is no doubt why such institutions as the
British Council seem to him futile and wasteful: the want of
critical balance in this attitude is shown in his almost complete ignoring of the Council's operations in British territories overseas, which even he might be expected to find
praiseworthy.

In an age which is neither an age of faith nor an age of

reason, most men seem content to live on the day-to-day treadmill of impulse: *ad maiorem Dei gloriam* and the *suprema ratio rerum* alike give way to the sovereignty of *ad hoc*. Yesterday's belief is as obsolete as yesterday's newspaper. Strong fixed principles, properly so called, are usually the result of religious conviction and training, or of an advanced education in science, history or the humanities. The biblical allusions, the snatches of metrical psalmody, the other relics of his Presbyterian upbringing with which this truant of the Manse has so often made play are not so much expressions of a coherent religious philosophy as nostalgic or superstitious ornaments of speech. Mr Philip Guedalla wrote of him: 'It is curious to observe how this sprightly observer is almost invariably baffled by men of education'. He instanced Asquith, Balfour, and Curzon. Beaverbrook himself has been at pains to show that, in his view, a traditional English university education can be a positive handicap in what is, to him, the real world. He once published an analysis of the educational backgrounds of all the editors of national daily newspapers: only one of them, he discovered triumphantly, had been to Oxford or Cambridge—and that one was Geoffrey Dawson, of *The Times*, whom he would not, in any case, have cared to commend as a model to young journalists. In 1923 he wrote of a young man he knew, working in the City, a young man of financial talent who was, he said, 'ruining himself' by self-indulgence: 'I attribute this failing to his education at Cambridge'. In defence of the hard-boiled worldly pragmatism of his book, *Success*, he wrote:

> It has been objected ... that the motives implied in the formation of such a character as I have depicted are purely materialistic. I am not afraid of the charge, which is a somewhat unreal one. Wealth and position and prestige are not ignoble ambitions. They are rough-and-ready but fairly accurate tests of the merits of individuals ...

It is presumably this want of principle, in the accepted

sense of the word, this obsession with persons and property, that accounts for his erratic political courses. The *National Review* once observed: 'No man has any right to be as wrong as Lord Beaverbrook manages to be on public affairs, personal and impersonal. His views strike his readers as being exclusively animated by the spirit of the vendetta.' Among the various policies which he and his newspapers have advocated, everybody could find some to agree and some to disagree with. At times they have been 'progressive': against hereditary titles and privilege (a matter in which he had a keen personal interest), for a levy on war fortunes, against Churchill's anti-Soviet intervention, for the Irish settlement (perhaps because of the friendship with Tim Healy), against Churchill's return to the gold standard, for a 'fair chance' for the first Labour Government, for the Second Front in 1942 (an argument still to be settled finally by the historians), against German rearmament during the controversy of the past few years. At other times they have been 'reactionary': against the League of Nations, for the 'Red letter' stunt which destroyed the first Labour Government, against a loan to Soviet Russia, against the General Strike of 1926, for the appeasement of Hitler and Mussolini, the carving-up of Czechoslovakia, and the whole Munich policy; the Laski scare in 1945, the propaganda against rationing during and after the Second World War... Dozens of examples in either category could be quoted. Beaverbrook himself would no doubt claim as his guiding 'principle' the one policy that he has advocated consistently through the years, the policy of imperial economic unity. Few would agree that it can be dignified by this term: in the form in which he has generally stated it, it has been dismissed, by people in all parties and all the dominions, as an infantile notion not worthy of serious consideration. 'Infantile' may, indeed, be an exact description; for it has already been noted as the one general idea which seems to have taken root in his mind, for local historical reasons, in childhood. Like Disraeli's Mr Kremlin, a modern Disraelian might say, he has been 'distinguished for ignorance, for he had only one idea—and that was wrong'. He himself argues—it is an arguable hypothesis—that at one moment there was a real chance that Empire Free Trade would become official Conservative policy. This was after Baldwin's Queen's Hall speech, when Neville Chamberlain was promoting a truce between Beaverbrook and the Party.[1] Had Chamberlain remained dominant in a Tory Cabinet, he might have furthered Beaverbrook's cause. But a few months later came the crisis and the MacDonald coalition; the Cabinet was diluted with Free Traders; the chance was lost.

In any man who achieves high position and therefore power to guide and to order the conduct of many of his fellows, to negotiate with them and to use them, a want of principle may be as dangerous to himself as to the community; for without it, paradoxically, however much he may fancy his own judgement of persons, it will be less sure than that of the man of principle. He may have a kind of horse-coper's nose for an obvious weakness that can be exploited; he will be able to pick an efficient accountant, valet, carpenter, or leader-writer; but he must depend on chance or 'hunch' in assessing the quality of men of affairs. Beaverbrook has suffered throughout his career from a twofold disability arising from this defect: he has failed—for instance, at the time of the Empire Crusade—to induce any politicians of indubitably first-class status and ability to enlist in his cause; and he has, again and again, either picked the wrong enemies or under-estimated those whom he has picked. The story of Haman and Mordecai should have warned him against despising the quiet man in the corner who will not doff his cap; Baldwin, with whom he could have made common cause, was such a man; of another, Attlee, who could never indeed have been his ally, he quite failed, too, to take the measure.

[1] See p. 216.

If his hatred of what they represented socially had been less compulsive, he could have collaborated usefully with such powerful politicians as the late Lord Salisbury or such 'men of Munich' as Geoffrey Dawson. Since their brief wartime alliance—whose *raison d'être* has been hinted at—his antipathy to Sir Anthony Eden has grown steadily. This alone would be enough to ensure a lessening of Beaverbrook's influence in the Conservative Party; and it is hardly surprising that, in January, 1949, the Conservative Central Office should have let it be known, without any apparent distress, that he had not renewed his subscription to the Epsom constituency Conservative Association, having told the agent there that he was 'no longer a Tory'. Even for practical purposes, caprice makes a poor substitute for principle; for the capricious man is apt to parade his wounded egotism, like a Mediterranean beggar's sores, and so to receive the contemptuous penny rather than genuine sympathy or the rigorous therapy that is needed. This is particularly so when caprice accompanies a want of formal English education, one of the chief worldly benefits of which is the skill that it imparts in concealing emotion.

Increasingly, therefore, intelligent readers came to disregard *Express* campaigns against foreign policies promoted by Eden (for they knew that probably, buried deep beneath them, was some real or fancied personal slight once inflicted by him on Beaverbrook); or even against the administration of the War Office (for one of the more recent victims of punishment by this modern version of the pillory is Mr Antony Head, Secretary of State for War, whose offence may be that, having obtained a safe Conservative seat in Parliament with Beaverbrook's help, he omitted to pay to his patron the assiduous attentions that might have been dictated by gratitude or caution).

Ultimate frustration, then—as he himself admits, with ostentatious candour—is his lot; and it must be the more galling to him because he is more than ever conscious of his strength of will and of his great practical abilities, and because he must have begun to realize that it is his own character or temperament alone—not ill luck, not the malevolence of others—that has debarred him from the supreme power to which those abilities might have carried him. He is a classic and, it may be said, a tragic example of the man who, in the hackneyed phrase, is 'his own worst enemy'.

It is hard to contemplate the bright, mischievous New Brunswick boy, hiding with his Scott romance in the hay-loft or catching trout in the Miramichi, without pity and a pang of regret—regret that, outside the gloomy Manse, none of the few older friends who had his confidence was able to touch his imagination with a sense of life's real values. If that abundant energy had been used for half a century in the service of nobler causes than the accumulation of wealth and the pursuit of power, the moments of recollection and intro-spection that occur in even the most laboriously crowded old age might be less leaden and dusty than, it may be surmised, his are now. Yet if some unfathomable, sharp resentment had not cut him off from normal family affection, inflamed his ego, and spurred his ambition, if he had not been a lone wolf-cub, he might have been merely a useful nonentity or local worthy, rarely venturing further than Saint John or Fredericton—and Britain might not have had a war-winning Prime Minister in 1916, or the aircraft that held the Nazis off in 1940; or, for that matter, the *Daily Express* as it is.

Such speculations are as idle as those which relate Keats's odes to his tuberculosis. All that need be said here, in sum-ming up, is that, for good and for evil, Beaverbrook is a unique and potent figure in the British public life of the twentieth century—potent, yet always just missing that supreme power whose attainment has obsessed him.

> He who bends to himself a joy
> Doth the wingéd life destroy . . .

It is, however, still necessary to write of him in the present tense. His versatile activity is hardly abated by time. He may yet strike out in many new directions. Within the past two years, satirists of his hostility to culture have been confounded by his suddenly intensified interest in modern painting. This interest is catholic, unprejudiced, and humble. 'I know nothing about it yet,' he said recently, 'but I'm learning.' As is invariable with him, the interest is expressed, as quickly as possible, in practical form. He took the best advice he could get, and bought—anonymously, through agents, so that he would not be overcharged too flagrantly—some hundred pictures by representative British artists of this century, from Sickert and Wilson Steer to Francis Bacon. These he has had conveyed to New Brunswick and placed on public exhibition there; and he proposes to build a gallery to house them permanently, together with a selection of paintings by European and Canadian masters.

So it may well go on for five or ten years more. Beaverbrook at seventy-six does not look like a machine running down: his mind is as resilient and as omnivorously curious as ever, his vital force is unimpaired. He can still, without discomfort, swim a leisurely three or four lengths of his pool at Aitken House, Nassau, talking of Bonar Law and Curzon and 'George' as he swims. If he could ever acquire equanimity, he might live to be a hundred. Even now he is sure to be 'cooking up' some new project, to tickle his cronies and to scandalize the orthodox. Perhaps he is revising for publication his closely secret Life of Christ, written some years ago and suppressed on the advice of Tim Healy. Its publication would be a piquant event in the world of theological literature; for it must be, in essence, an attempt to reconcile the stern dogmas of Calvinism with the Sermon on the Mount.

One of the legends about Beaverbrook is that he is afraid of death, that even the mention of it will upset and depress him. This may have been true a decade or more ago, in his hypochondriac period. It is no longer so. Quite recently someone dared to mention the legend to him: he denied the truth of it with vigour but without perturbation, saying: 'If it were true, would I have devoted so much time and care to making arrangements for my affairs after I'm gone?' Nor did he show any disposition to change the subject, discussing it easily, even merrily, and recalling occasions on which he had been near to death, such as a curious incident in 1917, when a friend of his, Robertson Lawson—a fellow-Presbyterian and an accountant who had risen to be deputy-chairman of Lipton's—lost his reason, locked himself into Beaverbrook's office with him, cried, 'On your knees, Beaverbrook!', produced a revolver, and intimated that he had been charged by God with the task of judging and, if necessary, destroying him.

Recently, too, another rich man, also more than seventy years of age, was dining with him. As often happens when rich men dine together, the talk was of money—market trends, investments, purchases of real estate, taxation. Beaverbrook's contemporary was spreading his money widely throughout the world: only that day he had bought a brewery in a remote colony. He spoke of death duties, and of his struggle to minimize the amount that would have to be paid on his estate. 'From the way he talks,' said Beaverbrook after he had gone, 'you'd think he had to pay it himself.'

So the tale of this turbulent life draws near to its end. Serenity seems as unattainable now as it was in the crowded Manse at Newcastle: the perennially familiar sound at La Capponcina as at Cherkley, in Nassau or in Arlington House, is the rushing mighty wind rather than the still small voice. But none may dare to anticipate the final Reckoning; for of all the utterances attributed to Max, first Baron Beaverbrook, the most characteristic is perhaps his defiant dictum: 'I *always* dispute the umpire's decision'.

Max , Lord Beaverbrook .

INDEX

INDEX

INDEX